THE MIGHTY THOR

BY WALTER SIMONSON

COLLECTION EDITOR: Mark D. Beazley
ASSISTANT EDITORS: Nelson Ribeiro & Alex Starbuck
EDITOR, SPECIAL PROJECTS: Jennifer Grünwald
SENIOR EDITOR, SPECIAL PROJECTS: Jeff Youngquist
PRODUCTION: ColorTek & M. Hands
BOOK DESIGN: Jeff Powell
SVP OF PRINT & DIGITAL PUBLISHING SALES: David Gabriel

EDITOR IN CHIEF: Axel Alonso
CHIEF CREATIVE OFFICER: Joe Quesada
PUBLISHER: Dan Buckley
EXECUTIVE PRODUCER: Alan Fine

Special Thanks to Ralph Macchio, Carolynn Calabrese, Steve Hoveke,
Nicolas Waldman, Jeff Amaxon, Michael Harriot & James Sokolowski

THOR BY WALTER SIMONSON VOL. 1. Contains material originally published in magazine form as THOR #337-345. First printing 2013. ISBN# 978-0-7851-8460-7. Published by MARVEL WORLDWIDE INC., a subsidiary of MARVEL ENTERTAINMENT, LLC. OFFICE OF PUBLICATION: 135 West 50th Street, New York, NY 10020. Copyright © 1983, 1984 and 2013 Marvel Characters, Inc. All rights reserved. All characters featured in this issue and the distinctive names and likenesses thereof, and all related indicia are trademarks of Marvel Characters, Inc. No similarity between any of the names characters, persons, and/or institutions in this magazine with those of any living or dead person or institution is intended, and any such similarity which may exist is purely coincidental. Printed in the U.S.A. ALAN FINE, EVP - Office of the President, Marvel Worldwide, Inc. and EVP & CMO Marvel Characters B.V.; DAN BUCKLEY, Publisher & President - Print, Animation & Digital Divisions; JOE QUESADA, Chief Creative Officer; TOM BREVOORT, SVP of Publishing; DAVID BOGART, SVP of Operations & Procurement, Publishing; C.B. CEBULSKI, SVP of Creator & Content Development; DAVID GABRIEL, SVP of Print & Digital Publishing Sales; JIM O'KEEFE, VP of Operations & Logistics; DAN CARR, Executive Director of Publishing Technology; SUSAN CRESPI, Editorial Operations Manager; ALEX MORALES, Publishing Operations Manager; STAN LEE, Chairman Emeritus. For information regarding advertising in Marvel Comics or on Marvel.com, please contact Niza Disla, Director of Marvel Partnerships, at ndisla@marvel.com. For Marvel subscription inquiries, please call 800-217-9158. **Manufactured between 6/14/2013 and 7/22/2013 by R.R. DONNELLEY, INC., SALEM, VA, USA.**

10 9 8 7 6 5 4 3 2 1

WRITER & ARTIST
WALTER SIMONSON

INKER
TERRY AUSTIN
(THOR #342)

REMASTERED COLORING
STEVE OLIFF & OLYOPTICS

LETTERER
JOHN WORKMAN

COVER ARTISTS
WALTER SIMONSON & STEVE OLIFF

EDITOR
MARK GRUENWALD

OF GODS AND THEIR SKALDS...

BY WALTER SIMONSON

Introduction from *Thor by Walter Simonson Omnibus*

The first Marvel comic I ever read was a well-thumbed copy of *Journey into Mystery #113*. It was lying on a chair in a friend's dorm room my freshman year in college. The issue was written by Stan Lee and penciled by Jack Kirby with inks by Chic Stone. It featured the tale of the mighty Thor's second go-round with his enemy, the Grey Gargoyle. I was caught by the rough, visceral art on the cover. The drawing exploded with energy, despite the fact that it was largely a picture of people standing around a doctor's office. It looked like no comic I'd ever seen before. And the interior art was just as rough, just as vital.

I had always loved the tales of the Norse myths, filled as they were with wild gods and tragic destinies. When I was a child, I discovered a 1895 edition of *Myths from Northern Lands* by H.A. Guerber on one of my parents' bookshelves. From that moment, I was hooked. Back then, there weren't a lot of books that related the Norse myths. But I read everything I could find, and loved it all. So it came as an extremely cool surprise to find a comic loosely based on one of the principal figures of the old stories. I tore through the tale, and remained untroubled by the differences I found between the original myths and this pop culture Thor. Blond hair, no beard, no Belt of Strength, no Iron Gloves, and an ordinary handle on Mjolnir? Who cared? I wasn't looking for stories I had already read in books. I was discovering a new world!

I didn't see any more of that world for six months. In those days before local comic shops, comic books were mostly available in drug stores, five-and-dimes, and mom-and-pop soda fountains that sported spinner racks. I quickly discovered that very few of them carried Marvel comics. But in the fall of 1965, I stumbled across the mother lode of Marvel titles in a drug store. *Journey into Mystery #120* and *121* were sitting side-by-side on the rack at a Drug Fair in Greenbelt, MD, a five-mile bike ride from home. I devoured them…but didn't buy them.

Naturally, as a sophisticated and worldly-wise sophomore in college, purchasing comics was, after all, somewhat beneath me. Comics were for kids. However, after I'd ridden back to the Drug Fair four or five times to reread the comic books, I finally decided that the wisest course of action was to buy the damn things.

With that, I was off.

Stan and Jack were just at the beginning of what I regard, in retrospect, as their finest run on the title. They told stories I read so many times that I can still remember them better than I can my own. Off the top of my head—the Trial of the Gods, Thor's evolving struggle against Loki, the Norn Stones and the Destroyer, the Absorbing Man, the coming of Hercules, the treachery of Seidring the Merciless (I do think Odin missed the boat there; would you trust your life to somebody on your staff named Seidring the Merciless?), Thor's titanic battle against Pluto and the forces of the Netherworld, the ultimate fate (at least for the first time) of Jane Foster, and the introduction of Sif coinciding with the War against Ulik, the Trolls, and their hidden ally, Orikal.

Reading comics didn't get any better than that.

That two-year run of Thor stories became the model for my own creative efforts on the title. Stan and Jack's inventiveness never flagged. New characters seemed to appear with practically every issue, the pace of the stories never let up, and Thor was in trouble most of the time. Perhaps the most powerful lesson I learned from those comics was that if you kept a straight face, you could do anything. The wildest stories were possible if you invited the readers to come along on the journey without breaking faith with them. No nudges in the ribs or sly winks to let them know that we were all in on the joke, that we were all too hip for our own good. The essence of a good story was to bind the reader with a spell broken only at the story's conclusion, and perhaps, not even then.

I was inspired as well by the original Norse myths. I tried to capture something of the range of those tales without simply going back and regurgitating them. I wanted to tell stories of epic scope; I wanted to tell stories of small scale with elements of humor in them; I wanted to tell stories of great deeds and dark treacheries, of misplaced loyalties and blasted hopes, seasoned with occasional unexpected laughter.

And of course, I mixed in my own interests as well. The story of Thor's magical transformation (I will say no more about that story here) was inspired in part by my love of the work of Carl Barks, the first comic book creator whose work I ever followed specifically, long before I knew his name.

I could not be more delighted to see these stories reprinted as a collection, remastered and recolored. I hope that they will please those readers already familiar with them, and perhaps find a new audience a quarter of a century after they were first told.

No project like this is the work of a single individual. The following is a lengthy though by no means exhaustive list of some of the folks I'd like to thank who helped make these stories and this book a reality, then and now:

Terry Austin, Mark Beazley, Sal Buscema, Dennis Calero, Mike Carlin, Howard Chaykin, Dan Didio, Mark Gruenwald, Steve Hoveke, Thomas Kintner, Jim Lee, Ralph Macchio, Howard Mackie, Frank Miller, Allen Milgrom, Steve Oliff and the entire Olyoptics crew, George Roussos, Christie (Max) Scheele, Jim Shooter, Louise Simonson, James Sokolowski, Bob Wiacek, and John Workman.

So be it.

Walter Simonson
New York
January 2011

WELL, YOU NEVER CAN TELL.

WHO KNOWS? SOME OF THEM MAY GROW UP TO BE SUPER-HEROES THEMSELVES.

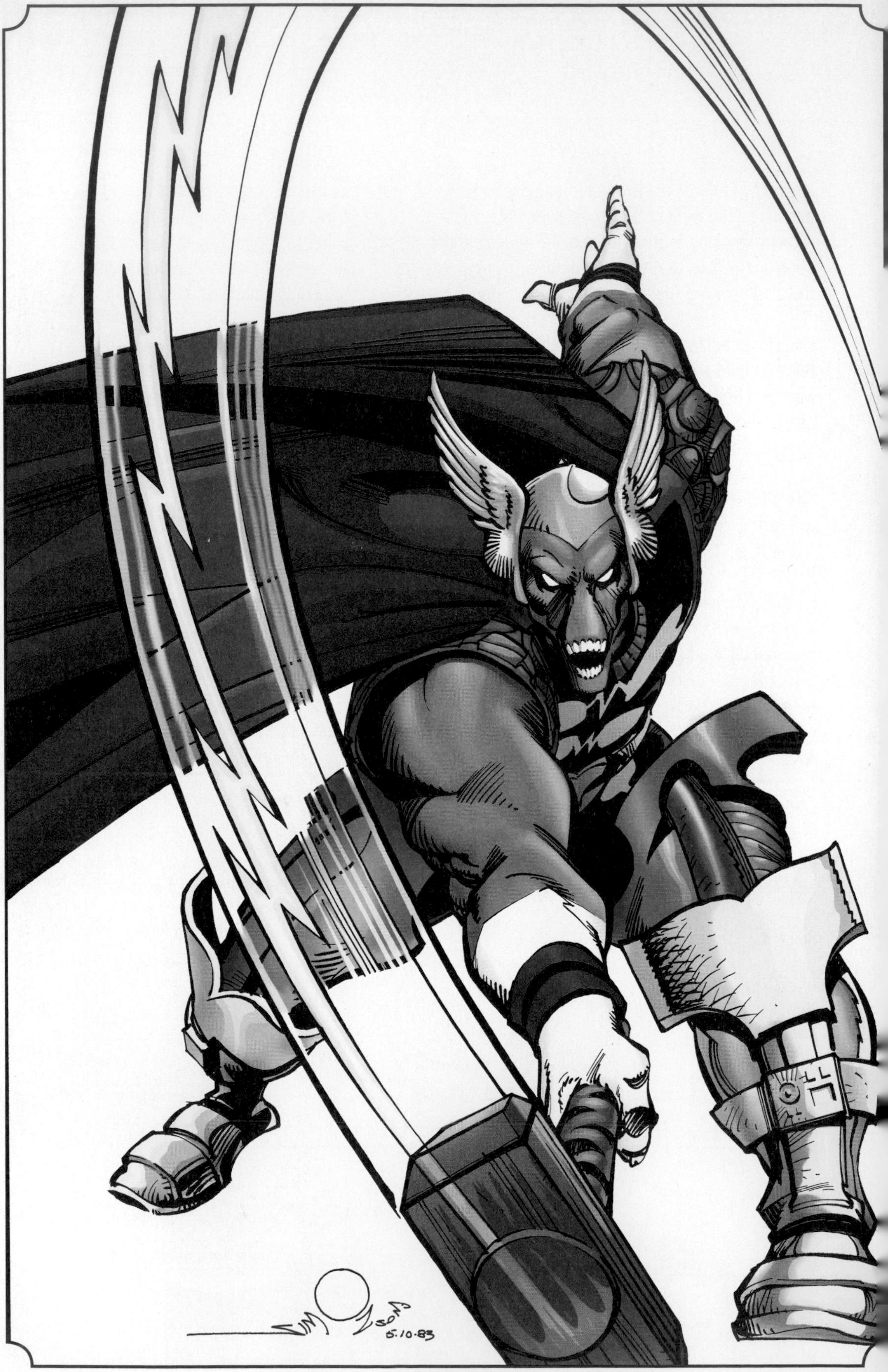

FAR BEYOND THE FIELDS WE KNOW, THE CORE OF AN ANCIENT GALAXY...

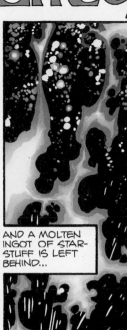

...EXPLODES!

AND A MOLTEN INGOT OF STAR-STUFF IS LEFT BEHIND...

...BUT NOT LEFT ALONE.

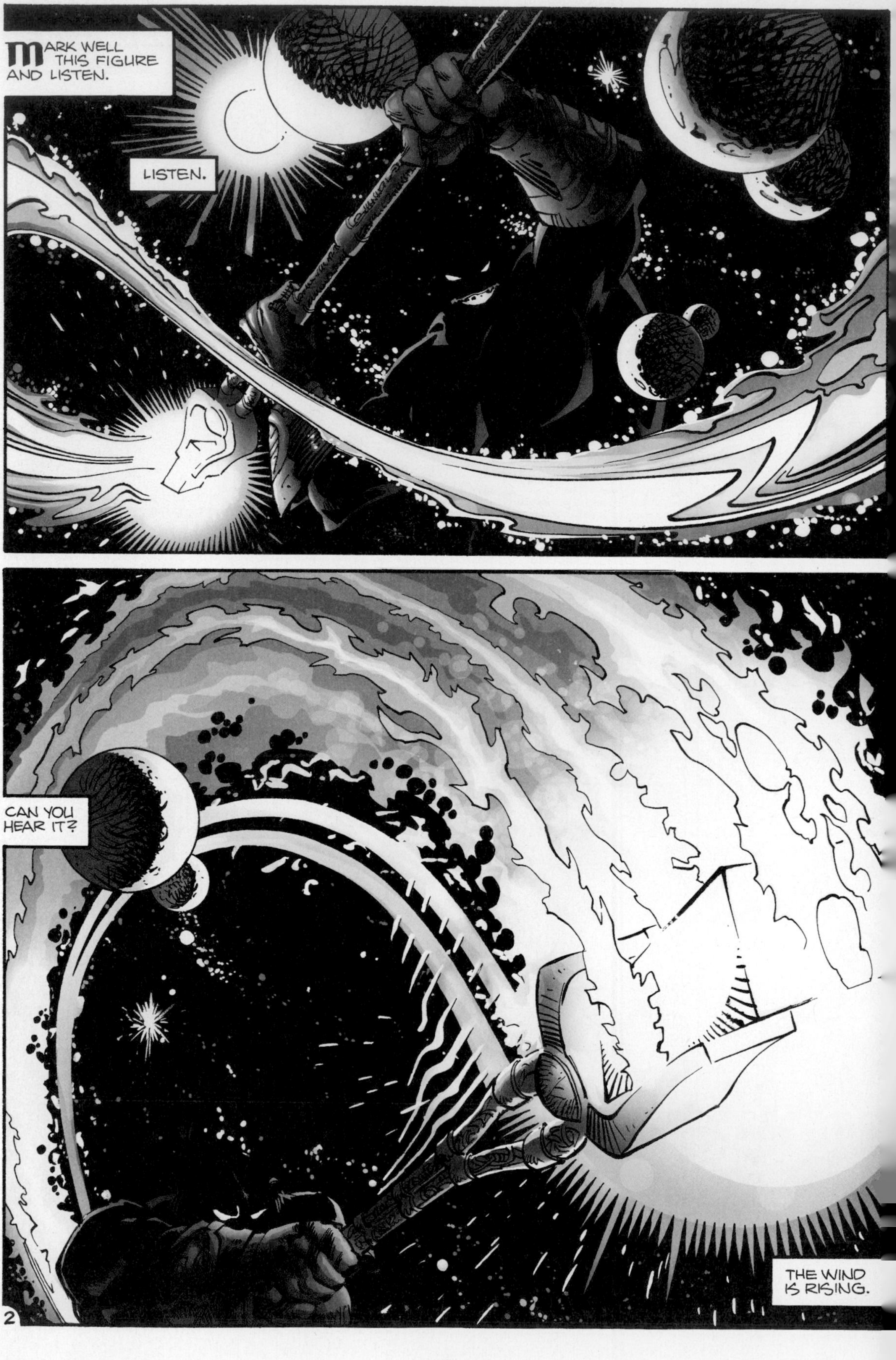
MARK WELL THIS FIGURE AND LISTEN.
LISTEN.
CAN YOU HEAR IT?
THE WIND IS RISING.
2

THE SOUND OF THUNDER REVERBERATES THROUGHOUT A BILLION BILLION WORLDS.

ON A BEAUTIFUL DAY LIKE TODAY, I ALMOST ENVY EVERY MORTAL I SEE.

FOR WHO COULD GUESS THAT WITHIN MY FRAIL BODY LIES THE SOUL AND POWER OF THE MIGHTY THOR, WAITING TO BE RELEASED BY A MERE TAP OF MY ENCHANTED CANE.

AND WITH THAT POWER COMES A MEASURE OF RESPONSIBILITY FAR BEYOND ANYTHING AN ORDINARY MAN COULD BEAR.

SOMETIMES, THE BURDEN IS SO HEAVY, I WISH I COULD SET ASIDE MY HERITAGE EVEN FOR A DAY AND BE A MAN, JUST A MAN.

YET EACH AND EVERY ONE OF THESE PEOPLE IS TIED TO THE EARTH, WHILE I AM FREE TO ROAM THE GLORY OF THE HEAVENS IF I CHOOSE.

TO SEE THINGS NO MORTAL HAS EVER DREAMED OF.

DESPITE ALL THE RESPONSIBILITIES IT IS NO BAD THING TO BE THE SON OF LORD ODIN.

WHA--?!

IS THIS SOME NEW ATTACK?

OH, GOOD GRIEF.

GEE, MISTER, SORRY ABOUT THAT. JOHN'S A LOUSY SHOT.

NO HARM DONE, MISS.

4

WHY NOT LET US BE THE JUDGES OF THAT, MISTER. A LAME GUY LIKE YOURSELF--YOU LOOK LIKE YOU COULD USE SOME HELP.

LET ME TAKE YOUR CANE.

HEY!

NOT TOO LOUD NOW, BUB. YOU'RE JUST GOING FOR A LITTLE RIDE.

THROW THE STICK IN, TOO, BOYS.

SURE THING, COLONEL.

YOU'RE ALL SET, SIR.

SLAM!

ANY IDEA WHAT'S GOING ON?

BEATS ME.

VARROOOOM!

WHAT DO YOU THINK YOU'RE--

COLONEL NICK FURY!

YOU WIN THE KEWPIE DOLL, DOCTOR BLAKE.

SORRY TA GRAB YA SO DRAMATIC-LIKE, BUT WE NEED YER HELP ...FAST!

HOLD ON TA YER HELMET.

I'M CONVERTIN' TA AERIAL MODE!

WHAT IS THIS, FURY? WHY DOES THE DIRECTOR OF SHIELD--

--NEED AN ORDINARY SAWBONES?

I DON'T. I NEED YOUR OTHER HALF!

WHAT DO YOU MEAN?

LOOK, DOC, I'LL LEVEL WITH YA.

WE GOT AN EMERGENCY ON OUR HANDS LIKE WE AIN'T SEEN BEFORE.

ONLY ONE GUY I KNOW OF CAN MAYBE HANDLE IT.

AND HE PACKS A HAMMER THAT MAKES OUR LATEST WEAPONS LOOK LIKE TINKERTOYS!

HOW...HOW DID YOU FIND OUT?

IT'S MY JOB, REMEMBER? I'M SUPPOSED TA KNOW STUFF.

BUT YA GOT MY WORD-- NOBODY ELSE IN OR OUT OF *SHIELD* KNOWS WHAT I KNOW.

SO WHAK YER MAGIC STICK THERE AND HANG ON, 'CAUSE WE'RE ALMOST HOME.

WHAK

BA-ROOMM!

YEEOW! WHY DIDN'T YA *WARN* ME ABOUT THE SPECIAL EFFECTS?

THOU DIDST NOT ASK.

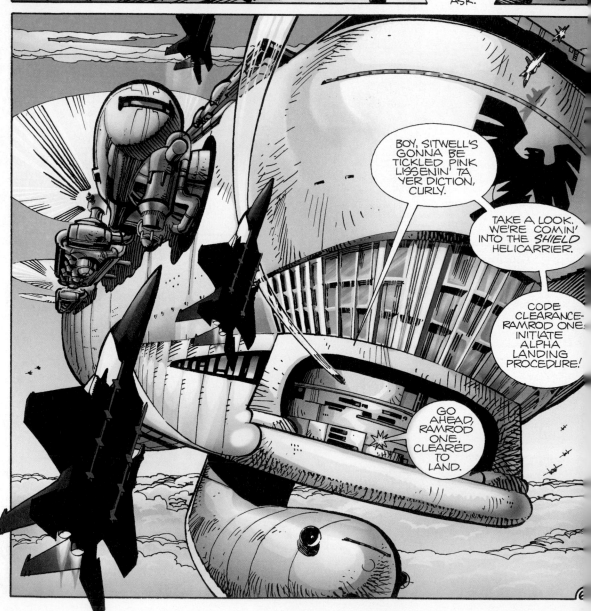

BOY, SITWELL'S GONNA BE TICKLED PINK LISSENIN' TA YER DICTION, CURLY.

TAKE A LOOK. WE'RE COMIN' INTO THE *SHIELD* HELICARRIER.

CODE CLEARANCE- RAMROD ONE. INITIATE ALPHA LANDING PROCEDURE!

GO AHEAD, RAMROD ONE, CLEARED TO LAND.

SHORTLY, IN A DARKENED SHIELD SCREENING ROOM...

SITWELL'S OUR LOCAL ENCYCLOPEDIA. IF HE DON'T KNOW IT, IT AIN'T A FACT!

OKAY, SITWELL, FILL IN OUR GUEST AND MAKE IT SNAPPY, HUH?

WELL, SIR, YOUR HONOR...AHEM...THIS IS THE VERY LATEST DEVELOPMENT FROM OUR TELEMETRY DIVISION.

AN EXPERIMENTAL WARP-DRIVEN PROBE CAPABLE OF COVERING UNIMAGINABLE DISTANCES AND TRANSMITTING PICTURES INSTANTANEOUSLY VIA HYPER-WAVE BACK TO A RECEIVER.

NAMELY US.

OPERATING ON AN ASSIGNED CARRIER FREQUENCY OF--

THE GUTS, SITWELL, JUST THE GUTS!

YESSIR! THESE ARE THE LAST PICTURES WE RECEIVED FROM THE PROBE. NOTE THE APPARENT VESSEL IN CENTER SCREEN.

AN ALIEN SHIP, UNLIKE ANYTHING WE'VE EVER SEEN BEFORE.

NOW WATCH THE STAR.

AS THE SHIP PASSED BY IT, THE STAR SUDDENLY FLARED TO LIFE...

...AND WAS SUCKED IN BY THE SHIP.

OUR EXPERTS THINK THE VESSEL WAS REFUELING AND DESTROYED AN ENTIRE STAR TO DO IT.

SHORTLY THEREAFTER, THE PROBE WAS DETECTED BY THE ALIEN SHIP AND ALL TRANSMISSION CEASED.

ACCORDING TO OUR BEST ESTIMATES, THE SHIP IS TRAVELING AT SEVERAL TIMES LIGHT SPEED...

...HEADING DIRECTLY FOR OUR SOLAR SYSTEM.

AND THE PROBE?

DEADER'N A DOORNAIL, THOR. BLOWN APART BY SOMETHING COMING OUR WAY.

SOMETHING REAL POWERFUL! AND DANGEROUS!

WE GOTTA FIND OUT WHAT IT IS! AND YER THE ONLY JOE WHO CAN DO IT!

WILL YA HELP US?

7

THE ANSWER IS NOT LONG IN COMING...

...YET EVEN AS THE MIGHTY THOR ARCS SKYWARD...

...FAR BEYOND THIS REALM OF SPACE AND TIME, IN THE GOLDEN HALLS OF ASGARD, HOME OF THE NORSE GODS, ALL IS NOT WELL.

AH, MILADY SIF, COME AND JOIN BALDER AND MYSELF IN A HEARTY REPAST.

WE'VE HARDLY BEGUN-- ONLY *SIXTEEN* COURSES SINCE BREAKFAST--AND BALDER IS LATELY GLUM COMPANY!

I CAN SCARCELY CREDIT IT!

8

BRAVE BALDER, I RETURN TO ASGARD FROM EARTH ONLY TO FIND YOU IN THE MEAD HALL WITH VOLSTAGG THE ENORMOUS, FEASTING WITHOUT RESPITE!

THOR HAS FORSAKEN ME FOR MIDGARD.*

*EARTH.

MY HEART, MY SOUL ARE EMPTY.

I NEED YOUR STRENGTH, YOUR UNDER-STANDING, YOUR TENDERNESS...

THEN SEEK SOLACE ELSEWHERE, LADY. BALDER THE BRAVE IS NO MORE.

HE WHO HAS RETURNED FROM HELA'S DARK DOMAIN IS NOT FIT TO BE A MAN MUCH LESS A GOD!

I HAVE FORSWORN ALL BATTLES SAVE THIS ONE--THAT I WILL FORGET EVERYTHING I HAVE EVER CHERISHED...

...DEFEATING AT LAST THE FEARFUL CURSE OF THE MEMORY OF THE GOD I ONCE WAS.

ETERNITY IS A LONG TIME, MILADY. BALDER THE BRAVE IS A MYTH I HAVE OUTLIVED.

SOMEONE APPROACHES HEIMDALL THE WATCHER.

BY WHOSE LEAVE DO YOU TREAD UPON BIFROST, THE RAINBOW BRIDGE?

IT IS I, SIF. I HAVE COME BECAUSE I HAVE NOWHERE ELSE TO TURN.

SIF, DEAR SISTER, I HAVE HEARD YOUR TROUBLES. WHAT WOULD YOU HAVE ME DO?

I AM A SHIELD MAIDEN, MY BROTHER. YOUR EYES AND EARS SEE AND HEAR ALL THINGS.

WHITHER CAN I FIND THE CLASH OF BATTLE TO MAKE ME HAPPY AND EASE MY EMPTINESS?

MY POOR DAR-LING. MAYHAP ONLY ODIN HIMSELF CAN HELP YOU NOW.

9

15

MEANWHILE, A LONG WAY FROM EARTH...

THE POWER OF MY ENCHANTED MALLET TO CROSS TIME AND SPACE HAS BROUGHT ME CLOSE TO THE ALIEN VESSEL...

...AND RESTORED MY FAITH IN MY HERITAGE! WHAT MORTAL COULD DO WHAT I HAVE DONE?

'TIS GOOD TO BE THE GOD OF THUNDER!

ODIN'S BLOOD! THE SHIP OUTRACES ME AS THE HARE OUTRACES THE TORTOISE!

I MUST INCREASE MY SPEED A HUNDREDFOLD IF I AM TO OVERTAKE YON VESSEL.

BUT OVERTAKE IT I SHALL!

ITS APPEARANCE REFLECTS A GRIM AND SERIOUS PURPOSE. T'WOULD SEEM TO BE A WARSHIP!

CHIKCHIKCHIK

SENSORS DETECT UNIDENTIFIED PURSUER ON INTERCEPT COURSE. ENERGY CONFIGURATIONS SIMILAR TO DEMON BREED. PREPARE TO OPEN FIRE.

MAIN BATTERIES CHARGED AND READY.

TARGET LOCKED MAGNIFICATION THREE.

TARGET CLOSING.

10

16

FIRE!

BY THE GOLDEN SPIRES OF ASGARD!

AN ENERGY BOLT OF PURE FORCE!

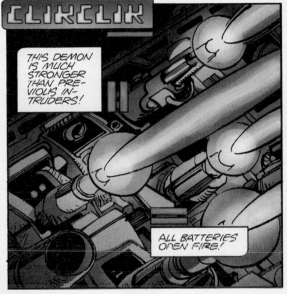

CLIKCLIK

THIS DEMON IS MUCH STRONGER THAN PREVIOUS INTRUDERS!

ALL BATTERIES OPEN FIRE!

AGAIN THE VESSEL DIRECTS AN UNPROVOKED ATTACK AT ME!

SO BE IT!

LET THE HAMMER OF THOR SPEAK FOR ME NOW!

THRAAKKT

AS EVER, MY HAMMER RETURNS TO ME...

...AND NOW, BEFORE A FURTHER ATTACK CAN BEGIN...

...I SHALL AVOID THE DEADLY WEAPONRY AND ENTER THE SHIP AS ONLY THE GOD OF THUNDER CAN!

PERHAPS INSIDE I CAN DISCOVER THE PURPOSE OF THIS DEADLY VESSEL.

ALL AROUND ME I CAN HEAR THE HUM OF THE MIGHTY STAR-DRIVEN ENGINES...

...WHILE BEHIND ME, THE HULL SEALS ITSELF SHUT LIKE A LIVING THING!

BUT IF THIS IS TRULY A LIVING MECHANISM, THEN SURELY THAT CRYSTAL MUST BE ITS HEART!

YET WHAT LIES HERE AT ITS VERY CENTER?

A FIGURE OF SOME SIZE.

PERHAPS-- EH?

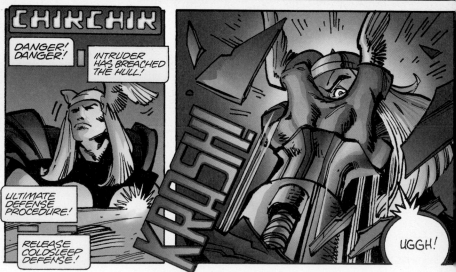

CHIKCHIK

DANGER! DANGER!

INTRUDER HAS BREACHED THE HULL!

ULTIMATE DEFENSE PROCEDURE!

RELEASE COLDSLEEP DEFENSE!

KRASH!

UGGH!

12

BUT EVEN AS THOR STRUGGLES FOR BREATH, LET US TURN TO A DESOLATE CORNER OF ASGARD TO FIND...

I AM BORED TO DEATH!

TO THINK THAT LOKI, PRINCE OF DARKNESS, SHOULD WASTE HIS TIME IN MONOTONOUS EXILE WHILE CHEER AND GOOD FELLOWSHIP ABOUND IN THE LAND.

BAH! I'VE HALF A MIND TO...

...BUT SOFTLY! WHAT'S THIS I HEAR?

WHO DARES TO PASS SO CLOSE TO LOKI'S LONELY ABODE?

"SO! A FEW LACKWIT WARRIORS VENTURE TO ENGAGE IN A FORBIDDEN TROLL HUNT!"

"I BELIEVE THE END OF MY BOREDOM IS AT HAND!"

PUFF PUFF

MUST HIDE! MUST HIDE! OR HUNTERS SLAY ME!

DID YOU SEE?

YES, HELGI, THE TROLL'S GONE TO COVER IN THOSE THISTLES!

BY YMIR'S BEARD, WE MAY NEVER FLUSH HIM NOW!

LITTLE ONE! PSST! LITTLE ONE!

HUH?

DO NOT BE AFRAID, LITTLE TROLL. I CAN HELP YOU. I CAN HIDE YOU.

IT! GIRL! SHE...SHE BEAUTIFUL!

COME. LOOK AT ME. GIVE ME YOUR HAND...

...AND FEAR NOTHING.

LOOK AT ME.

I...

WHITHER AWAY, MY LORDS?

WHA--?

IT'S LORELEI! WITH THE TROLL! SHE'S WON THE HUNT!

JUST AS I FORETOLD YOU!

WEAPONS AND STRENGTH ARE NOT EVERYTHING, MY LORDS.

INDEED, MILADY. AS NONE KNOW BETTER THAN I.

I THINK WE SHOULD DISCUSS THIS FURTHER. WILL YOU NOT ACCOMPANY ME BACK TO MY HUMBLE DWELLING?

PERHAPS I SHALL, MY LORD.

LORELEI, YOU'D BEST LEAVE WITH US. THE OPEN HAND OF LOKI IS NOT SAFE!

NOR WILL YOU BE SAFE IF ODIN LEARNS OF THIS HUNT! LEAVE US AND FORGET WHAT HAS HAPPENED HERE...

...OR THE NEXT HAND OF LOKI YOU SEE WILL BE FILLED WITH MENACE

14

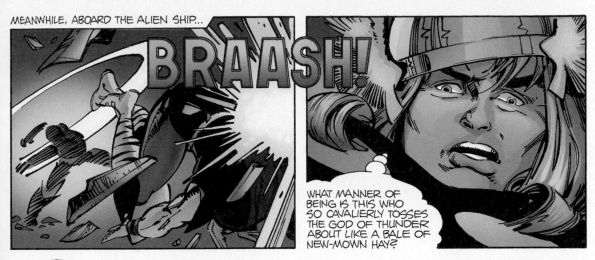

BRAASH!

WHAT MANNER OF BEING IS THIS WHO SO CAVALIERLY TOSSES THE GOD OF THUNDER ABOUT LIKE A BALE OF NEW-MOWN HAY?

RISE UP, DEMON!

YOU HAVE PURSUED ME ONLY TO FIND DEATH!

AND WHEN I AM THROUGH WITH YOU, YOU WILL WELCOME IT!

I AM CALLED BILL--*BETA RAY BILL!*

15

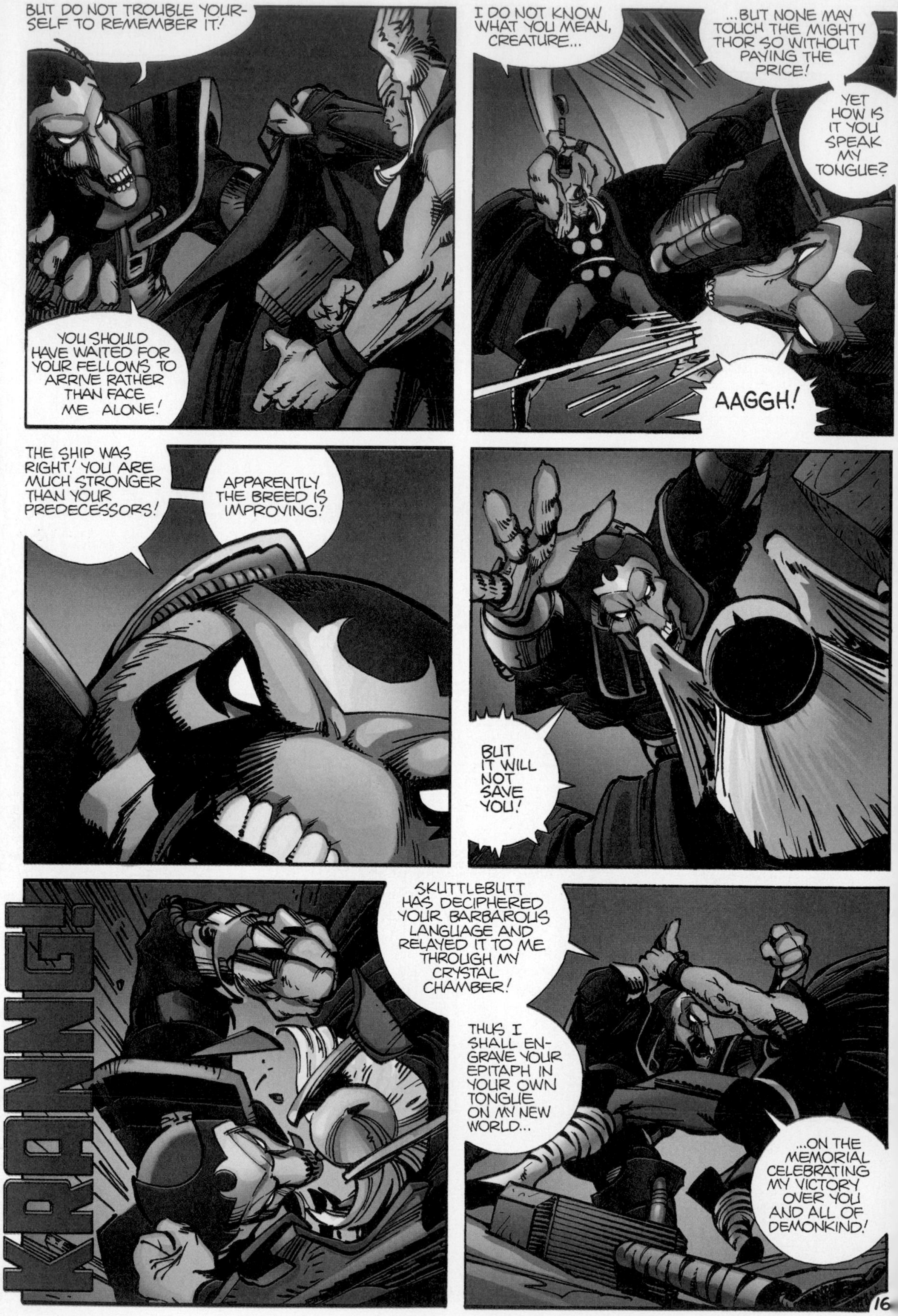
BUT DO NOT TROUBLE YOURSELF TO REMEMBER IT!
YOU SHOULD HAVE WAITED FOR YOUR FELLOWS TO ARRIVE RATHER THAN FACE ME ALONE!
I DO NOT KNOW WHAT YOU MEAN, CREATURE...
...BUT NONE MAY TOUCH THE MIGHTY THOR SO WITHOUT PAYING THE PRICE!
YET HOW IS IT YOU SPEAK MY TONGUE?
AAGGH!
THE SHIP WAS RIGHT! YOU ARE MUCH STRONGER THAN YOUR PREDECESSORS!
APPARENTLY THE BREED IS IMPROVING!
BUT IT WILL NOT SAVE YOU!
KRANG!
SKUTTLEBUTT HAS DECIPHERED YOUR BARBAROUS LANGUAGE AND RELAYED IT TO ME THROUGH MY CRYSTAL CHAMBER!
THUS I SHALL ENGRAVE YOUR EPITAPH IN YOUR OWN TONGUE ON MY NEW WORLD...
...ON THE MEMORIAL CELEBRATING MY VICTORY OVER YOU AND ALL OF DEMONKIND!
16

YOU STILL SPEAK IN RIDDLES, WARRIOR...

...BUT IT IS CLEAR TO ME THAT I CAN NEVER PERMIT SUCH A DANGEROUS ENTITY TO REACH EARTH...

...EVEN IF I MUST DESTROY THIS SHIP FROM WITHIN TO STOP YOU!

CHIKCHIK

INTERNAL MONITORS INDICATE GRAVE DAMAGE TO SURVIVAL AND WEAPONS SYSTEMS.

IMMEDIATE LANDING NECESSARY TO EFFECT REPAIRS. BEGIN INSTRUMENT SEARCH FOR POTENTIAL SITES!

CURSÉD DEMON! YOUR DEATH WILL BE AN UNCLEAN ONE FOR THIS DELAY!

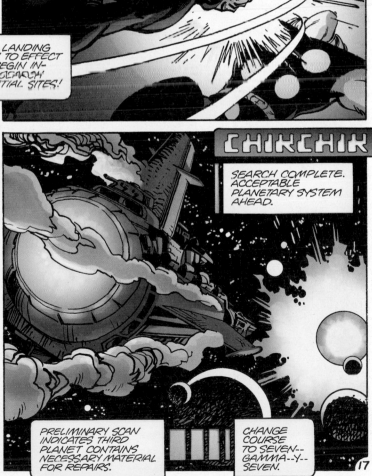

CHIKCHIK

SEARCH COMPLETE. ACCEPTABLE PLANETARY SYSTEM AHEAD.

PRELIMINARY SCAN INDICATES THIRD PLANET CONTAINS NECESSARY MATERIAL FOR REPAIRS.

CHANGE COURSE TO SEVEN-- GAMMA--Y-- SEVEN.

17

NEVER HAVE I BEEN SO WELL MATCHED BY ANY MORTAL, BUT THOUGH I RELISH THE STRUGGLE, IT MUST END NOW!

WILL YOU YIELD, WARRIOR?

ONLY IN DEATH!

CHIKCHIK

LANDING MODE CONFIRMED.

SHIP NOW ENTERING THE PLANE OF THE ECLIPTIC OF THE THIRD PLANET.

YOU LEAVE ME NO CHOICE. I MUST--

BY MY TROTH!

WHAT WEAKNESS SUDDENLY ASSAILS ME?

OH, NO! NOT NOW! NOT LIKE THIS!

WE MUST BE CLOSING FAST WITH EARTH AND WITHOUT MY HAMMER IN MY HAND, I'VE REVERTED TO MY BLAKE FORM!

I'VE GOT TO--

YOU'LL DO NOTHING, DEMON!

YOU MAY HAVE CHANGED YOUR SHAPE... BUT IT CERTAINLY SEEMS ILL SUITED FOR COMBAT!

UHHH!

18

24

I DO NOT UNDERSTAND THE DEMON'S TRANSFORMATION...

...BUT IT WOULD BE UNWISE TO QUESTION SUCH A GIFT HORSE TOO CLOSELY!

CHIKCHIK

ATTENTION! ATTENTION! CRASH LANDING PROCEDURES INITIATED!

PLANETFALL IN THIRTY SECONDS!

QUICKLY, SKUTTLEBUTT.

ENERGIZE A STASIS EGG AROUND ME NOW!

MOMENTS LATER, THE FURIOUS FLIGHT OF THE ALIEN SHIP THUNDERS TO A FIERY END...

AND INSIDE...

THE STASIS FIELD HELD. I AM ALIVE AND UNHARMED.

AND IT WOULD SEEM THAT THE DEMON HAS SURVIVED WITHIN THE FIELD AS WELL.

SOMETHING I WILL ATTEND TO IN A MOMENT.

SKUTTLEBUTT, REPORT STATUS.

CHIKCHIK

WEAPONS CAPABILITY DOWN TO 5%--REPAIR TIME IS 40 HOURS TO LIFTOFF. SCANNERS DETECT APPROACHING VEHICLES WITH CLASS 3 LIFE FORMS.

IN OUR CURRENT STATE, THEY COULD DESTROY US.

I AM ALSO RECEIVING A BROADCAST FROM ONE OF THE VEHICLES IN A VARIANT OF THE DEMON'S LANGUAGE.

19

HEADS UP IN THE SHIP! THIS IS NICK FURY, DIRECTOR OF SHIELD TALKIN' AT YA!

WE GOT YA SURROUNDED! WADDYA SAY YOU COME OUT PEACE-ABLE AND WE'LL TALK!

THE DEMON'S WEAPON! THE HAMMER HE WIELD-ED SO POWERFULLY!

IT COULD BE MY ONLY CHANCE TO SAVE MY MISSION!

BUT WHERE...?

WHAT'S THIS? A STICK?

THE HAMMER HAS VANISHED!

THUNDER AND LIGHTNING!

THAK!

WHA--?!

I...I HAVE THE POWER! THE STICK WAS THE HAMMER!

AND NOW I...I CAN FEEL THE POWER OF THE DEMON HIM-SELF ADDED TO MY OWN!

POWER ENOUGH TO SHAKE THIS PLANET TO ITS FOUNDATIONS!

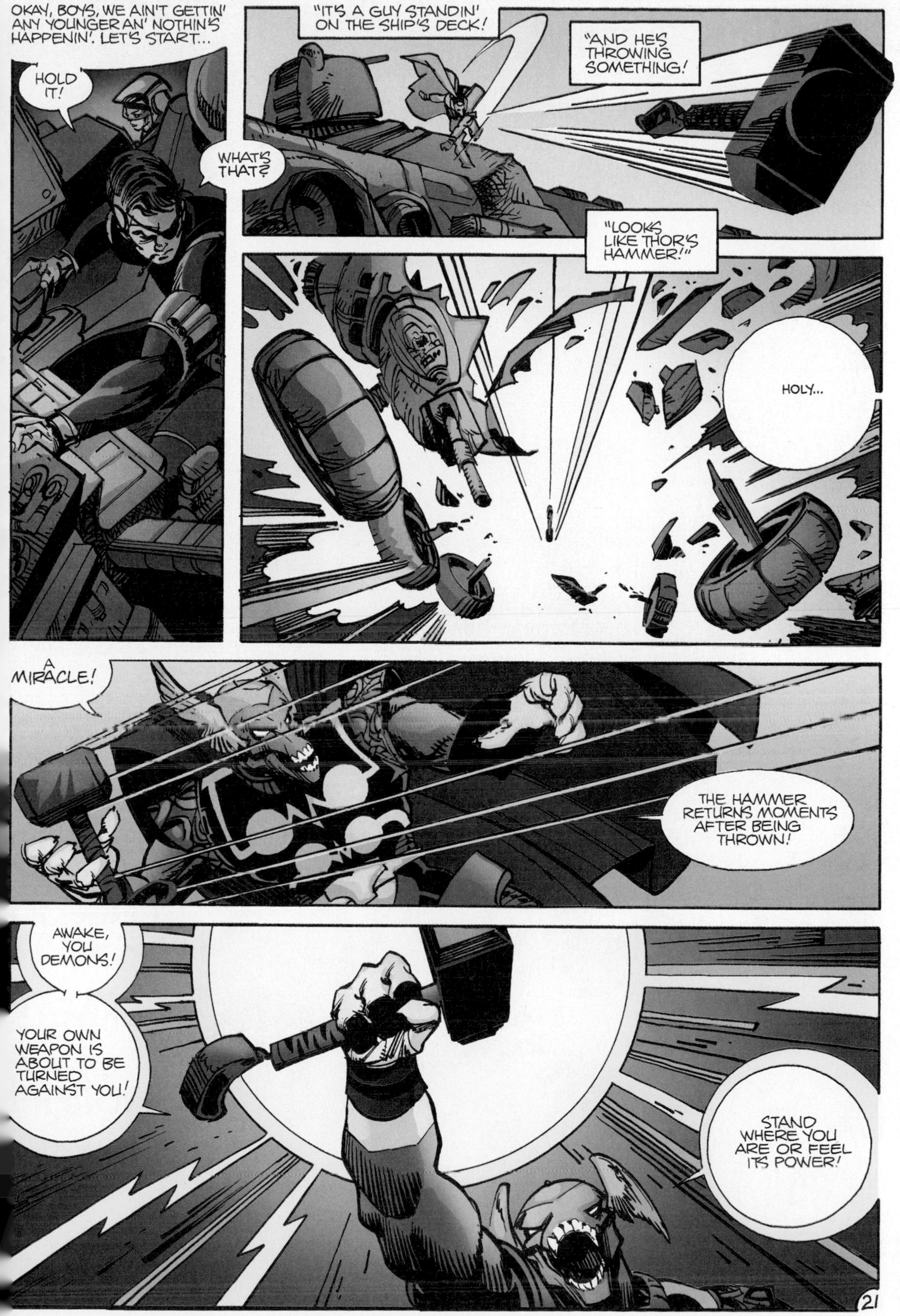
OKAY, BOYS, WE AIN'T GETTIN' ANY YOUNGER AN' NOTHIN'S HAPPENIN'. LET'S START...
HOLD IT!
WHAT'S THAT?
"IT'S A GUY STANDIN' ON THE SHIP'S DECK!
"AND HE'S THROWING SOMETHING!
"LOOKS LIKE THOR'S HAMMER!"
HOLY...
A MIRACLE!
THE HAMMER RETURNS MOMENTS AFTER BEING THROWN!
AWAKE, YOU DEMONS!
YOUR OWN WEAPON IS ABOUT TO BE TURNED AGAINST YOU!
STAND WHERE YOU ARE OR FEEL ITS POWER!
21

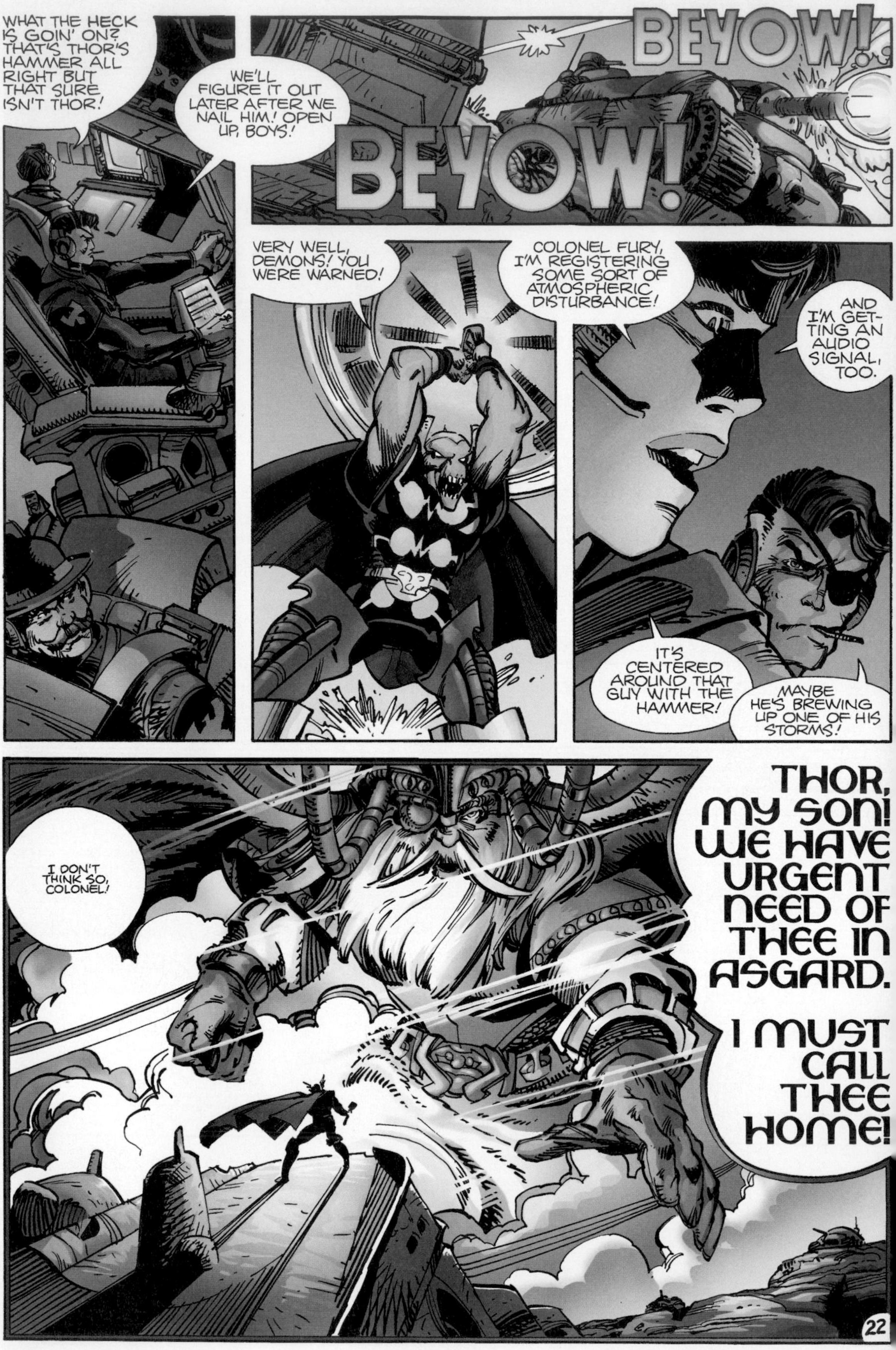

WHAT THE HECK IS GOIN' ON? THAT'S THOR'S HAMMER ALL RIGHT BUT THAT SURE ISN'T THOR!
WE'LL FIGURE IT OUT LATER AFTER WE NAIL HIM! OPEN UP, BOYS!
BEYOW!
BEYOW!
VERY WELL, DEMONS! YOU WERE WARNED!
COLONEL FURY, I'M REGISTERING SOME SORT OF ATMOSPHERIC DISTURBANCE!
AND I'M GETTING AN AUDIO SIGNAL, TOO.
IT'S CENTERED AROUND THAT GUY WITH THE HAMMER!
MAYBE HE'S BREWING UP ONE OF HIS STORMS!
I DON'T THINK SO, COLONEL!
THOR, MY SON! WE HAVE URGENT NEED OF THEE IN ASGARD.
I MUST CALL THEE HOME!
22

BARROOOOM!

HE'S GONE! THEY'RE BOTH GONE!

AND I GOT A FEELIN' SOMEBODY'S GETTIN' THE SURPRISE OF THEIR LIFE RIGHT ABOUT NOW!

BUT THAT SHIP'S STILL HERE...

...AND IT COULD STILL BE DANGEROUS!

SIGNAL EVERYBODY TA ADVANCE... REAL CAREFUL LIKE.

LOOK, SIR! THERE'S SOMEBODY ELSE CRAWLING OUT OF THE SHIP!

HOLD YER FIRE! IF THAT'S WHO I THINK IT IS, WE COULD ALL BE IN BIG TROUBLE!

MY CANE IS GONE! AND SOMEHOW I KNOW THAT THAT ALIEN IS RESPONSIBLE.

BUT THE ATMOSPHERE, THE STORM! ODIN WAS HERE!

HIS PRESENCE STILL LINGERS! AND HE DID NOT TAKE ME!

ONLY A FEW HOURS AGO, I NEARLY ENVIED THE MORTALS AROUND ME!

AND NOW, I MAY HAVE TO JOIN THEM... FOREVER!

FATHER! HEAR ME!

DO NOT FORSAKE ME HERE!

23

29

FATHER!

BUT THE LASHING STORM DOES NOT LISTEN.

AND ONLY THE WIND AND RAIN REPLY.

ART AND STORY: WALTER SIMONSON · LETTERING: JOHN WORKMAN, JR. · COLORS: GEORGE ROUSSOS
EDITING: MARK GRUENWALD · EDITOR-IN-CHIEF: JIM SHOOTER

NEXT--A FOOL AND HIS HAMMER...

BE HERE!
'CAUSE WE'LL MISS YOU IF YOU'RE NOT AROUND.

WHOSOEVER HOLDS
THIS HAMMER, IF HE BE
WORTHY, SHALL
POSSESS THE POWER OF
THOR

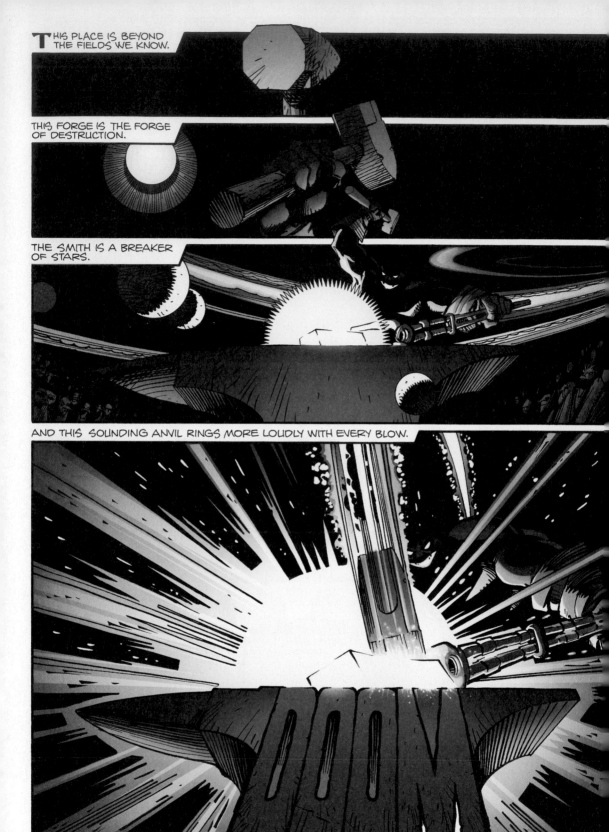

THIS PLACE IS BEYOND THE FIELDS WE KNOW.

THIS FORGE IS THE FORGE OF DESTRUCTION.

THE SMITH IS A BREAKER OF STARS.

AND THIS SOUNDING ANVIL RINGS MORE LOUDLY WITH EVERY BLOW.

DOOM

STAN LEE PRESENTS: the MIGHTY THOR

ORDINARILY, DR. DONALD BLAKE CAN SIMPLY TAP HIS ENCHANTED CANE AND BE TRANSFORMED INTO THE MIGHTY THOR, AS THE CANE BECOMES HIS MIGHTY HAMMER, MJOLNIR.

BUT THE HAMMER HAS BEEN CARRIED OFF BY THOR'S RECENT FOE, BETA RAY BILL, WHO WAS HIMSELF TRANSFORMED BY THE MAGIC WEAPON...

...LEAVING A DESPERATE DONALD BLAKE STRANDED ON EARTH, TRAPPED WITHIN HIS MORTAL IDENTITY...

ODIN! FATHER ODIN!

HEAR ME!

A FOOL AND HIS HAMMER...

HEAR ME.

IT'S NO USE. THE HAMMER'S GONE AND WITHOUT IT, I'M DOOMED TO REMAIN A MORTAL, UNABLE TO CONTACT ASGARD OR ODIN, MY FATHER.

WHAT WILL I DO? WHAT WILL I DO? ODIN, HELP ME.

DON'T TAKE IT TOO HARD, DOC. I EXPECT IT'LL ALL WORK OUT EVENTUALLY.

COLONEL FURY! I... I SHOULD HAVE KNOWN YOU'D BE HERE.

I'VE LOST EVERYTHING, NICK! THERE WAS AN ALIEN ON BOARD THIS SHIP. WE FOUGHT AND I TURNED BACK INTO DON BLAKE AT THE WRONG MOMENT.

HE KNOCKED ME OUT AND NOW IT LOOKS AS THOUGH HE'S TAKEN MY HAMMER. THAT'S NEVER HAPPENED BEFORE. AND WITHOUT MJOLNIR, I'M MAROONED HERE, PERHAPS FOREVER.

MAYBE NOT, DOC. AN OLD GUY WITH ONE EYE APPEARED AND THEN VANISHED, TAKING THE ALIEN WITH HIM.

SURE THING, DOC. SHIELD'S BEEN TRACKIN' THIS SHIP ALL THE WAY. THOUGHT YA MIGHT NEED A LITTLE HELP WHEN IT CRASHED ON EARTH.

LOOKS LIKE WE WERE RIGHT. YOU OKAY?

IF THAT WAS YER OLD MAN, HE AIN'T GONNA BE REAL HAPPY TO SEE SOMEBODY ELSE WEARIN' YER THREADS AND HEFTIN' YER HAMMER

34

ELSEWHERE IN ASGARD, LEGENDARY HOME OF THE NORSE GODS...

'TIS THOR!

LORD ODIN HAS RECALLED HIM FROM MIDGARD.*

TRULY ONLY HE CAN HELP US NOW IN THIS, OUR HOUR OF NEED.

*EARTH.

BACK, DEMONS! YOU'VE MORE TRICKS ABOUT YOU THAN I DREAMED OF BUT IT WILL AVAIL YOU NAUGHT!

WHO... WHO ARE YOU THAT WEARS THE COSTUME AND CARRIES THE HAMMER OF THE MIGHTY THOR?

NO ASGARDIAN COULD EVEN LIFT THE ENCHANTED MALLET, LET ALONE DEFEAT THOR IN BATTLE.

IT IS NOT FOR YOU TO QUESTION ME! TELL ME RATHER WHERE THIS PLACE IS... AND WHO YOU DEMONS SERVE.

BETA RAY BILL'S ONSLAUGHT IS DEADLY AND OVERWHELMING! BUT THE SHOCK OF THE ATTACK SCARCELY EQUALS THE ASGARDIAN'S SUBSEQUENT SURPRISE!

35

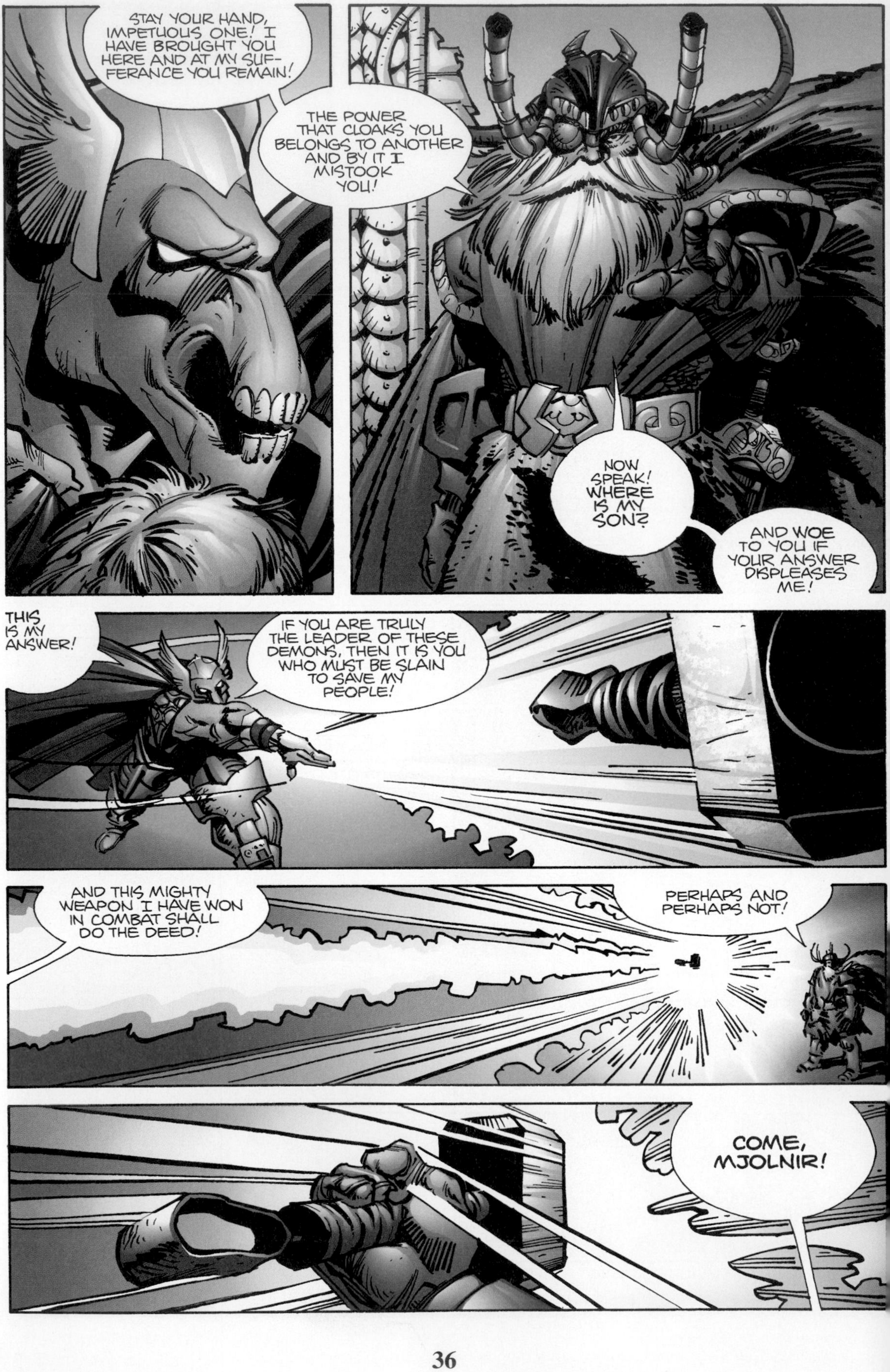
STAY YOUR HAND, IMPETUOUS ONE! I HAVE BROUGHT YOU HERE AND AT MY SUF-FERANCE YOU REMAIN!
THE POWER THAT CLOAKS YOU BELONGS TO ANOTHER AND BY IT I MISTOOK YOU!
NOW SPEAK! WHERE IS MY SON?
AND WOE TO YOU IF YOUR ANSWER DISPLEASES ME!
THIS IS MY ANSWER!
IF YOU ARE TRULY THE LEADER OF THESE DEMONS, THEN IT IS YOU WHO MUST BE SLAIN TO SAVE MY PEOPLE!
AND THIS MIGHTY WEAPON I HAVE WON IN COMBAT SHALL DO THE DEED!
PERHAPS AND PERHAPS NOT!
COME, MJOLNIR!

STRIKE NOT YOUR CREATOR NOR RETURN TO THIS FALSE MASTER!

WHERE IS THOR?

WHERE IS MY SON?

I KNOW NOT WHO YOU MEAN!

BUT I FAIRLY WON THE HAMMER IN COMBAT AND NOT ALL YOUR POWER CAN CHANGE THAT!

YOUR VOICE HAS THE RING OF TRUTH!

LET ME STAY MY WRATH A MOMENT AND SEEK TO KNOW MORE OF THIS MATTER.

EVEN THOR'S PRODIGIOUS STRENGTH WOULD BE HARD PUT TO SHATTER A VESSEL OF ETHEREAL FORCE.

AND NOW WE SHALL LEARN WHAT WE MUST, NO MATTER THE COST!

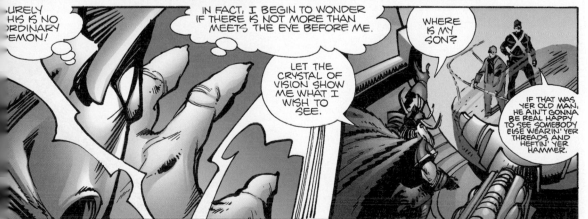

SURELY THIS IS NO ORDINARY DEMON!

IN FACT, I BEGIN TO WONDER IF THERE IS NOT MORE THAN MEETS THE EYE BEFORE ME.

LET THE CRYSTAL OF VISION SHOW ME WHAT I WISH TO SEE.

WHERE IS MY SON?

IF THAT WAS YER OLD MAN, HE AIN'T GONNA BE REAL HAPPY TO SEE SOMEBODY ELSE WEARIN' YER THREADS AND HEFTIN' YER HAMMER.

FACT IS, I'M SURPRISED HE HASN'T...

IS IT MY IMAGINATION OR IS IT GETTIN' DARKER?

I HOPE IT WASN'T SOMETHIN' I SAID.

BARROOM

YEOW! NOT AGAIN!

NOW DOC'S GONE, TOO. BROTHER, THIS IS GONNA MAKE ONE HECK OF A REPORT!

WELL, GOOD LUCK, BLAKE, I THINK YER GONNA NEED IT.

IT LOOKS LIKE IT'S STARTIN' TO RAIN AGAIN, TOO.

SWELL. DON'T THESE GUYS EVER TRAVEL IN DRY WEATHER?

AT THAT MOMENT, ON ASGARD...

FATHER!

WELCOME HOME, MY SON. HOW STANDS THY ZEST FOR ADVENTURE NOW?

UNABATED, MY LORD. THOUGH I CONFESS THAT A MOMENT AGO, I FEARED THAT PERHAPS ALL MY ADVENTURES WERE OVER.

AH, MY YOUTHFUL SON, DOES THIS MEAN THAT YOUR MORTAL FRIEND HAS MORE FAITH IN A ONE-EYED VISION THAN MY BOY HAS IN HIS OWN FATHER?

38

THAT FRIEND HAD NOT HAD HIS WITS KNOCKED ABOUT BY A SUPERB FIGHTER.

MY MORTAL GUISE IS POORLY EQUIPPED FOR BATTLE.

AYE, WE MAY HAVE TO ATTEND TO THAT. BUT NOW IT IS TIME TO LEARN MORE OF THIS AFFAIR.

FIRST, I MUST FREE THE WARRIOR.

MIGHTY STRANGER, WILL YOU FORGIVE MY ANGER OF A MOMENT AGO?

IT WAS THE HONEST REACTION OF A FRIGHTENED PARENT.

I ASK YOU PLEASE TO ACCEPT THE HOSPITALITY OF MY HOME.

SUCH BONDS OF LOVE AS I SEE BETWEEN FATHER AND SON PERSUADE ME THAT WHATEVER YOU ARE, YOU ARE NOT DEMONS.

I ACCEPT.

THEN FOLLOW ME UP THE MOUNTAINS. WE WILL CONVERSE ON HLIDSKJALF, THE HIGH SEAT, ITSELF!

FROM THERE, WE CAN SEE ALL THE NINE WORLDS AND PERHAPS WE SHALL LOOK CLEARLY INTO EACH OTHER'S HEARTS.

LET ME BEGIN. I AM ODIN, SON OF BOR, SON OF BURI, AND LORD OF ASGARD. THIS IS MY SON, THOR.

SINCE THE DAWN OF TIME, NONE BUT WE HAVE EVER LIFTED MJOLNIR, THE ENCHANTED HAMMER.

UNTIL NOW.

SIT BESIDE US, STRANGER, AND TELL US OF YOURSELF.

MEANWHILE, BELOW THE HIGH SEAT, AT THE GARDEN ENTRANCE TO ODIN'S NOBLE HALL, WE FIND THE LADY SIF...

AND THOUGH MY LOVE SURPASSES UNDERSTANDING, I CANNOT SHARE THOR'S JOY FOR EARTH.

BUT WHAT'S THIS I HEAR?

MY BROTHER, HEIMDALL THE WATCHER, MAY BE RIGHT. ONLY ODIN HIMSELF CAN HELP ME EASE MY EMPTY HEART NOW THAT THOR AND I ARE NO LONGER PROMISED TO EACH OTHER.

WOULD THAT ODIN HAD NEVER GIVEN THOR HIS MORTAL IDENTITY SO LONG AGO. I STILL LOVE THE NOBLE WARRIOR BUT HIS HEART MAY EVER BE DIVIDED BETWEEN ASGARD AND MIDGARD.

SURELY MY SENSES DECEIVE ME!

AH, LADY LORELEI, TO FEEL YOUR ARMS ENTWINED ABOUT ME, YOUR SWEET BREATH UPON MY FACE, YOUR LIPS PRESSED TO MINE... 'TIS ALL THAT I DESIRE.

FOR SUCH KISSES, I WOULD FORSAKE EVEN MIDGARD ITSELF!

SO.

I..., UH... I... MILADY SIF?

THOUGH MY OWN BREATH IS LESS SWEET, MY LORD THOR, ACCEPT THIS PARTING KISS...

THE KISS OF A WARRIOR BORN AND NO SOFT PLAYTHING!

AS FOR YOU, YOU BAWD, I LEAVE THOR TO YOUR TENDER EMBRACES! BUT HAVE A CARE!

FALSE HEART ONCE IS FALSE HEART FOREVER!

SPUTTER SPUT

HAHAHA! WHAT A RARE JEST! A WONDERFUL FOLLY!

AH, LORELEI, I WOULD HOLD YOU IN MY ARMS FOR-EVER FOR SUCH SPORT AS THIS.

PERHAPS, MY LORD, I WOULD NOT HAVE UNDER-TAKEN THIS JEST HAD I KNOWN BEFORE-HAND THAT IT WOULD BE SO DANGEROUS!

NONSENSE!

THE LADY SIF WILL NOW SHORTLY DEPART THIS IMMORTAL SPHERE.

AND YOU, MY SWEETLING...

...MAY YET SUCCEED WHERE YOUR SISTER, THE ENCHANTRESS...

...HAS EVER FAILED.

BUT EVEN AS LOKI CHORTLES IN HIS GLEE, WE RETURN TO THE HIGH SEAT AND ITS OCCUPANTS...

LISTEN WELL THEN, LORDS, AND I WILL TELL MY TALE, THE STORY OF BETA RAY BILL.

MINE IS AN ANCIENT AND NOBLE RACE THAT HAS LIVED IN THE HEART OF A GALAXY FROM TIME IMMEMORIAL.

WE BUILT OUR CITIES IN THE BURNING SKIES AND DANCED IN THE SUNLIGHT.

41

"FOR LONG AGES WE DWELT THERE IN HARMONY, UNTIL WITHOUT WARNING, THE CORE OF OUR GALAXY EXPLODED, DESTROYING MUCH OF OUR CIVILIZATION.

"I ALONE WAS CHOSEN BY OUR LEADERS TO BE THE GUARDIAN OF THE EXODUS...

"... AND SO I WAS... CHANGED TO SUIT MY TASK.

"OUR SCIENTISTS TOOK THE MOST FEROCIOUS CARNIVORE OF OUR EMPIRE AND BIO-ENGINEERED IT TO PRODUCE A WARRIOR OF SURPASSING SKILL AND STRENGTH.

"WHEN ALL WAS MADE READY, MY SOUL WAS FITTED TO THE BODY AND I BECAME THE PROTECTOR OF MY PEOPLE.

"THE SURVIVORS WERE FORCED TO FLEE FOR, AS TIME PASSED, THE REMAINING GALACTIC CORE GREW HOTTER THAN WE COULD WITHSTAND.

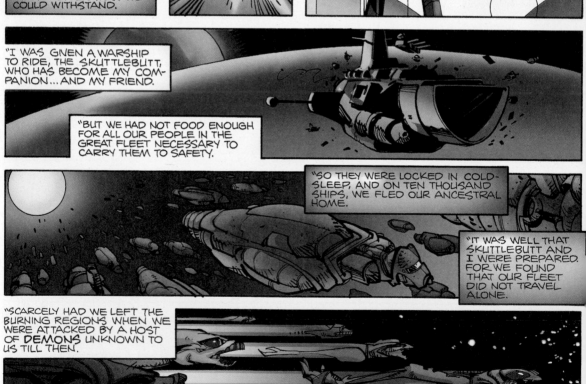

"I WAS GIVEN A WARSHIP TO RIDE, THE SKUTTLEBUTT, WHO HAS BECOME MY COMPANION... AND MY FRIEND.

"BUT WE HAD NOT FOOD ENOUGH FOR ALL OUR PEOPLE IN THE GREAT FLEET NECESSARY TO CARRY THEM TO SAFETY.

"SO THEY WERE LOCKED IN COLD-SLEEP, AND ON TEN THOUSAND SHIPS, WE FLED OUR ANCESTRAL HOME.

"IT WAS WELL THAT SKUTTLEBUTT AND I WERE PREPARED, FOR WE FOUND THAT OUR FLEET DID NOT TRAVEL ALONE.

"SCARCELY HAD WE LEFT THE BURNING REGIONS WHEN WE WERE ATTACKED BY A HOST OF **DEMONS** UNKNOWN TO US TILL THEN.

"THEY CAME OUT OF THE FIERY CORE HARD ON OUR HEELS AND HARRIED US AND DESTROYED THOSE THEY CAUGHT.

"SKUTTLEBUTT AND I FOUGHT THEM UNTIL OUR PEOPLE HAD DRAWN AWAY SAFELY. THEN WE FLED AND ESCAPED BUT THE DEMONS TURNED AND FOLLOWED US.

"I SPED ON AHEAD OF THE FLEET, SEARCHING FOR SANCTUARY AND FINDING NONE.

THE PURSUIT STILL GOES ON ACROSS COUNTLESS LIGHT-YEARS. THEY ARE SLOWLY OVERTAKING US BUT WE CANNOT FIND A HAVEN.

NOW I HAVE FOUND A WEAPON THAT MAY PROTECT MY PEOPLE FOR ALL TIME, AND I AM LOATH TO GIVE IT UP.

ESPECIALLY AS I HAVE WON IT IN FAIR COMBAT.

WHAT?

I SAY THEE **NAY**, NOBLE WARRIOR.

IT WAS **NOT** THOR THOU DID DEFEAT BUT A MORTAL SHELL! I--!

BE STILL, MY SON. HE HAS A POINT.

YET, TRULY, MIGHTY BILL, THE COMBAT YOU SPEAK OF WAS NOT ENTIRELY FAIR.

IN THOSE DAYS, THOR WAS PROUD AND HEADSTRONG. I SOUGHT TO TEACH HIM THE WISDOM OF PATIENCE.

IN MY OWN PRIDE, I FASHIONED A MAGIC ABOUT THE HAMMER.

FOR MY SON FOUGHT UNDER THE HANDICAP OF A SPELL THAT I MY-SELF CREATED MANY YEARS AGO, BOUND UP IN THIS VERY HAMMER.

43

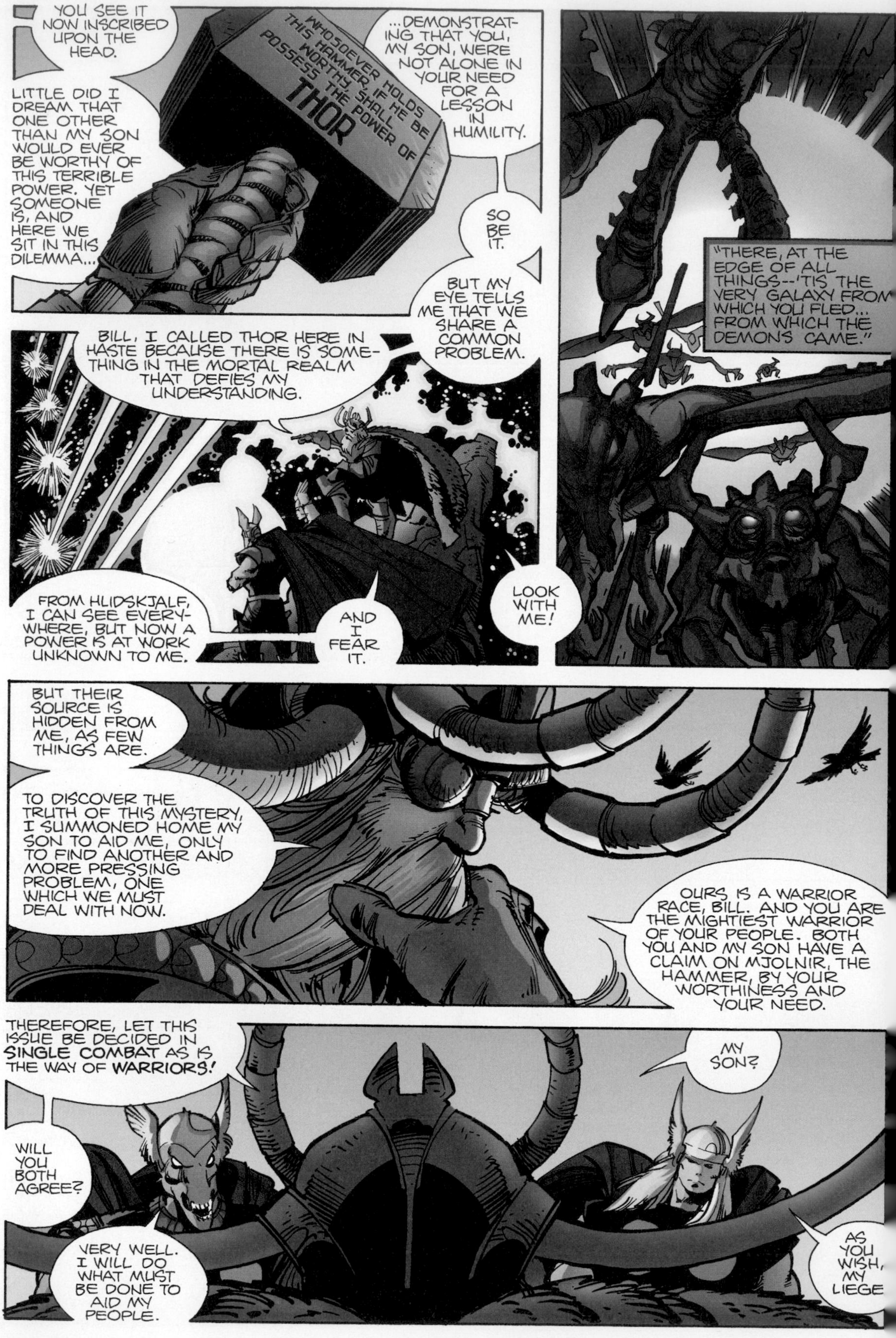
YOU SEE IT NOW INSCRIBED UPON THE HEAD.
WHOSOEVER HOLDS THIS HAMMER, IF HE BE WORTHY, SHALL POSSESS THE POWER OF THOR
LITTLE DID I DREAM THAT ONE OTHER THAN MY SON WOULD EVER BE WORTHY OF THIS TERRIBLE POWER. YET SOMEONE IS, AND HERE WE SIT IN THIS DILEMMA...
...DEMONSTRATING THAT YOU, MY SON, WERE NOT ALONE IN YOUR NEED FOR A LESSON IN HUMILITY.
SO BE IT.
BUT MY EYE TELLS ME THAT WE SHARE A COMMON PROBLEM.
BILL, I CALLED THOR HERE IN HASTE BECAUSE THERE IS SOMETHING IN THE MORTAL REALM THAT DEFIES MY UNDERSTANDING.
FROM HLIDSKJALF, I CAN SEE EVERYWHERE, BUT NOW A POWER IS AT WORK UNKNOWN TO ME.
AND I FEAR IT.
LOOK WITH ME!
"THERE, AT THE EDGE OF ALL THINGS--'TIS THE VERY GALAXY FROM WHICH YOU FLED... FROM WHICH THE DEMONS CAME."
BUT THEIR SOURCE IS HIDDEN FROM ME, AS FEW THINGS ARE.
TO DISCOVER THE TRUTH OF THIS MYSTERY, I SUMMONED HOME MY SON TO AID ME, ONLY TO FIND ANOTHER AND MORE PRESSING PROBLEM, ONE WHICH WE MUST DEAL WITH NOW.
OURS IS A WARRIOR RACE, BILL. AND YOU ARE THE MIGHTIEST WARRIOR OF YOUR PEOPLE. BOTH YOU AND MY SON HAVE A CLAIM ON MJOLNIR, THE HAMMER, BY YOUR WORTHINESS AND YOUR NEED.
THEREFORE, LET THIS ISSUE BE DECIDED IN SINGLE COMBAT AS IS THE WAY OF WARRIORS!
MY SON?
WILL YOU BOTH AGREE?
VERY WELL. I WILL DO WHAT MUST BE DONE TO AID MY PEOPLE.
AS YOU WISH, MY LIEGE

SHORTLY, IN ODIN'S MIGHTY HALL, BEFORE ASGARD ASSEMBLED...

MIGHTY THOR, BETA RAY BILL-- STAND FORTH AND HEAR MY CHARGE TO YOU.

YOU WILL FIGHT WEAPONLESS, BUT FOR THE POWER OF YOUR OWN RIGHT ARMS. TO THIS END, I HAVE REMOVED ALL ENCHANTMENTS FROM THE COMBATANTS... ALL THE POWERS OF STORM AND LIGHTNING, TEMPEST AND THUNDER!

EVEN SO, THE COMBINED MIGHT OF TWO SUCH DOUGHTY WARRIORS MIGHT WELL LAY WASTE TO ASGARD ITSELF.

THEREFORE, THE STRUGGLE SHALL TAKE PLACE IN THE RUINED LANDS OF SKARTHEIM FAR BEYOND THE ABODE OF GODS OR MEN.

THE VICTOR'S REWARD SHALL BE MJOLNIR, THE ENCHANTED HAMMER.

THE LOSER'S REWARD SHALL BE A FUNERAL PYRE.

FOR STAKES SO HIGH, THE PRICE MUST BE GREAT.

THIS FIGHT... IS TO THE **DEATH!**

I HAVE SPOKEN!

GET THEE TO SKARTHEIM!

FFSHHAMMM!

45

AN INSTANT LATER, THOR MATERIALIZES ABOVE A FORBIDDING LANDSCAPE...

SKARTHEIM! WHERE EVEN GODS MAY PERISH!

MY FATHER SURELY HAS ENTRUSTED OUR FATES TO THE NORNS* THEMSELVES!

*THE THREE FATES!

BUT I DO NOT SEE MY OPPONENT.

NO DOUBT LORD ODIN CAUSED HIM TO APPEAR ELSEWHERE IN THIS DANGEROUS REALM.

I FEEL THE HEAT OF THE EARTH ITSELF!

THE VERY GROUND ERUPTS BENEATH MY FEET!

I MUST TAKE MYSELF TO A SAFER PERCH!

UHGG!

NAY, THUNDER GOD, THERE IS NO SAFETY IN ALL THIS LAND AS LONG AS ONE OF US REMAINS ALIVE!

RASH WARRIOR! SO BOOTLESS AN ATTACK UPON A PRINCE OF ASGARD WILL SCARCELY WIN YOU THE HAMMER!

NOT EVEN WHEN THE PRINCE WILL CUSHION OUR DEADLY PLUNGE FROM THE CLIFFS WITH HIS OWN BODY?

KRAKKSH

WHAT? DO YOU SUPPOSE A SIMPLE FALL WILL INJURE ME? THOUGH I AM WITHOUT THE GODLY POWER OF MY HERITAGE, I DO POSSESS THE STRENGTH THAT IS MY BIRTHRIGHT!

STILL I AM STRONG ENOUGH TO GIVE THEE PAUSE.

BUT PAUSE IS NOT A VICTORY, THUNDERER!

AND VICTORY WILL SOON BE MINE!

THOUGH I DO GRIEVE TO DO THIS DEED, YOUR OWN FATHER HAS COMMANDED IT.

HIS WILL BE DONE!

47

BALDER, MY FRIEND, I FEAR YOU DO NOT PROPERLY APPRECIATE THE TRUE PHILOSOPHY OF EATING!

TAKE ME, FOR INSTANCE. SOME SAY I EAT BECAUSE I HAVE A WIFE WHO COULD SINK A LONGSHIP AND EIGHTEEN SCREAMING OFFSPRING WHOSE FURY WOULD DAUNT NOBLE ODIN HIMSELF!

SCURRILOUS LIES! I EAT BECAUSE I ENJOY IT. IT IS POSSIBLY THE GREATEST PLEASURE IN LIFE! AND ONE OF THE FEW I HAVE LEFT, IF I MAY SAY SO.

BUT NOBLE FRIEND, EATING SHOULD BE AN AFFIRMATION OF LIFE, NOT AN ESCAPE FROM IT.

SHOULD YOU NOT TASTE MORE KEENLY THE JOYS OF LIVING, BALDER, YOU WHO ALONE AMONG US HAS TASTED DEATH ITSELF?

ONE WOULD THINK SO, VOLSTAGG, MY FRIEND.

BUT THE VISIONS I HAVE SEEN TROUBLE ME CEASELESSLY.

THE FACES OF THOSE I HAVE SLAIN IN HONORABLE COMBAT ARE NOW MORE REAL TO ME THAN THE BRIGHT BLUE SKIES OF ASGARD.

AND THE SAVOR OF LIVING SEEMS FOREVER DUST TO ME NOW. AN EMPTY DREAM.

EH? WHO--?

THEN PERHAPS THE DREAMER SHOULD RETURN TO HIS FINAL REST!

I AM AGNAR, SON OF HROTHGAR! I HAVE COME FROM VANAHEIM SEEKING BALDER, WHOSE FAME TELLS OF HIS PROWESS IN BATTLE.

I WOULD CHALLENGE HIM TO FIGHT IF HE BE NOT A COWARD...

...AND PROVE TO ME THAT HE IS A BETTER WARRIOR THAN I!

NAY, AGNAR, I AM DONE WITH FIGHTING. I'LL FIGHT NO MORE FOREVER.

SPURN ME, WILL YOU? THEN DIE WHERE YOU STAND! I'LL... HUH?

WHAT TRICKERY IS THIS THAT ALLOWED YOU TO ESCAPE MY BLOW?

COME BACK! I'LL NOT LET YOU WALK AWAY AS THOUGH I WERE SOME THRALL!

COME BACK! OR BY THE MOTHER THAT BORE ME, I'LL SPLIT YOU WHERE YOU STAND!

HOLD, MY YOUNG FRIEND. PERMIT ME TO SPEAK ON BEHALF OF THE NOBLE BALDER.

OWW! MY FOOT! GET OFF, YOU CLUMSY OAF!

CRUNCH!

TUT, TUT, AGNAR, I AM BEYOND SUCH INSULTS! IN FACT, TO DEMONSTRATE MY GENEROUS NATURE, LET ME SHOW YOU SOME OF THE WONDERS OF THE ETERNAL REALM WHILE BALDER CONTINUES HIS WALK.

NO. I WANT TO... OW, MY FOOT! I THINK IT'S BROKEN!

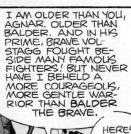

I AM OLDER THAN YOU, AGNAR. OLDER THAN BALDER. AND IN HIS PRIME, BRAVE VOLSTAGG FOUGHT BESIDE MANY FAMOUS FIGHTERS! BUT NEVER HAVE I BEHELD A MORE COURAGEOUS, MORE GENTLE WARRIOR THAN BALDER THE BRAVE.

HERE'S A SHADY SPOT.

OOF!

SURELY THOSE OF VANAHEIM ARE MADE OF STERNER STUFF. ALLOW ME TO CARRY YOU. WE'LL VISIT THE PALACE GARDENS. VERY SOOTHING AND WE CAN CONVERSE THERE AT OUR LEISURE.

HIS DEEDS ARE LEGENDARY-- THE SLAYING OF THE UTGARD DRAGON, THE BINDING OF THORN OF THE FOUR RINGS-- THE SAVING OF ASGARD A HUNDRED TIMES! NOW ALL THAT HAS CHANGED-- PERHAPS FOREVER!

OFF! GET OFF!

PATIENCE, LITTLE ONE. YOU FEEL YOU'RE BRAVE ENOUGH TO FACE DEATH, DO YOU? WELL, BALDER IS THE ONLY GOD AMONG US WHO HAS HIMSELF DIED AND RETURNED TO TELL THE TALE...

...AND A BLOOD-CHILLING TALE IT IS, TOO! JUST THE SORT OF STORY FOR A SUMMER'S AFTERNOON.

IT IS, HOWEVER, A TALE WE WILL HEAR ANOTHER TIME, FOR IN THE REMOTE LAND OF SKARTHEIM, WE FIND...

BACK, WARRIOR! THE HAMMER IS NOT YET THINE!

NEVER BEFORE HAVE I FOUGHT ONE SO WORTHY OR NOBLE! BUT IF I FAIL...

NEITHER HERO SURRENDERS AN INCH AS THE BATTLE RAGES ACROSS THE ANCIENT LAND, TEARING THE VERY MOUNTAINS FROM THEIR ROOTS UNTIL...

SHKKKTT!

...WHAT OF MY GUARDIANSHIP OF EARTH? WHO SHALL BE HER CHAMPION IN TIME OF NEED?

I SENSE THAT MY FOE IS TIRING EVEN AS I! THE MOMENT OF DECISION IS UPON US!

WILL THE THUNDER GOD NEVER BREAK? AGAIN HE LEAPS TO DO BATTLE WITH UNDIMINISHED FERVOR!

BUT NOW, HE HAS LEFT HIMSELF OPEN...

...FOR THIS!

KA-BHTHOOM!

BY THE BRISTLING BEARD OF ODIN! HE HAS SHATTERED THE HILLSIDE ITSELF TO CREATE A RAIN OF BOULDERS!

I CANNOT CHANGE MY DIRECTION IN TIME-- UHH!

TRULY HIS STRENGTH IS BEYOND COMPREHENSION!

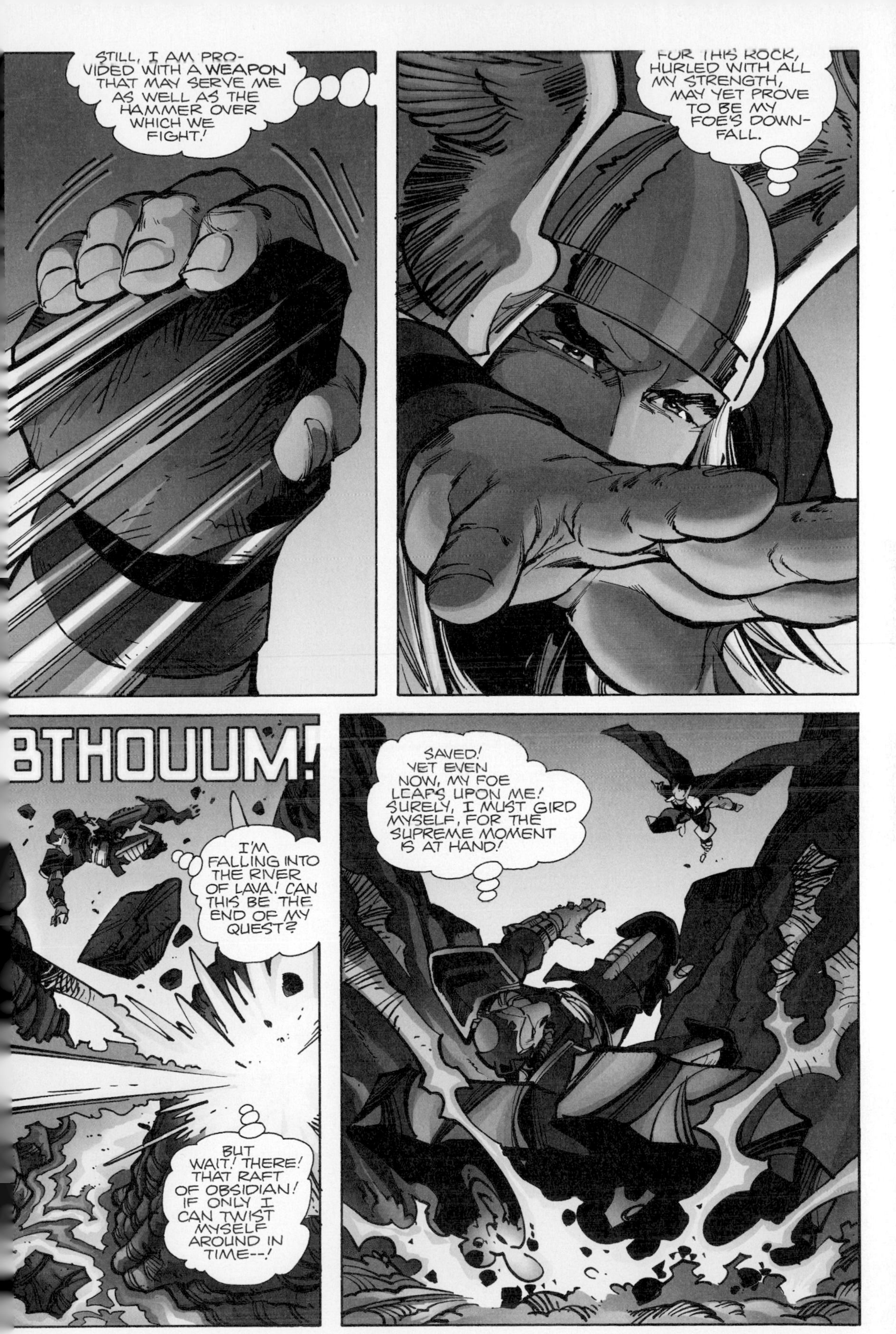
STILL, I AM PROVIDED WITH A WEAPON THAT MAY SERVE ME AS WELL AS THE HAMMER OVER WHICH WE FIGHT!
FOR THIS ROCK, HURLED WITH ALL MY STRENGTH, MAY YET PROVE TO BE MY FOE'S DOWNFALL.
BTHOUUM!
I'M FALLING INTO THE RIVER OF LAVA! CAN THIS BE THE END OF MY QUEST?
BUT WAIT! THERE! THAT RAFT OF OBSIDIAN! IF ONLY I CAN TWIST MYSELF AROUND IN TIME--!
SAVED! YET EVEN NOW, MY FOE LEAPS UPON ME! SURELY, I MUST GIRD MYSELF, FOR THE SUPREME MOMENT IS AT HAND!

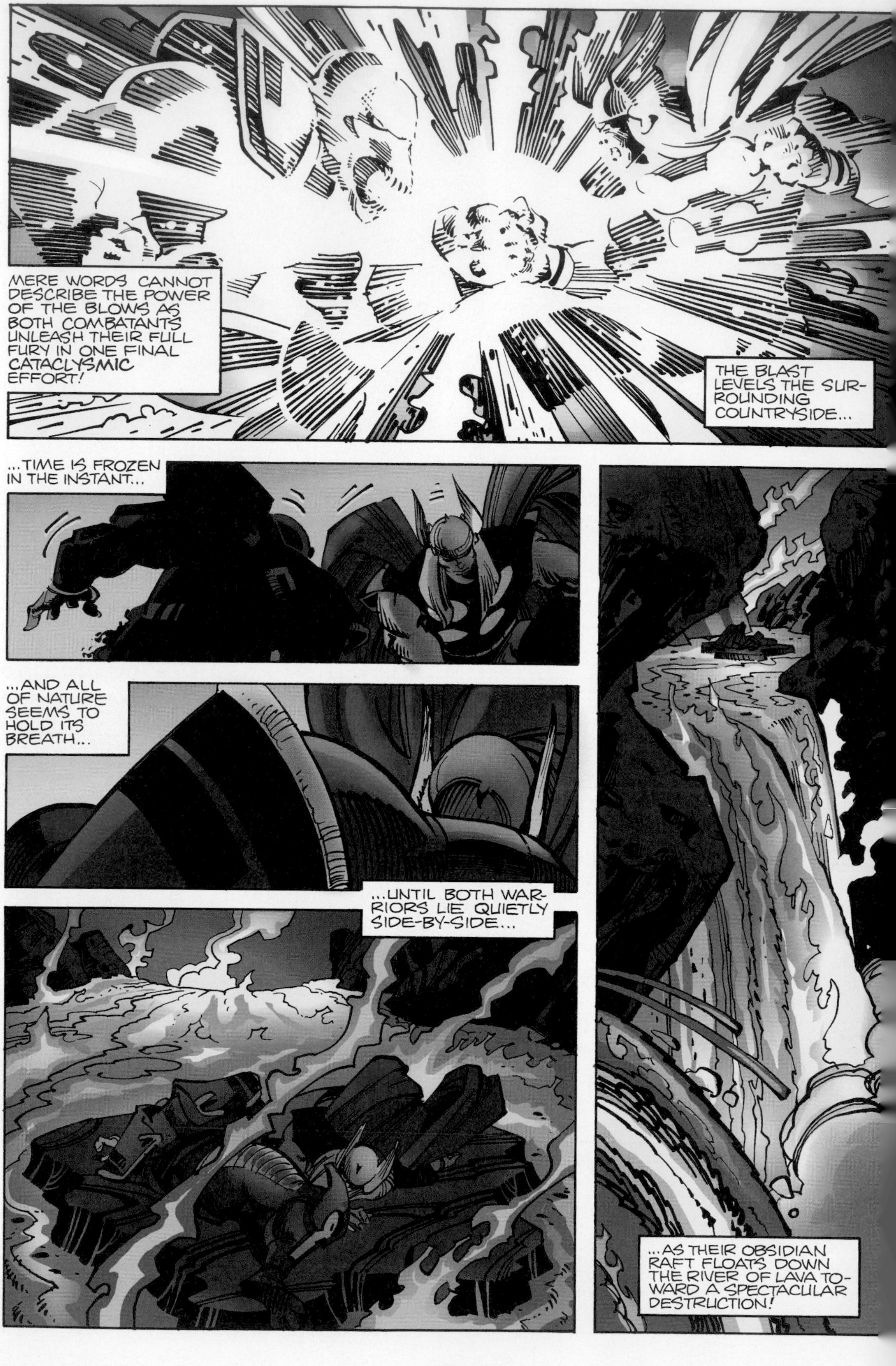
MERE WORDS CANNOT DESCRIBE THE POWER OF THE BLOWS AS BOTH COMBATANTS UNLEASH THEIR FULL FURY IN ONE FINAL **CATACLYSMIC** EFFORT!
THE BLAST LEVELS THE SURROUNDING COUNTRYSIDE...
...TIME IS FROZEN IN THE INSTANT...
...AND ALL OF NATURE SEEMS TO HOLD ITS BREATH...
...UNTIL BOTH WARRIORS LIE QUIETLY SIDE-BY-SIDE...
...AS THEIR OBSIDIAN RAFT FLOATS DOWN THE RIVER OF LAVA TOWARD A SPECTACULAR DESTRUCTION!

FINALLY...

I...I LIVE! THE HEAT REVIVES ME. YET I AM BROKEN INSIDE. I FEEL IT.

THOR LIES UNCONSCIOUS STILL. I HAVE BUT TO LEAP TO THE SHORE AND SAFETY AND THE HAMMER IS *WON!*

QUICKLY-- THE FALLS ARE JUST AHEAD!

NO! MY FOE IS TOO BRAVE TO PERISH SO MEANLY IN THIS FORSAKEN WILDERNESS.

I...UGH...I MUST CARRY US BOTH TO SAFETY.

TOO LATE! THE RAFT ALREADY PLUNGES O'ER THE FIERY BRINK! BUT I MUST TRY!

AND WITH A FINAL GROAN, BETA RAY BILL LEAPS FOR THE SHORE...

...ONLY TO BE ENVELOPED BY A BLINDING FLASH OF ENERGY...

...THAT TRANSPORTS HIM IN THE WINK OF AN EYE TO THE GLEAMING HALLS OF ASGARD BEFORE A SHOCKED AND SILENT GATHERING.

LORD ODIN, YOUR SON YET LIVES. THE FINEST FOE I HAVE EVER FOUGHT. BUT I HAVE BESTED HIM.

THE HAMMER... IS *MINE!*

NEXT: SOMETHING OLD, SOMETHING NEW...!

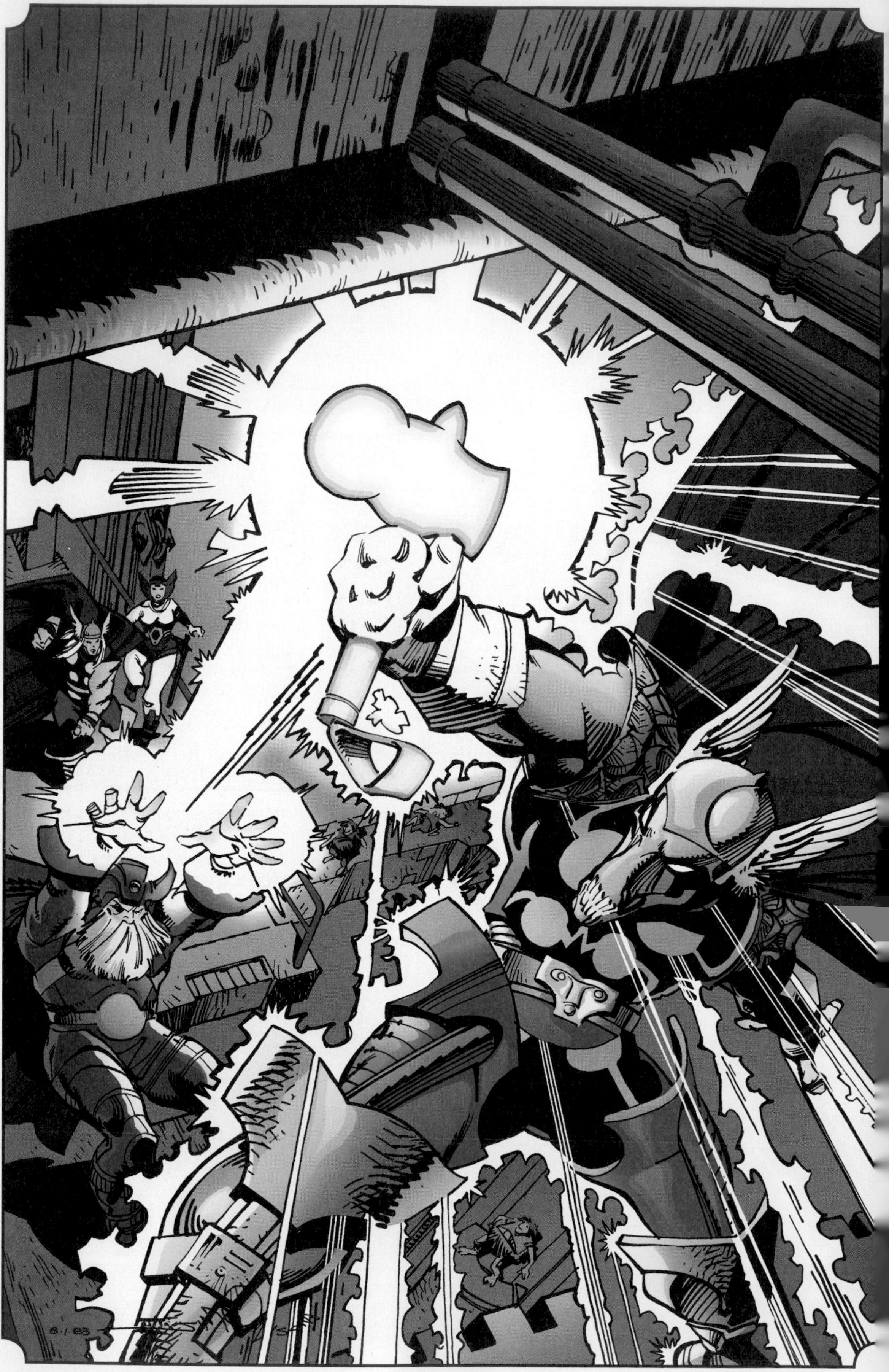

MOMENTS AGO, **BETA RAY BILL**, A BIONIC ALIEN, BESTED THE MIGHTY THOR IN SINGLE COMBAT AND SO WON THE RIGHT TO POSSESS THOR'S ENCHANTED HAMMER, MJOLNIR.*

BUT EVEN AS HE ANNOUNCES HIS VICTORY BEFORE THE STUNNED ASGARDIANS...

SOMETHING OLD, SOMETHING NEW...

UGGHG...

*AS SEEN IN OUR LAST COUPLE OF ISSUES.

ART AND STORY: WALTER SIMONSON • LETTERING: JOHN WORKMAN, JR. • COLORS: GEORGE ROUSSOS
EDITING: MIKE CARLIN • EDITOR-IN-CHIEF: JIM SHOOTER

...AND FOR A LONG MOMENT, THERE IS SILENCE!

AROUSE YOURSELVES! LET THE IMPERIAL GUARD CARRY BOTH COMBATANTS TO THE HOUSE OF HEALING WITHOUT DELAY! AND BID THE ROYAL PHYSICIANS APPLY ALL THEIR ARTS!

THESE BRAVE WARRIORS MUST **NOT** PERISH!

BUT THOUGH THE ARMS OF **HELA,** THE DEATH GODDESS, BECKON TO EACH, NEITHER THOR NOR BETA RAY BILL IS DESTINED TO SURRENDER TO HER EMBRACE THIS DAY.

FOR THE SKILLS OF ODIN'S PHYSICIANS ARE UNMATCHED IN ALL THE NINE WORLDS.

STILL, THE HEROES' HURTS ARE GRIEVOUS AND EACH RESTS QUIETLY UNDER THE WATCHFUL (AND CURIOUS) EYES OF THEIR ATTENDANTS.

THE ALIEN SLEEPS PEACEFULLY.

BUT HE IS A STRANGE MIXTURE OF STRENGTH AND SORROW. THOUGH HE HAS WON THE HAMMER, HE TAKES NO JOY IN HIS VICTORY.

THEY SAY BILL RE- GAINS HIS STRENGTH AS QUICKLY AS THE MIGHTY THOR. DO YOU SUPPOSE HE WILL REMAIN LONG IN ASGARD?

I FOR ONE WOULD WOULD BE INTEREST- ED TO LEARN JUST HOW MECHANICAL HE REALLY IS.

WELL, I FOR ONE COULD CARE LESS. I'VE SEEN HIM...

...AND HE'S REPULSIVE!

I'D SOONER KISS A DOG THAN BE IN THE SAME ROOM WITH HIM!

RECALLING SOME PAST TRIUMPH, LORELEI?

THOR IS NO DOG, BUT THE HANDSOMEST GOD IN ALL ASGARD, LADY SIF. AND AFTER THIS DEFEAT, HE MAY WELCOME SUCH COM- FORT AS ONLY I CAN GIVE.

HANDSOME IS AS HANDSOME DOES. BILL HAS LIFTED THE HAMMER AND FOUGHT AGAINST THOR AS NO ONE EVER HAS BEFORE. TO SEE LESS THAN THAT IS TO MISTAKE HIM.

THEN PERHAPS **YOU** SHOULD EMBRACE THE ALIEN! HE MIGHT WELCOME SUCH COMFORT AS YOU COULD GIVE.

SOME, HOWEVER, ARE MORE PARTICULAR!

AND WITH THAT, LORELEI LEAVES, UNAWARE OF THE WATCHING EYE THAT SEES ALL THINGS...

"SOME ARE MORE PARTICULAR!" FAGH!

PAY NO HEED TO HER, SIF. EVERY DOG HAS ITS DAY.

EVEN LORELEI.

BUT YOU MUST EXCUSE ME. I HAVE COME TO SEE OUR PATIENTS.

HOW FARES THE SON OF MY HEART?

DISGRACED BEFORE YOUR EYES, MY LORD.

I HAVE DECIDED. I WILL RENOUNCE MY GODHOOD AND LEAVE ASGARD FOREVER! NO LONGER AM I WORTHY TO BE THE GOD OF THUNDER!

YES, WELL... WE SHALL SEE. I THINK I OUGHT TO SPEAK WITH BILL.

HE IS NOT HAPPY ABOUT THE OUTCOME OF THIS BATTLE EITHER, I UNDERSTAND.

AS YOU WISH, FATHER. BUT TALKING WILL NOT CHANGE THE PAST.

ALL THINGS ARE POSSIBLE, MY SON.

MY MIND IS MADE UP. WHEN I AM WELL, I SHALL DEPART AND JOURNEY AMONG THE STARS.

PERHAPS DISCUSSION MAY BE ABLE TO HELP US WHERE BRUTE STRENGTH SEEMS TO HAVE FAILED.

LORD ODIN, I AM HONORED. AND GRATEFUL. YOUR PHYSICIANS AND YOUR SMITHS HAVE WORKED WONDERS. I AM NEARLY HEALED. HOW IS YOUR SON?

WELL ENOUGH, THANK YOU. ALL THINGS CONSIDERED.

AND YOU? THE GOSSIP OF THE HOUSE TELLS OF YOUR SINGULAR LACK OF ENTHUSIASM CONCERNING YOUR VICTORY.

I AM DEEPLY TROUBLED, MY LORD. FOR MYSELF AND MY PEOPLE. THEY NEED THE POWER OF THE HAMMER DESPERATELY. BUT MY HEART MISGIVES ME.

THOUGH I HAVE WON THIS BATTLE, IS MY CLAIM TO THE HAMMER'S POWER ESTABLISHED FOREVER, OR ONLY UNTIL I, MYSELF, MEET SOME STRONGER CHALLENGER?

THE HAMMER WAS FORGED IN THE BEGINNING OF TIME TO BE CARRIED BY THOR ALONE. MY VICTORY DOES NOT ALTER THAT, NOR PERMIT ME TO FORGET IT.

AND, IN TRUTH, I COULD NOT BRING MYSELF TO SLAY THOR, ALTHOUGH SUCH WAS THE ESTABLISHED CONDITION OF THE CONTEST.

YOU ARE A HIGH AND PUISSANT LORD. IS THERE NO WAY OUT OF THIS DILEMMA OF HONOR AND NEED?

YOU HAVE BUT TO ASK.

CAN YOU... HELP ME?

IN THE PAST, IN RETURN FOR HELP, THE GODS DEMANDED A SACRIFICE. YOU HAVE ALREADY GIVEN ME SOMETHING MORE PRECIOUS—THAN ANYTHING—THE LIFE OF MY SON.

YOU HAVE PROVEN YOURSELF ABLE TO WIELD GREAT POWER AND WIELD IT WISELY. AND, YOU HAVE ASKED FOR HELP.

THEREFORE, I WILL GIVE YOU WHAT AID I CAN. I SHALL BESTOW UPON YOU A **GIFT** THAT CARRIES AN AWESOME RESPONSIBILITY.

THE GIFT MAY YET SAVE YOUR PEOPLE... THE RESPONSIBILITY MIGHT DESTROY YOU!

THROO BOOOM

IT IS DUSK WHEN A SOLITARY RIDER CRESTS THE DIVIDE THAT OVERLOOKS NIDAVELLIR, THE REALM OF THE DWARFS...

EITRI, LOOK! SOMEONE HAS CROSSED THE FORBIDDEN PATH THROUGH THE MOUNTAINS OF ULLTHANG!

GREETINGS, NOBLE DWARFS.

EVENING COMES ON AND THIS WANDERER HAS JOURNEYED FAR. MIGHT I SHARE YOUR FIRE AND FELLOWSHIP THIS NIGHT? YOU'LL FIND ME A GENIAL COMPANION.

WEL- COME, **MOST HIGH.** PLEASE ACCEPT OUR HOSPITALITY.

YOU KNOW ME, EITRI?

HAD I BUT ONE EYE, LORD ODIN, I SHOULD RECOGNIZE YOUR MANTLED POWER EVEN IN THE DARK.

AND I WOULD KNOW THAT YOU HAD SOUGHT ME OUT FOR A PURPOSE, NOT MERELY TO SHARE A FIRE.

WHAT DOES THE LORD OF ASGARD SEEK IN NIDAVELLIR?

YOUR SKILL, EITRI. FOR A TASK THAT ONLY YOU CAN PERFORM.

COME THEN. SIT BESIDE ME AND TELL ME WHAT THE DWARFS CAN DO FOR THE GODS.

YOU ASK MUCH, LORD ODIN. MORE THAN WE DWARFS CAN EASILY GIVE.

IF THE TASK WERE SIMPLE, EITRI, I WOULD NOT HAVE SOUGHT OUT THE GREATEST OF ALL DWARF SMITHS.

SO YOU SAY!

LONG AGO, WE DWARFS WERE HUMBLED AND DRIVEN FROM THE LIGHT BY THE GODS!

WE LIVE NOW BENEATH THE GROUND AND SEEK OUT THE EARTH'S TREASURES, BUT WE HAVE NOT FORGOTTEN OLD HURTS AND OUR HEARTS ARE BITTER.

YET THE GODS ALSO GAVE US OUR FORM AND OUR THOUGHTS.

SO WE WILL DO THIS NEW TASK YOU SET US BUT ON ONE CONDITION AND ONE CONDITION ONLY.

WE HAVE A CHAMPION AMONG US NOW, A MIGHTY FIGHTER.

SEND US A WOMAN WHO CAN DEFEAT HIM AND WE WILL DO THIS THING YOU ASK. BUT IF SHE LOSES, SHE MUST REMAIN WITH THE DWARFS FOREVER, TO SERVE OUR CHAMPION AS HIS CHATTEL!

THUS DO WE REPAY THE GODS FOR ANCIENT WRONGS!

TWO DAYS LATER, IN THE HOUSE OF HEALING IN ASGARD...

I AM GLAD TO SEE YOU NEARLY RE-COVERED, BILL. YOU WILL NEED ALL YOUR STRENGTH TO CARRY THE HAMMER PROUDLY. AS I KNOW YOU WILL.

MY THANKS, THOR. BUT BE NOT TOO HASTY TO GIVE MJOLNIR AWAY.

I LOST, BILL. I COULD NOT WISH FOR A MORE HON-ORABLE FOE. I AM NO LONGER WORTHY TO CARRY THE ENCHANTED MALLET.

NEVER AGAIN WILL I BE ABLE TO SAVOR THE PLEASURE OF GLIDING THROUGH THE COSMIC OCEAN AS THE GOD OF THUNDER.

NO? THINK BACK, MY FRIEND, TO MY STORY.* I WAS BORN IN A GALACTIC INFERNO. AND FIERY SKARTHEIM WHERE WE FOUGHT WAS NOT SO DIFFERENT A PLACE.

A PLACE CHOSEN FOR OUR BATTLE BY YOUR FATHER, I MIGHT ADD.

IN NO OTHER REALM COULD I HAVE WON SO CLOSE A CONTEST. AND EVEN SO, I HAD THE LUCK.

*TOLD LAST ISSUE.

YOU THINK SO, BILL? MY FATHER IS SUBTLE AND HIS PURPOSES OFTEN HIDDEN. PERHAPS I SHOULD SPEAK TO HIM WHEN HE RETURNS. FOR HE IS AWAY-- BUT HOLD.

WHAT'S THIS I SEE?

IT IS SIF! IN FULL ARMOR! AND RIDING AS THOUGH THE WOLF HIMSELF PURSUED HER.

NURSE! WHAT DO YOU KNOW OF THIS? WHERE DOES THE LADY SIF TRAVEL IN SUCH HASTE?

HAD YOU NOT HEARD? SHE'S GONE TO FIGHT A CHAMPION WARRIOR ON BEHALF OF YOU BOTH.

WHAT?

THEY SAY HER THOUGHTS NOW ARE ONLY FOR BATTLE. AND THAT SHE MAY NEVER RETURN!

BUT AS SIF PASSES THROUGH ASGARD'S GOLDEN GATES, THE COMING BATTLE IS ONLY ONE OF MANY THOUGHTS THAT SPIN THROUGH HER MIND...

...AS SHE SEES AGAIN HER MEETING WITH THE ALL-FATHER THAT VERY MORNING.

SUCH WAS MY BARGAIN, SIF. THE DWARFS WANT A GODDESS TO FIGHT THEIR CHAMPION AND I KNOW THAT YOU HAVE SOUGHT DISTRACTION TO EASE YOUR HEART'S ACHE.

BUT I DO NOT COMMAND THIS THING.

THE DECISION RESTS WITH YOU.

MY LORD, 'TIS TRUE I AM EMPTY AND THOUGHT THAT BATTLE WOULD FILL MY NEED.

NOW, FOR REASONS OF MY OWN, I WOULD GLADLY TRAVEL TO HELA'S PALLID DOMAIN ITSELF TO DEMONSTRATE MY PROWESS.

VERY WELL, CHILD. ARM THY-SELF STRONGLY AND KNOW THAT I SHALL BE WATCHIN OVER YOU FROM AFAR.

AND AS HER THOUGHTS RETURN TO THE PRESENT...

I DARED NOT TELL EVEN ODIN THAT I RIDE NOW EAGER TO BATTLE BE-CAUSE OF A DESIRE SO SECRET THAT NONE MUST KNOW. I CAN SCARCELY BELIEVE IT MYSELF.

THERE IS ANOTHER WARRIOR IN THIS WORLD WHO IS AS BRAVE, AS VALIANT AS THE MIGHTY THOR!

AND THOUGH HE WEARS A GUISE AS ALIEN AS ANY I HAVE EVER SEEN, STILL I WOULD FIND FAVOR IN HIS EYES.

STILL I WOULD SHOW HIM THAT I, TOO AM A WARRIOR BORN.

SO! THE CRAVEN ASGARDIANS HAVE DELIVERED A WIFE TO ME AT LAST AS I KNEW THEY WOULD! AND ABOUT TIME!

I KNEW THEY'D BE TOO AFRAID TO RESIST!

I MUST REMEMBER TO THANK EITRI... EVENTUALLY!

NOW, MY PRETTY, BID FAREWELL TO THE SUN AND PREPARE TO LIVE WITH ME FOREVER IN THE DARK BENEATH THE AGELESS MOUNTAINS OF NIDAVELLIR.

THINK AGAIN, BRAGGART!

OWWW!

THE GODDESS HAS A STING, EH? NO MATTER!

NONE CAN OVER-COME **THROGG THE DWARF!**

63

BUT EVEN AS THROGG LEAPS HIGH INTO THE AIR ABOVE SIF, WE TURN ELSEWHERE TO FIND, IN THE GARDENS OF ASGARD, VOLSTAGG THE ENORMOUS CHATTING WITH AGNAR OF VANAHEIM...

MARK WELL THESE WORDS, MY YOUNG FRIEND, AND I WILL TELL THE STORY OF BALDER THE BRAVE AND HIS TRAGIC DEATH AS ONLY VOLSTAGG CAN!

FROM THIS CAUTIONARY TALE, YOU WILL LEARN MORE THAN YOU EVER WISHED TO ABOUT MUCH THAT IS HIDDEN EVEN FROM THE GODS.

"IT BEGAN WITH AN ARROW MAGICALLY CREATED BY THE ARCH DECEIVER LOKI, HIMSELF, MADE OF THE LITTLE PLANT MISTLETOE. AND ON A BLACK DAY FOR ASGARD, THAT ARROW SLEW BRAVE BALDER.

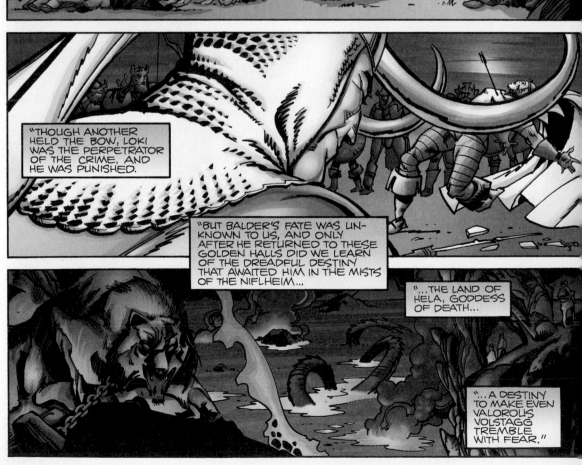

"THOUGH ANOTHER HELD THE BOW, LOKI WAS THE PERPETRATOR OF THE CRIME, AND HE WAS PUNISHED.

"BUT BALDER'S FATE WAS UN-KNOWN TO US, AND ONLY AFTER HE RETURNED TO THESE GOLDEN HALLS DID WE LEARN OF THE DREADFUL DESTINY THAT AWAITED HIM IN THE MISTS OF THE NIFLHEIM...

"...THE LAND OF HELA, GODDESS OF DEATH...

"...A DESTINY TO MAKE EVEN VALOROUS VOLSTAGG TREMBLE WITH FEAR."

ALAS, THE REST OF THE TALE MUST WAIT FOR WE JOURNEY NOW TO A PLACE BEYOND THE FIELDS WE KNOW, PERHAPS BEYOND THE NINE WORLDS THEMSELVES...

...TO WATCH AS A FIGURE WHO DWARFS THE STARS LOOMS OVER A MIGHTY ANVIL AND RAISES HIS SINEWED ARM HIGH ABOVE HIS HEAD.

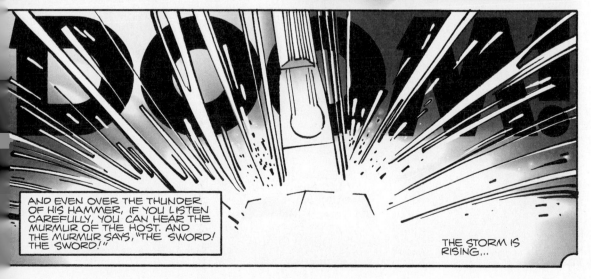

DOOM

AND EVEN OVER THE THUNDER OF HIS HAMMER, IF YOU LISTEN CAREFULLY, YOU CAN HEAR THE MURMUR OF THE HOST. AND THE MURMUR SAYS, "THE SWORD! THE SWORD!"

THE STORM IS RISING...

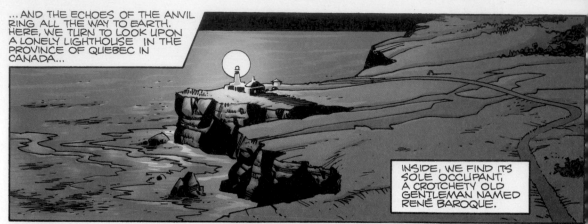

...AND THE ECHOES OF THE ANVIL RING ALL THE WAY TO EARTH. HERE, WE TURN TO LOOK UPON A LONELY LIGHTHOUSE IN THE PROVINCE OF QUEBEC IN CANADA...

INSIDE, WE FIND ITS SOLE OCCUPANT, A CROTCHETY OLD GENTLEMAN NAMED RENÉ BAROQUE.

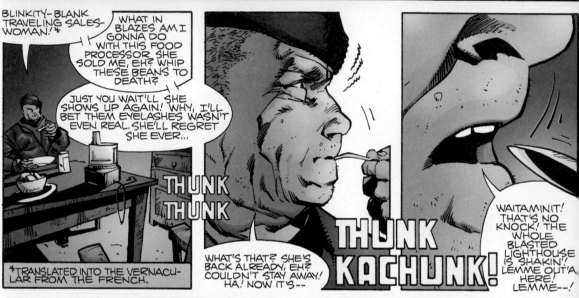

BLINKITY-BLANK TRAVELING SALESWOMAN!*

WHAT IN BLAZES AM I GONNA DO WITH THIS FOOD PROCESSOR SHE SOLD ME, EH? WHIP THESE BEANS TO DEATH?

JUST YOU WAIT'LL SHE SHOWS UP AGAIN! WHY, I'LL BET THEM EYELASHES WASN'T EVEN REAL. SHE'LL REGRET SHE EVER...

*TRANSLATED INTO THE VERNACULAR FROM THE FRENCH.

THUNK THUNK

THUNK KACHUNK!

WHAT'S THAT? SHE'S BACK ALREADY, EH? COULDN'T STAY AWAY! HA! NOW IT'S--

WAITAMINIT! THAT'S NO KNOCK! THE WHOLE BLASTED LIGHTHOUSE IS SHAKIN'! LEMME OUT'A HERE! LEMME--!

BUT RENÉ IS DESTINED NEVER TO REACH THE DOOR FOR AT THAT MOMENT THE VERY EARTH SPLITS ASUNDER...

FREE! FREE! AFTER ALL THE MILLENNIA! NOW AT LAST I WILL DESTROY THOSE WHO THOUGHT THEY HAD IMPRISONED ME FOREVER!

VENGEANCE WILL BE MINE!

MEANWHILE IN NIDAVELLIR...

HOLD STILL, WOMAN! YOU'RE NO MATCH FOR ME AND I DON'T WANT TO DAMAGE YOU!

BTHKASSH!

VERY THOUGHTFUL OF YOU. BUT SURELY YOU'D HAVE A BETTER CHANCE OF CATCHING ME IF YOU USED BOTH HANDS!

WHY NOT DROP THE CLUB?

GAAHHG!

MY HAND! YOU'VE CUT MY HAND!

ARE WE THROUGH OR DO YOU STILL THINK YOU CAN CATCH ME?

ROAARR!

SO YOU'VE DECIDED TO OUTTHINK ME AFTER ALL!

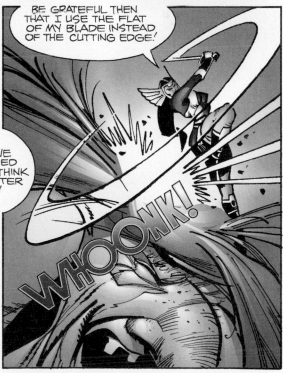

BE GRATEFUL THEN THAT I USE THE FLAT OF MY BLADE INSTEAD OF THE CUTTING EDGE!

WHOONK!

THE DWARFS HAVE CHOSEN A SINGULARLY INEPT CHAMPION IN THEIR CAUSE. BUT NO MATTER. THE BARGAIN IS COMPLETE AND THEY MUST FULFILL THEIR PART OF IT.

BUT WHAT DO I DO WITH THIS USELESS CREATURE? TO SLAY HIM WOULD SEEM ALMOST A WASTE OF TIME.

AND CERTAINLY NO LONGER NECESSARY, LADY SIF. IT IS THE LADY **SIF**, IS IT NOT? FOREMOST WARRIOR WOMAN AMONG THE ASGARDIANS. I HAD HOPED ODIN WOULD CHOOSE YOU TO FIGHT THROGG!

EITRI!

WHAT'S THIS? I HAVE DEFEATED YOUR CHAMPION. THE BARGAIN STANDS.

MOST CERTAINLY, VALIANT LADY. AND A GOOD BARGAIN IT WAS.

TOO LONG HAS THROGG LORDED OVER THE DWARFS AIDED BY HIS FREAKISH SIZE, MAKING LIFE MISERABLE FOR MYSELF AND MY BROTHERS.

NOW, DEFEATED BY A WOMAN, HE'LL NOT SHOW HIS FACE AGAIN FOR AGES AND WE'LL BE RID OF HIS BULLYING WAYS.

WE DWARFS SHALL BE **HAPPY** TO AID LORD ODIN FOR THIS DELIVERANCE AND OUR CHILDREN WILL RELISH THE TALE OF MY BARGAIN WITH THE WANDERER.

RETURN TO YOUR LIEGE AND TELL HIM TO COME QUICKLY. WE SHALL BE READY ERE HE ARRIVES.

MAKE HASTE, LADS!

LEAP TO THE FIRES! STOKE THE FURNACES!

WE GO TO WORK!

SO SIF RETURNS TO ASGARD AND THE WORD GOES OUT FROM ODIN THAT HE AND THREE OTHERS WILL JOURNEY TO THE FORGES OF NIDAVELLIR...

...THERE TO PARTICIPATE IN A CREATION SUCH AS HAS NOT BEEN SEEN SINCE THE BEGINNING OF TIME.

BUT AS ALL IS MADE READY FOR THE TRIP WE FIND HIGH ATOP THE TOWERS OF ASGARD, TWO FIGURES DEEP IN CONVERSATION.

I AM WORRIED, LADY SIF, FOR MY PEOPLE. EVEN NOW, THEY MAY HAVE BEEN OVERTAKEN BY THE DEMONS THAT PURSUE THEIR FLEET. AND I AM HERE, UNABLE TO DEFEND THEM.

I THINK, BILL, THAT LORD ODIN HAS BEEN WATCHING OVER THEM.

IF ANY HARM HAD BEFALLEN THEM ERE NOW, WE WOULD KNOW.

THAT MAY BE, BUT MY PLACE IS WITH THEM AND AS I AM NOW FULLY RECOVERED, I LONG TO BE GONE FROM HERE.

IN THE GLORY OF ITS MANY BEAUTIES, ASGARD ONLY SERVES TO REMIND ME JUST HOW MUCH I HAVE GIVEN UP FOREVER.

IF... IF YOUR PEOPLE FIND SAFE HAVEN EVENTUALLY, WILL YOU EVER THINK OF RETURNING TO... US, SOMEDAY?

LOOK AT ME, LADY SIF. MY BROTHERS ARE THE BEASTS OF THE FORESTS, MY SISTERS THE MACHINES THAT DRIVE THE GREAT STARSHIPS.

WHEN I WAS REMADE AS A WARRIOR TO SAVE MY PEOPLE, I SURRENDERED ALL MY HUMANITY. I HAVE NONE LEFT... FOR ANYONE.

I DO NOT THINK I COULD BEAR THE PROSPECT OF RETURNING TO SUCH A PERFECT WORLD... NO MATTER HOW MUCH I MIGHT LONG TO.

THESE ARE THE **FURNACES** OF **NIDAVELLIR**, THE GREAT FORGES OF THE DWARFS, WHERE FOR AGES, THEY HAVE CREATED THE MOST WONDERFUL DELIGHTS OF THEIR IMAGINATIONS.

NOW THE FURNACES GLOW BLUE HOT AS WITHIN THE BOILING CAULDRONS, THE METAL IS MADE LIQUID WHILE THE DWARFS SCURRY ABOUT...

...AND THE FINAL PREPARATIONS ARE COMPLETED...

THE RAKING OF THE SLAG IS FINISHED. PREPARE TO TAP THE CHARGE!

...ALL UNDER THE WATCHFUL EYES OF ODIN AND HIS GUESTS.

THE URU IS NEARLY READY TO BE CAST. SEE HOW THEY LIFT THE GREAT LADLE ABOVE THE MASTER MOLD. EITRI IS INDEED THE GENIUS OF HIS CRAFT.

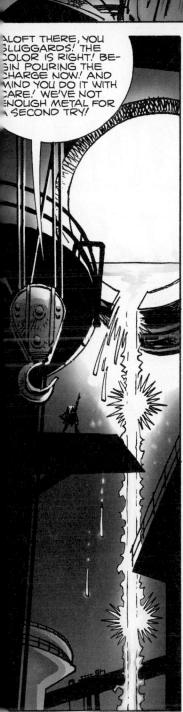

ALOFT THERE, YOU SLUGGARDS! THE COLOR IS RIGHT! BEGIN POURING THE CHARGE NOW! AND MIND YOU DO IT WITH CARE! WE'VE NOT ENOUGH METAL FOR A SECOND TRY!

BUT THE OPERATOR'S AIM IS PERFECT AND THE MOLTEN METAL URU THUNDERS INTO THE MOLD WITH A DEAFENING ROAR!

BAREDOOM!

NOW, LORD ODIN, BEFORE THE MOLD IS COOLED! RELEASE THE ENCHANTMENT NOW!

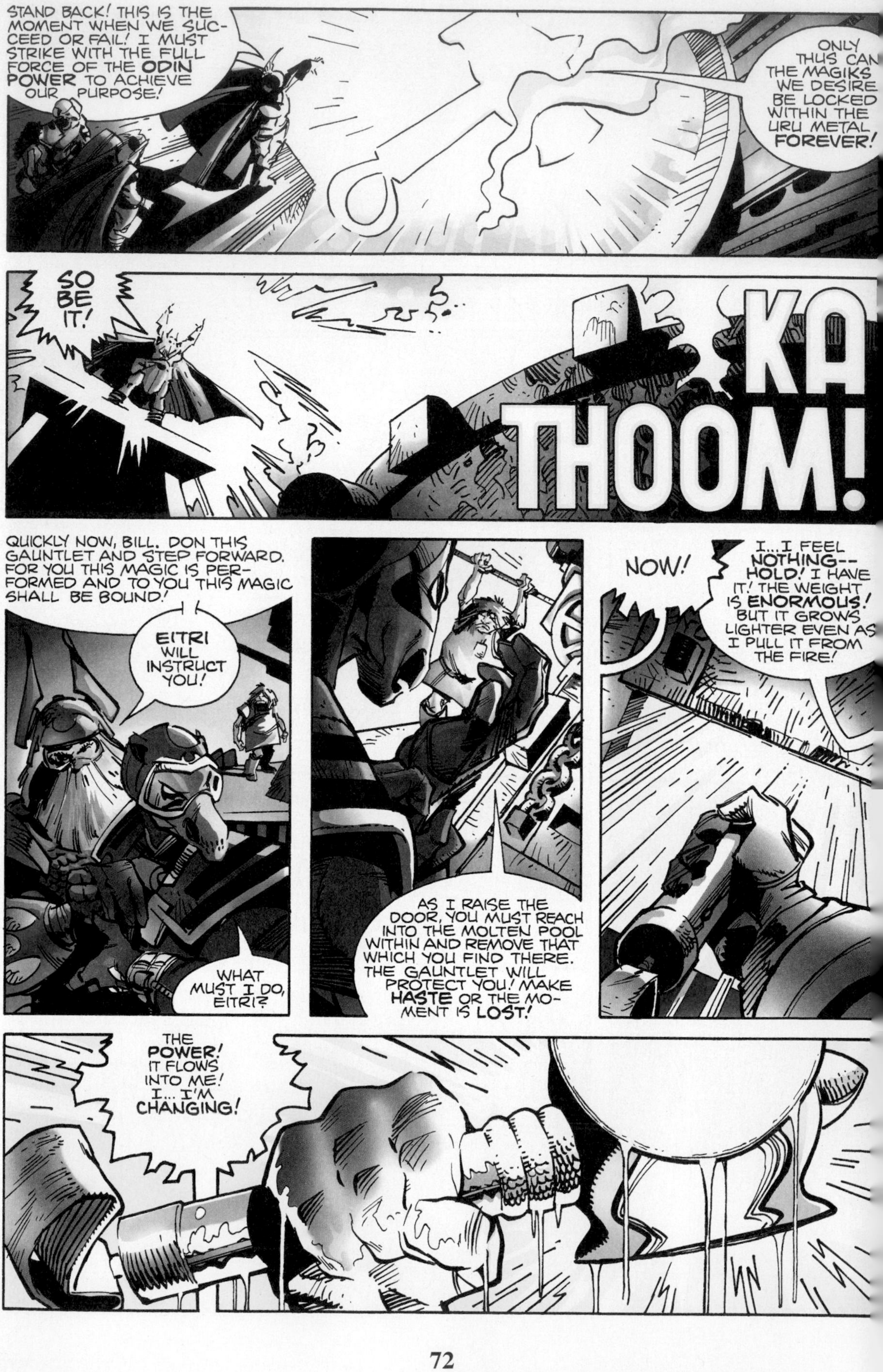

STAND BACK! THIS IS THE MOMENT WHEN WE SUCCEED OR FAIL! I MUST STRIKE WITH THE FULL FORCE OF THE ODIN POWER TO ACHIEVE OUR PURPOSE!
ONLY THUS CAN THE MAGIKS WE DESIRE BE LOCKED WITHIN THE URU METAL FOREVER!
SO BE IT!
KA THOOM!
QUICKLY NOW, BILL. DON THIS GAUNTLET AND STEP FORWARD. FOR YOU THIS MAGIC IS PERFORMED AND TO YOU THIS MAGIC SHALL BE BOUND!
EITRI WILL INSTRUCT YOU!
WHAT MUST I DO, EITRI?
AS I RAISE THE DOOR, YOU MUST REACH INTO THE MOLTEN POOL WITHIN AND REMOVE THAT WHICH YOU FIND THERE. THE GAUNTLET WILL PROTECT YOU! MAKE HASTE OR THE MOMENT IS LOST!
NOW!
I...I FEEL NOTHING-- HOLD! I HAVE IT! THE WEIGHT IS ENORMOUS! BUT IT GROWS LIGHTER EVEN AS I PULL IT FROM THE FIRE!
THE POWER! IT FLOWS INTO ME! I... I'M CHANGING!

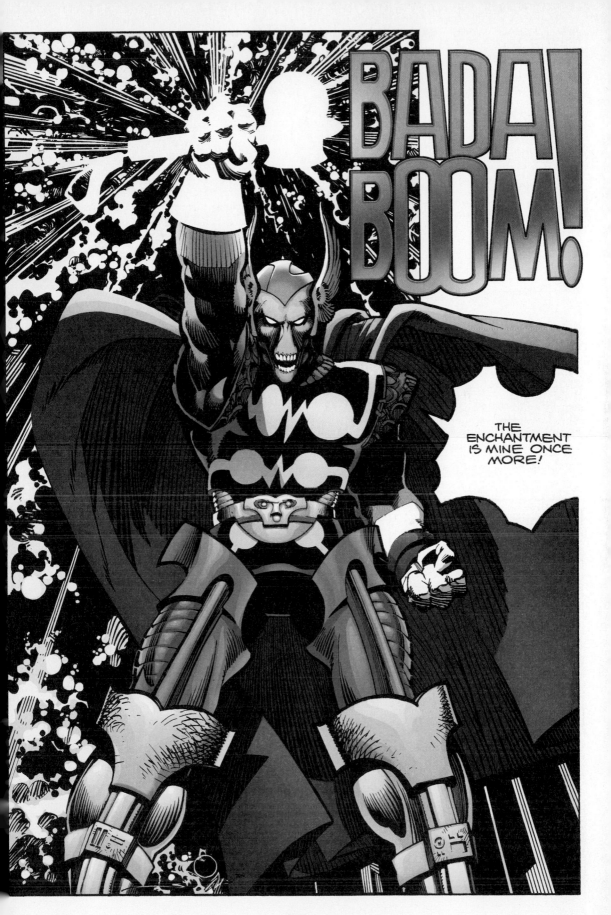

BADA! BOOM!

THE ENCHANTMENT IS MINE ONCE MORE!

AND SO SHALL IT EVER BE FOR AS LONG AS YOU LIVE. THE FORGING IS COMPLETE.

I DO ACCEPT IT, WITH ALL MY HEART.

BUT I MUST ASK YOU ONCE AGAIN, NOW THAT YOU FEEL THE POWER AND RESPONSIBILITY THAT YOU MUST SHOULDER, DO YOU TAKE THIS BURDEN OF YOUR OWN FREE WILL? FOR, ONCE UNDERTAKEN, IT WILL BE YOURS TO CARRY **FOREVER!**

VERY WELL. THIS HAMMER SHALL BE CALLED **STORM BREAKER!** MAY YOU BEAR THE BURDEN AS WELL AS MY SON, WHO HAS CARRIED SUCH RESPONSIBILITY NEARLY ALL THE DAYS OF HIS LIFE.

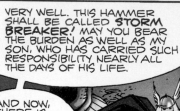

AND NOW, THERE IS YET ONE FURTHER TASK TO DISCHARGE.

STEP FORWARD, THOR AND RECEIVE FROM MY HANDS THE HAMMER, MJOLNIR...

...WHICH IS NOW AND FOREVER **YOURS** ALONE!

CARRY IT AS YOU ALWAYS HAVE, WITH **HONOR!**

THERE IS NOT MUCH TIME. I MUST RETURN TO ASGARD FOR I AM WEARY AND SPENT FROM THE EFFORT OF THIS DAY.

BUT BEFORE WE LEFT THE GOLDEN REALM, I SAT IN THE HIGH SEAT AND SOUGHT OUT A VISION OF YOUR PEOPLE, BILL.

ARE THEY...?

YOU MUST MAKE HASTE. THE DEMONS ARE NEARLY UPON THEM AND EVEN NOW I FEAR IT MAY BE TOO LATE. BUT WITHOUT SUCH POWER AS YOU NOW POSSESS, YOU COULD NOT HAVE WITHSTOOD THEIR FURY.

FATHER, LET **ME** GO WITH HIM.

IF, AS YOU HAVE SAID, THE DEMONS' POWER RIVALS YOUR OWN EVEN BILL MAY NOT SUCCEED AGAINST THEM.

YET **TOGETHER** WE MAY PREVAIL!

THIS WAS MY HOPE. BUT REMEMBER, MY SON, THE POWER OF THE DEMONS COMES FROM THEIR **SOURCE.** YOU MUST DESTROY IT OR THERE WILL BE **NO** VICTORY!

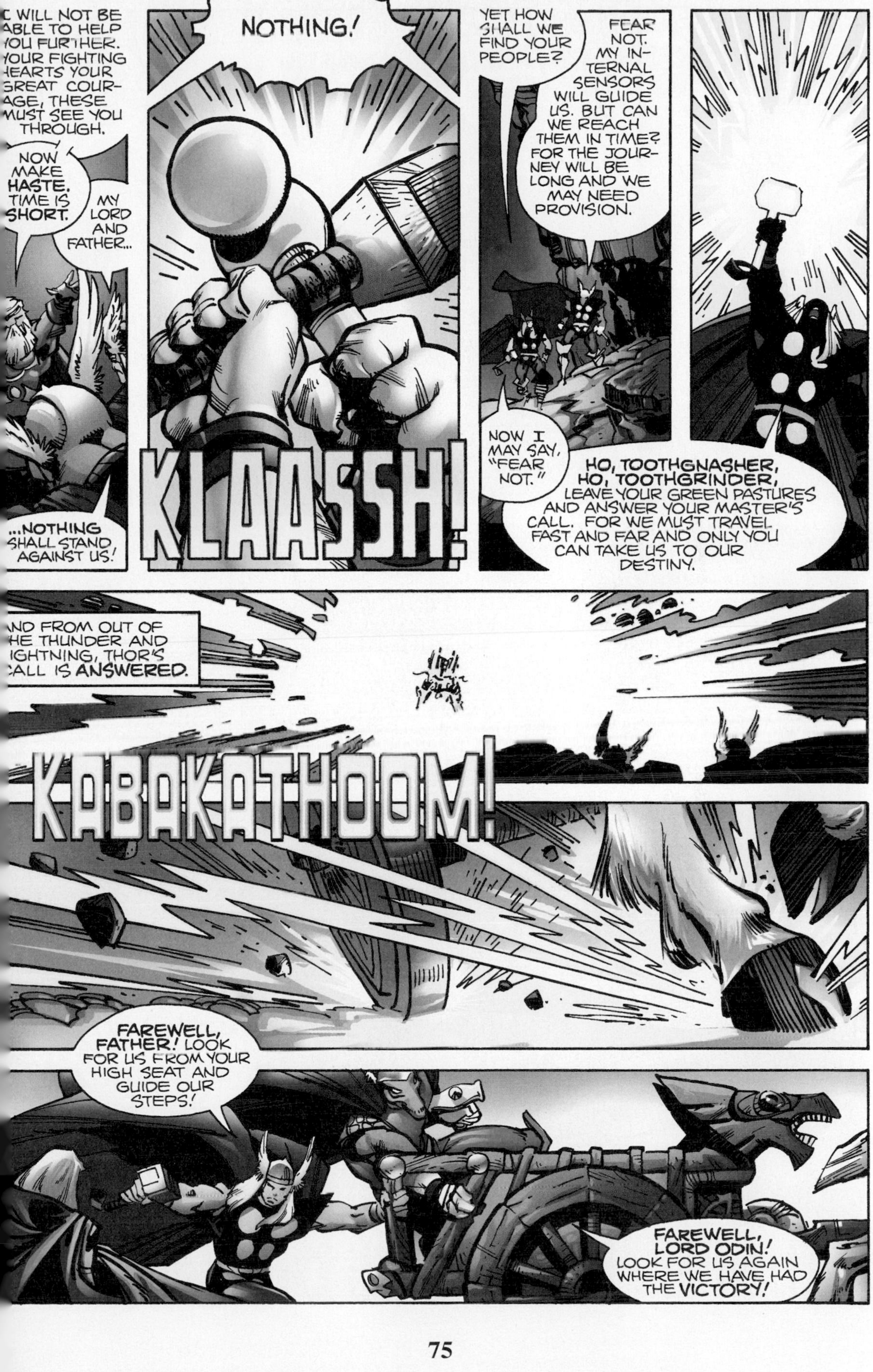
I WILL NOT BE ABLE TO HELP YOU FURTHER. YOUR FIGHTING HEARTS YOUR GREAT COURAGE, THESE MUST SEE YOU THROUGH.
NOW MAKE HASTE. TIME IS SHORT.
MY LORD AND FATHER...
NOTHING!
...NOTHING SHALL STAND AGAINST US!
KLAASSH!
YET HOW SHALL WE FIND YOUR PEOPLE?
FEAR NOT. MY INTERNAL SENSORS WILL GUIDE US. BUT CAN WE REACH THEM IN TIME? FOR THE JOURNEY WILL BE LONG AND WE MAY NEED PROVISION.
NOW I MAY SAY, "FEAR NOT."
HO, TOOTHGNASHER, HO, TOOTHGRINDER, LEAVE YOUR GREEN PASTURES AND ANSWER YOUR MASTER'S CALL. FOR WE MUST TRAVEL FAST AND FAR AND ONLY YOU CAN TAKE US TO OUR DESTINY.
AND FROM OUT OF THE THUNDER AND LIGHTNING, THOR'S CALL IS ANSWERED.
KABAKATHOOM!
FAREWELL, FATHER! LOOK FOR US FROM YOUR HIGH SEAT AND GUIDE OUR STEPS!
FAREWELL, LORD ODIN! LOOK FOR US AGAIN WHERE WE HAVE HAD THE VICTORY!

AND THEE, LADY?

FAREWELL, MY LIEGE! LOOK **NOT** FOR ME AGAIN TILL THE SUN STANDS UPON YON HILL!

SIF!

DO NOT TRY TO PREVENT ME, THOR. I HAVE **EARNED** THE RIGHT TO COME.

SO BE IT, AS THEY SAY.

LOOK TO THY WEAPONS, YOU DEMONS!

UP, TOOTHGNASHER! UP, TOOTHGRINDER! PULL FOR THE STARS! THE FOE AWAITS AND JOYOUS BATTLE IS BEFORE US!

THABAROOM!

NEXT: THOUGH HEL SHOULD BAR THE WAY

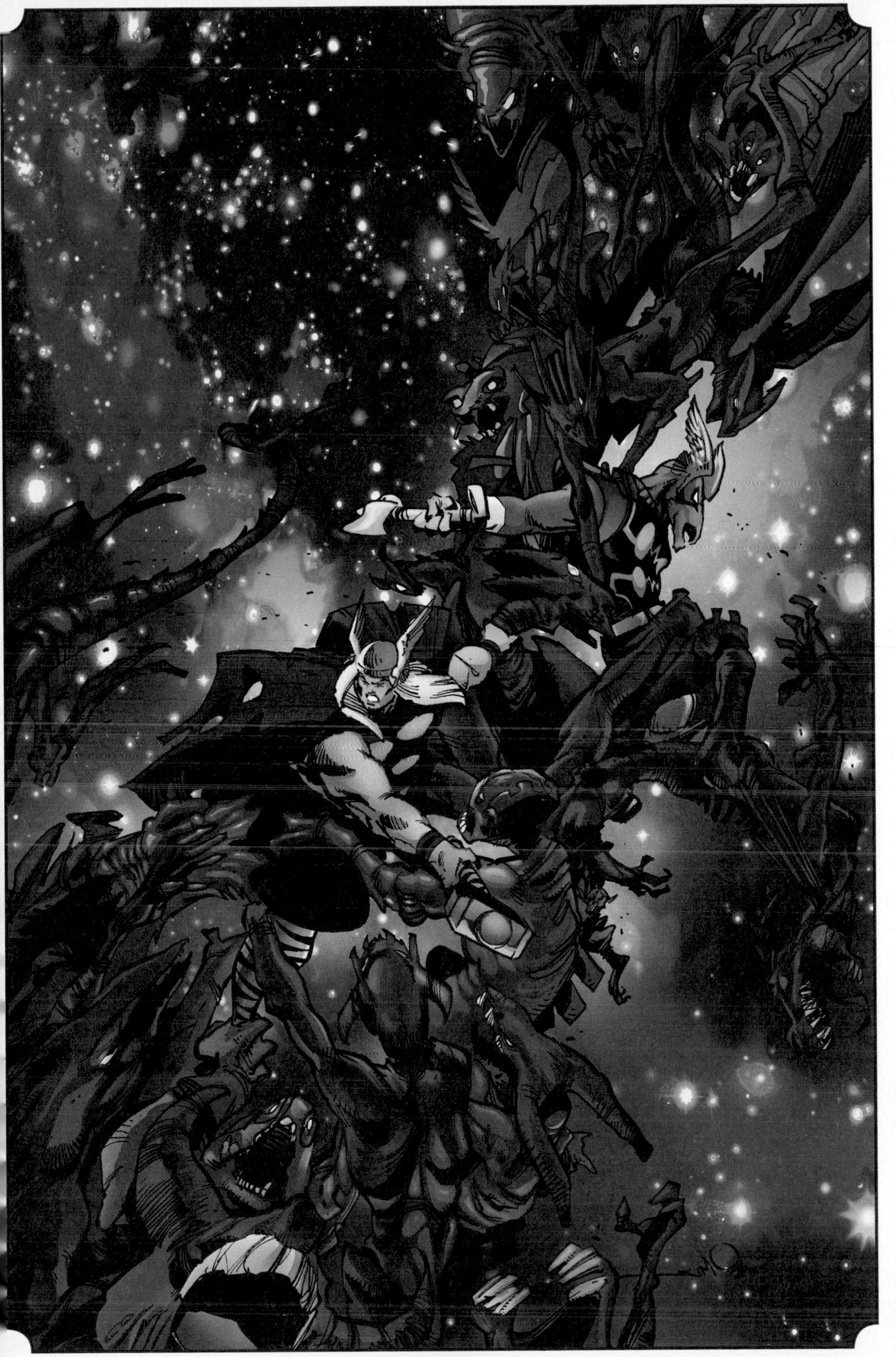

• 340 •

STAN LEE PRESENTS: the MIGHTY THOR

THOUGH HEL SHOULD BAR THE WAY!

THOR, SIF, AND BETA RAY BILL HAVE LEFT ASGARD FAR BEHIND AS THEY RIDE THE TIDES OF SPACE SEARCHING FOR BILL'S PEOPLE AND THE DEMONS WHO PURSUE THEM.

THE JOURNEY HAS BEEN LONG AND HAZARDOUS BUT AT LAST, THE FLEET OF STARSHIPS LIES LIKE A GREAT RIVER BELOW THEM...

ART AND STORY: WALTER SIMONSON · LETTERING: JOHN WORKMAN, JR. · COLORS: GEORGE ROUSSOS · EDITING: MARK GRUENWALD · EDITOR-IN-CHIEF: JIM SHOOTER

AND THE DEMONS ARE CLOSE AT HAND!

I SEE THEM! THEY HAVE CAUGHT THE LAST SHIP IN LINE!

MY PEOPLE! LOCKED IN COLD-SLEEP AS THEY WERE, THEY HAD NO CHANCE AGAINST THOSE CREATURES!

WE ARE TOO LATE!

TO SAVE THIS ONE SHIP...

WHAROOM WHAROOM

...BUT WE WILL AVENGE THEM AS ONLY THE MIGHTIEST WARRIORS OF ASGARD CAN!

OUR HAMMERS SHALL STRIKE WITHOUT MERCY!

LADY SIF!

RIDE ON! RIDE ON! ODIN SAID THAT ONLY BY DESTROYING THE SOURCE OF THESE DEMONS CAN WE WIN THE BATTLE!

I WILL REMAIN HERE AND PROTECT THE FLEET UNTIL YOU CAN REACH THE DEMON'S CRADLE AND SHATTER IT!

BUT, SIF...

RIDE ON! DO NOT WASTE WHAT LITTLE TIME WE HAVE! FOLLOW THE DEMONS HOME AND DO WHAT MUST BE DONE!

PRO-TECTING BILL'S PEOPLE IS MY DUTY!

WE CANNOT LEAVE HER THUS!

NO, SHE IS RIGHT. ONLY YOU AND I MIGHT WIN AGAINST THE DEMON HORDES ON THEIR OWN GROUND.

AND WE MUST LEARN ALL WE CAN ABOUT THEM SINCE EVEN MY FATHER, ODIN, CANNOT SEE INTO THEIR DOMAIN TO LEARN THEIR PURPOSE.

ON, TOOTH-GNASHER! ON, TOOTH-GRINDER! RACE THE LIGHTNING!

80

SO THOR AND BILL THUNDER PAST THE STARS, TRACKING THE DEMON WAVE THAT SEEMS TO FLOW ENDLESSLY PAST THEM...

...MOVING AT SUCH GREAT SPEED THAT THEY ARE INVISIBLE TO EVERY DEMONIC EYE...

...UNTIL AT LAST THEY REACH THE CORE OF THE GALAXY THAT ONCE HOUSED THE CIVILIZATION OF BILL'S PEOPLE.

BY THE BRISTLING BEARD OF ODIN!

MY HOME! MY HOME! WHAT HAVE THEY DONE TO YOU?

FOR BEFORE THEM LIE NOT THE RADIANT STARS OF AN ANCIENT AND WISE RACE...

...BUT A GLOWING PORTAL, PULSING WITH EVIL, OUT OF WHICH STREAMS A NUMBER-LESS HORDE OF DEMONS INTO THE UNIVERSE OF MEN!

WOE THAT THE VERY STARS WHICH GAVE ME LIFE SHOULD BE HARNESSED NOW TO CREATE SUCH EVIL!

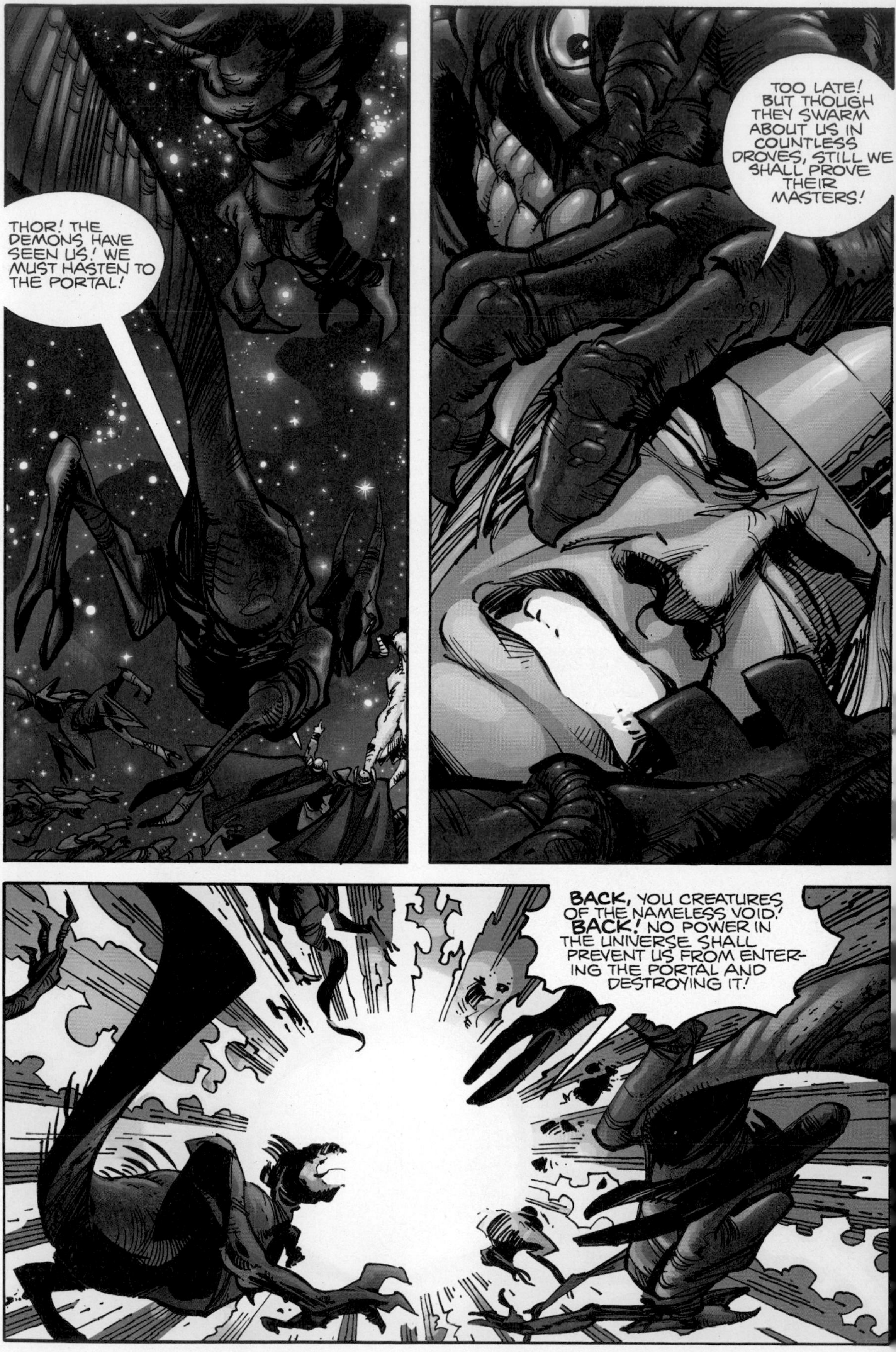
THOR! THE DEMONS HAVE SEEN US! WE MUST HASTEN TO THE PORTAL!
TOO LATE! BUT THOUGH THEY SWARM ABOUT US IN COUNTLESS DROVES, STILL WE SHALL PROVE THEIR MASTERS!
BACK, YOU CREATURES OF THE NAMELESS VOID! BACK! NO POWER IN THE UNIVERSE SHALL PREVENT US FROM ENTERING THE PORTAL AND DESTROYING IT!

MEANWHILE, BEYOND THE FIELDS WE KNOW, A MIGHTY FIGURE, SURROUNDED BY A SHADOW HOST, SWINGS AGAIN HIS MALLET HIGH ABOVE THE GLOWING ANVIL...

...AND THE ECHOES OF HIS BLOW RING ACROSS THE COSMOS.

DOOM!

IN THE DEEPS OF THE EARTH, THE MONSTERS ARE WAKING.

NO DEMON HAS YET GOTTEN PAST ME, BUT THEIR NUMBERS INCREASE WITH EVERY SECOND.

AND NOW THEY HAVE BEGUN TO MASS TOGETHER FOR THEIR FINAL ATTACK!

VERY WELL! IF TODAY I MUST JOURNEY TO THE HALLS OF HELA, I SHALL NOT TRAVEL ALONE!

COME, DEMONS! WHO WILL BE THE FIRST TO TASTE THIS SWEET STEEL?

BADDOOM! BADDOOM!

WHA--!

84

THAT SHIP! IT MUST BE BILL'S SKUTTLE-BUTT!

INDEED I AM, MILADY. REPAIRED AND RETURNED TO DUTY. JUST IN TIME IT WOULD SEEM.

AND THOUGH I DO NOT RECOGNIZE YOU, YOU MUST BE A FRIEND OF MY MASTER TO FIGHT HIS BATTLES.

LEAP ABOARD AND WE SHALL FIGHT TOGETHER.

WELL SAID. I AM SIF, WARRIOR MAID OF ASGARD.

BILL AND HIS COMPANION—THOR—HAVE JOURNEYED OFF TO FIND THE SOURCE OF THESE DEMONS AND DESTROY IT.

IN THE MEANTIME, I REMAIN BEHIND TO GUARD THE FLEET AND ITS PRECIOUS CARGO.

THEN LET US BEGIN. THESE CREATURES SEEM SINGLE-MINDEDLY DETERMINED TO DESTROY US.

PERHAPS WE CAN LEAD THEM AWAY FROM THE FLEET FOR A TIME AND GIVE BILL AND HIS COMPANION A CHANCE TO FINISH THEIR JOB!

BUT AS THE DEMONS TURN FROM THE FLEET IN HOT PURSUIT, LET US TURN TO THE GARDENS OF ASGARD TO LISTEN TO VALOROUS VOLSTAGG CONCLUDE HIS CHILLING TALE OF THE DEATH OF BALDER...

SO, MY YOUNG FRIEND, NOBLE BALDER WENT DOWN TO NIFLHEIM, HELA'S DARK DOMAIN.

HE FOUND THAT THE LEGENDS OF THE AFTER-LIFE WERE TRUE.

BEFORE HIM, DANK AND CHEERLESS, LAY THE CORPSE STRAND, THE HALLS OF THE TORTURED...

...AND THE DRAGON, NID-HOGG, THE EATER OF THE DEAD...

...CONSUMING THE SOULS OF THOSE WHO HAVE FLED IN TERROR DEEP INTO NIFLHEIM PAST THE GREAT WOLF GARM.

WHEN HE LOOKED UPON THE DEAD, HE WAS FILLED WITH HORROR...

...FOR THERE BEFORE HIM WERE THE VERY WARRIORS WHOM HE HIMSELF HAD SLAIN AND SENT TO NIFLHEIM IN BATTLES PAST!

THESE WERE THE FRUITS OF HIS MANY VICTORIES!

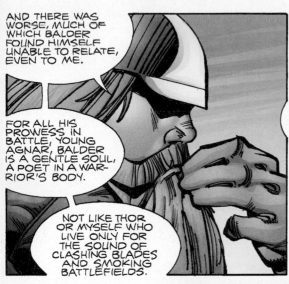

AND THERE WAS WORSE, MUCH OF WHICH BALDER FOUND HIMSELF UNABLE TO RELATE, EVEN TO ME.

FOR ALL HIS PROWESS IN BATTLE, YOUNG AGNAR, BALDER IS A GENTLE SOUL, A POET IN A WARRIOR'S BODY.

NOT LIKE THOR OR MYSELF WHO LIVE ONLY FOR THE SOUND OF CLASHING BLADES AND SMOKING BATTLEFIELDS.

OF COURSE I HAVE—UMMPH—GROWN SO—UGGH—LARGE THAT NO ORDINARY FOE IS WORTHY OF MY GREAT ABILITIES.

GROAN.

SURELY IF SOME HARM CAME NOW TO BALDER AND YOU WERE RESPONSIBLE, WHY I MIGHT EVEN FIND IT IN MY HEART, SO MUCH LARGER THAN THAT OF ORDINARY MEN, TO FORGIVE YOU.

LET ME DUST YOU OFF.

Paf Paf

OWOWOW.

WHY, EVEN THOR OR FANDRAL THE DASHING MIGHT FORGIVE YOU BECAUSE THEY WERE ONCE YOUNG AND DARING THEMSELVES.

POMPOUS OLD WINDBAG!

BUT HOGUN THE GRIM?

URK!

HOGUN WAS NEVER YOUNG. HE WOULD NEVER FORGET...

...OR FORGIVE!

87

MEANWHILE, IN THE DISTANT GALACTIC CORE...

IT IS NO GOOD, THOR! EVEN OUR COMBINED MIGHT IS UNABLE TO FORCE AN ENTRANCE THROUGH THE PORTAL!

THE POWER WITHIN IS TOO GREAT!

AND THE HEAT IS MORE THAN EVEN I CAN BEAR!

YOU ARE RIGHT, FRIEND BILL!

I NEVER THOUGHT SUCH POWER EXISTED BEYOND THE HALLS OF ODIN IN ASGARD!

YET THOUGH WE CANNOT ENTER, WE MAY STILL BE ABLE TO CLOSE THE PORTAL FOREVER TO THE DEMON HORDE AND SAVE YOUR PEOPLE!

STAND BESIDE THE PORTAL HERE AND AWAIT MY CALL.

I WILL TAKE MYSELF TO THE OTHER SIDE AND TOGETHER, WE MAY DO WHAT NEITHER OF US COULD ACCOMPLISH ALONE!

NOW, BILL! THROW YOUR HAMMER EVEN AS I THROW MJOLNIR AT THE PORTAL'S CENTER.

IF THE HAMMERS CAN COLLIDE WITHIN THE PORTAL ITSELF, PERHAPS--

SAY NO MORE, THUNDERER!

LET STORM BREAKER AND MJOLNIR SPEAK AS ONE!

BARRAHAMM!

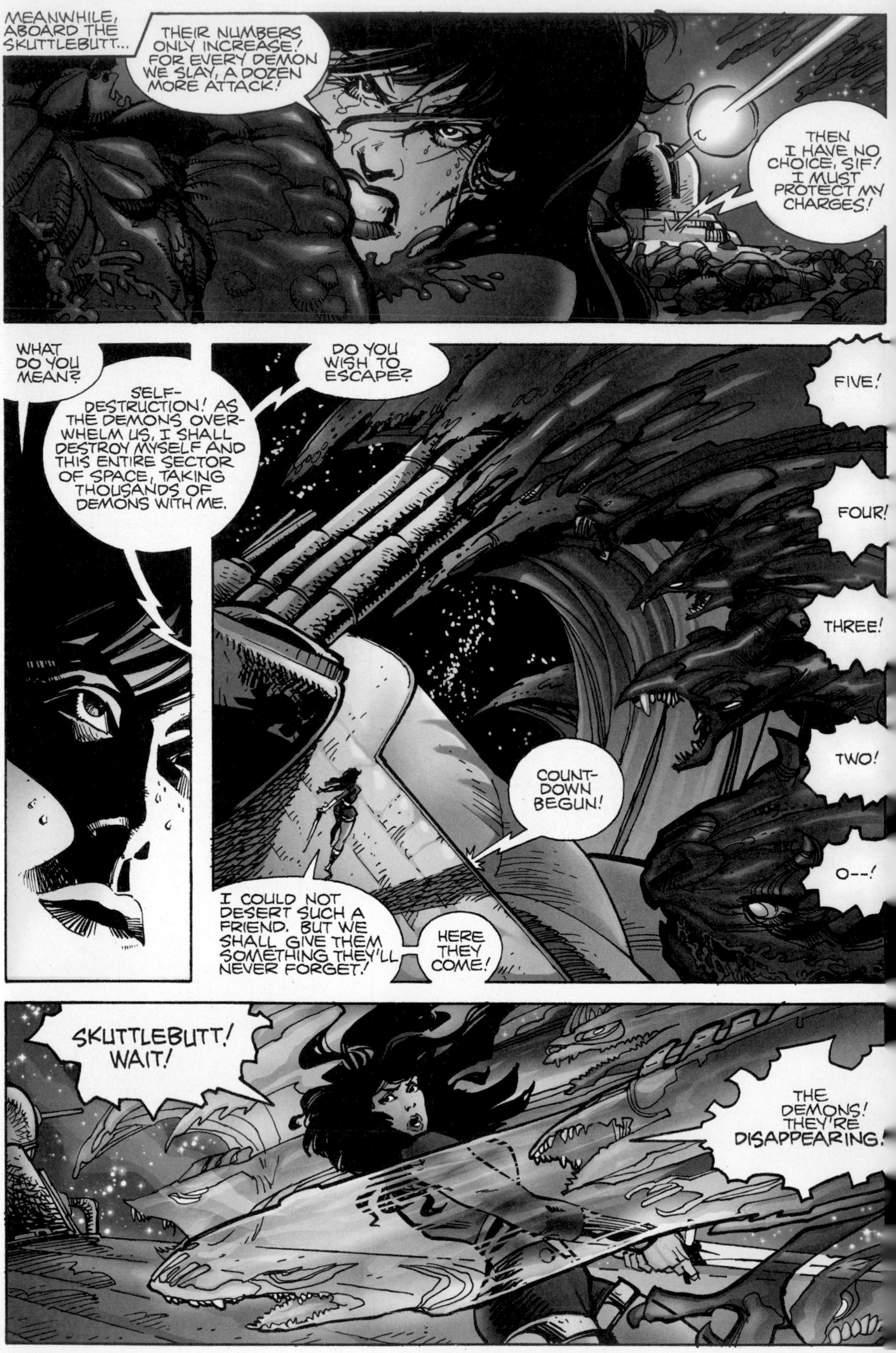
MEANWHILE, ABOARD THE SKUTTLEBUTT...
THEIR NUMBERS ONLY INCREASE! FOR EVERY DEMON WE SLAY, A DOZEN MORE ATTACK!
THEN I HAVE NO CHOICE, SIF! I MUST PROTECT MY CHARGES!
WHAT DO YOU MEAN?
SELF-DESTRUCTION! AS THE DEMONS OVERWHELM US, I SHALL DESTROY MYSELF AND THIS ENTIRE SECTOR OF SPACE, TAKING THOUSANDS OF DEMONS WITH ME.
DO YOU WISH TO ESCAPE?
I COULD NOT DESERT SUCH A FRIEND. BUT WE SHALL GIVE THEM SOMETHING THEY'LL NEVER FORGET!
HERE THEY COME!
COUNT-DOWN BEGUN!
FIVE!
FOUR!
THREE!
TWO!
O--!
SKUTTLEBUTT! WAIT!
THE DEMONS! THEY'RE DISAPPEARING!

THEY'RE GONE!

BILL...AND THOR...MUST HAVE DESTROYED...THE DEMONS' SOURCE...

...WE'VE...WON...

SIF?

I'LL BE ALLRIGHT, SKUTTLEBUTT. I'M JUST...SO TIRED. BUT BILL...AND THOR?

STILL ALIVE, MY SENSORS TELL ME. AND RE-TURNING HERE.

BUT THERE IS MORE TO YOUR STORY THAN A SIMPLE FRIENDSHIP WITH BILL. THE OFFER-ING OF ONE'S LIFE FOR ANOTHER IS NO SMALL GIFT. AS I WELL KNOW.

LET US TALK AS WE RETURN TO THE FLEET TO WAIT. I, TOO, WOULD LEARN MORE ABOUT YOU ...AND BILL.

AT THAT MOMENT, IN A PENTHOUSE OVERLOOKING CENTRAL PARK, IN NEW YORK CITY...

YOU NEEDN'T WORRY. I AM NOT UNSKILLED IN GETTING WHAT I WANT.

I DARE SAY. BUT HAVE A CARE, LORELEI.

THOR IS NO ORDINARY BUMPKIN TO SWOON AT YOUR FEET.

PERHAPS NOT. STILL, I HAVE MANY CHARMS WHICH I AM CERTAIN WILL ASSIST ME IN HIS DIRECTION.

BUT YOU, LOKI. YOU HAVE AIDED ME IN THIS ENDEAVOR.

WHAT REWARD DO YOU LOOK TO RECEIVE OUT OF THIS GAME?

IT WILL AMUSE ME, LADY.

IT WILL AMUSE ME GREATLY.

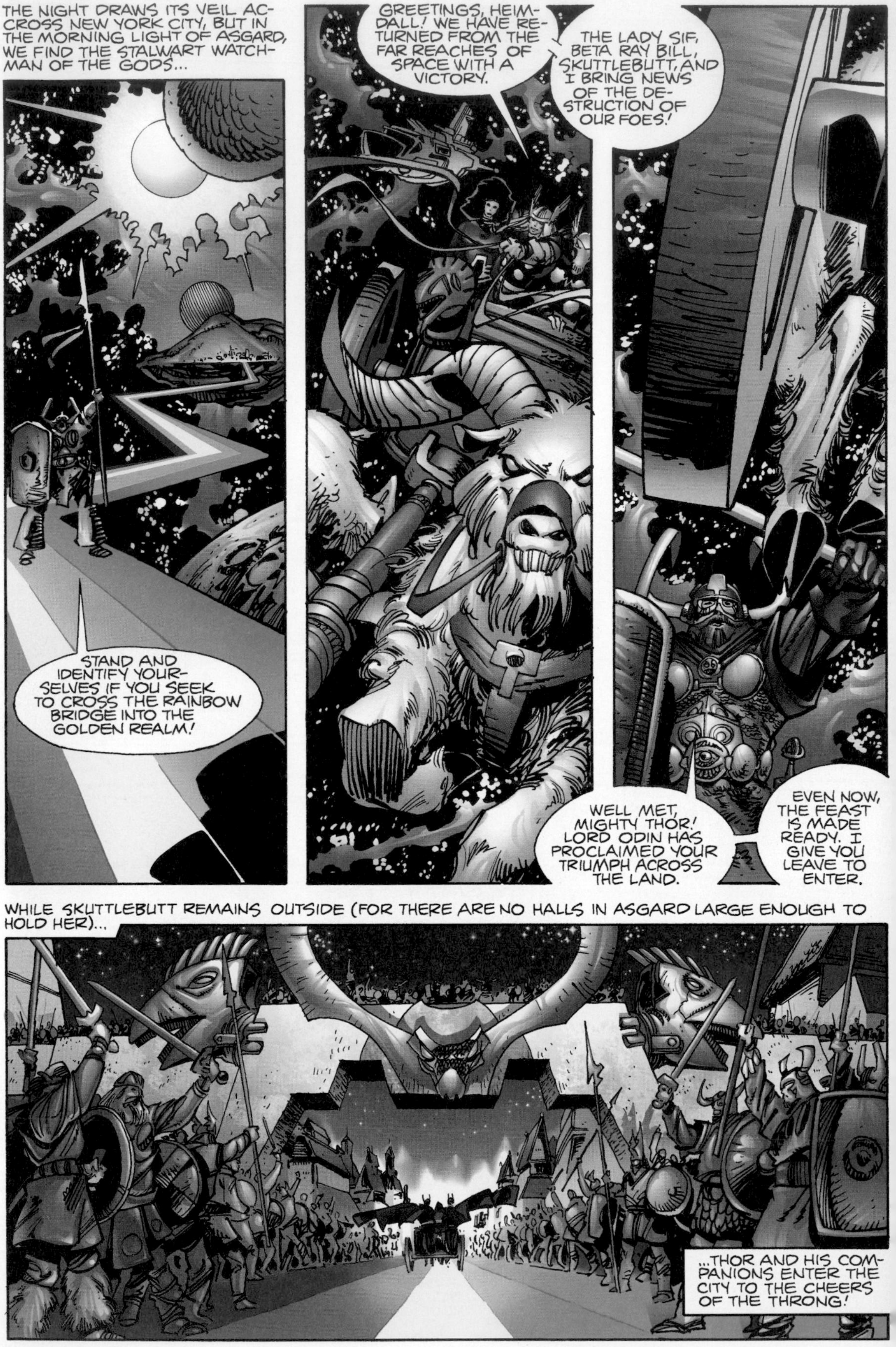
THE NIGHT DRAWS ITS VEIL ACCROSS NEW YORK CITY, BUT IN THE MORNING LIGHT OF ASGARD, WE FIND THE STALWART WATCHMAN OF THE GODS...
STAND AND IDENTIFY YOURSELVES IF YOU SEEK TO CROSS THE RAINBOW BRIDGE INTO THE GOLDEN REALM!
GREETINGS, HEIMDALL! WE HAVE RETURNED FROM THE FAR REACHES OF SPACE WITH A VICTORY.
THE LADY SIF, BETA RAY BILL, SKUTTLEBUTT, AND I BRING NEWS OF THE DESTRUCTION OF OUR FOES!
WELL MET, MIGHTY THOR! LORD ODIN HAS PROCLAIMED YOUR TRIUMPH ACROSS THE LAND.
EVEN NOW, THE FEAST IS MADE READY. I GIVE YOU LEAVE TO ENTER.
WHILE SKUTTLEBUTT REMAINS OUTSIDE (FOR THERE ARE NO HALLS IN ASGARD LARGE ENOUGH TO HOLD HER)...
...THOR AND HIS COMPANIONS ENTER THE CITY TO THE CHEERS OF THE THRONG!

STILL, EVEN HEROES NEED BATHS AND AS OUR COMRADES CHANGE INTO FRESH CLOTHING TO PREPARE FOR THE FEAST...

YOU ARE STRANGELY SILENT, FRIEND BILL. I HOPE YOU DO NOT FEEL THAT I HOLD A GRUDGE AGAINST YOU FOR YOUR VICTORY EARLIER AGAINST ME.*

AND AS FOR **YOUR** PEOPLE, WE DID WIN, YOU KNOW.

FEAR NOT, MY FRIEND. YOUR FRIENDSHIP IS BEYOND RE-PROACH. AS IS OUR VICTORY.

BUT I MUST SHORTLY RETURN TO GUIDE MY PEOPLE TO A NEW HOME AND THOUGH I CAN HARDLY BELIEVE IT, I AM LOATH TO LEAVE ASGARD...

...AND THAT ALL THAT I HAVE FOUND HERE.

THOR 338—NO POINTS IF YOU MISSED IT.

THE UNCOMPROMISING ACCEPTANCE I HAVE HAD WHEN EVEN MY OWN PEOPLE CAN SCARCELY LOOK AT ME, THE JOY OF COMRADESHIP, EVEN THE TOUCH OF A WOMAN'S HAND...

BUT I SAY TOO MUCH.

I AM WHAT I AM AND CANNOT CHANGE IT.

I SHALL SEE YOU AT DINNER.

ELSEWHERE...

YOU SENT FOR ME, MY LORD.

THANK YOU FOR COMING SO QUICKLY, SIF.

I WOULD LIKE A FEW WORDS WITH YOU... ABOUT BILL.

I KNOW MORE THAN YOU MIGHT THINK, LADY, ABOUT YOUR FEELINGS FOR HIM. I, TOO, FIND HIM A MATCH FOR MY OWN SON IN MORE WAYS THAN ONE.

BUT THERE IS IN BILL A CORE OF MELANCHOLY THAT EVEN I CANNOT FATHOM.

I THOUGHT PERHAPS A WOMAN'S HEART WOULD KNOW WHAT I DO NOT.

93

MY HEART WOULD KNOW NO MORE THAN YOU, LORD ODIN, WERE IT NOT FOR SKUTTLEBUTT. FOR BILL'S SHIP AND I HAVE HAD A LONG TALK AND SHARED MANY SECRETS.

SHE HAS BEEN WITH HIM ON THEIR ODYSSEY AND KNOWS HIM BETTER THAN ANYONE. SHE KNOWS WHAT HE DID **NOT** TELL US HIMSELF.

FOR THOUGH HIS STORY WAS TRUE, IT WAS IN-COMPLETE!

"WHEN HE WAS CHOSEN TO BE THE GUARDIAN OF HIS PEOPLE, HE NEGLECTED TO TELL US OF THE GREAT GAMES THAT WERE HELD TO PICK THE MIGHTIEST CHAMPION.

"HOW HE WON OVER THOUSANDS OF OTHERS IN GRUELING TESTS OF POWER AND ENDURANCE.

"HOW, FROM AMONG THE PHYSICALLY ACCEPTABLE CANDI-DATES, THE BEST WERE CHOSEN IN A SERIES OF PSYCHO-LOGICAL EXAMINA-TIONS...

"THAT LEFT MOST OF THEM DEAD OR INSANE!

"OR HOW THE CREATION OF BETA RAY BILL WAS ACCOMPLISHED WITH PAIN BEYOND IMAGINING...

"...UNTIL OF ALL THOSE COURAGEOUS WARRIORS, ONLY HE SURVIVED THE DREADFUL PROCESS."

AND THE CHANGE WAS IRREVERSIBLE. HE WILL ALWAYS BE WHAT HE HAS BECOME.

WORST OF ALL, HIS OWN PEOPLE COULD HARDLY BEAR THE SIGHT OF HIM ONCE HE HAD BEEN FINISHED. YET HE WOULD DO IT ALL AGAIN IF NECESSARY.

OH, ALL-FATHER, HOW DO MORTALS ENDURE IT?

BE AT PEACE, SIF. LET US SEE WHAT WE CAN DO.

THAT EVENING, AFTER THE FEASTING IS NEARLY THROUGH...

LET ALL NOW BE SILENT! LORD ODIN WOULD ADDRESS THE HEROES!

MY CHILDREN, WE STAND NOW TO HONOR THESE TWO WHO HAVE GONE TO THE ENDS OF THE UNIVERSE AND RETURNED VICTORIOUS.

WHAT CAN WE GIVE SUCH WARRIORS THAT THEY DO NOT ALREADY POSSESS?

VERY LITTLE, FOR THE TRUE WARRIOR CARRIES WITHIN HIMSELF ALL THAT IS NECESSARY.

YET MY HEART TELLS ME THAT WE MAY STAND HERE TOGETHER FOR THE LAST TIME AND SOME TOKEN, TO REMIND A DISTANT TRAVELER OF HIS FRIENDS, SEEMS APPROPRIATE.

STEP FORWARD AND RAISE YOUR HAMMERS THAT I MAY BESTOW UPON YOU EACH A GIFT THAT I HOPE WILL BE WORTHY OF YOU.

TO YOU, MY SON, AND TO YOU, BILL, LET EACH RECEIVE WHAT IS NEEDFUL.

SO SPEAKS ODIN!

KRACALACTAKA!

I...I FEEL NO DIFFERENT!

PERHAPS NOT. BUT I HAD AN OLD ENCHANTMENT THAT HAS OUTLIVED ITS ORIGINAL PURPOSE.

WITH MINOR ALTERATIONS, I THOUGHT YOU MIGHT FIND IT USEFUL.

STRIKE YOUR HAMMER, STORM BREAKER, UPON THE GROUND.

GO ON!

STRIKE IT!

BARROOM

96

AND SUDDENLY, THERE IS A DEAD SILENCE WITHIN THE HALL...

UNTIL AT LAST...

I...I AM MYSELF AGAIN!

I AM MYSELF AGAIN!

AND STORM BREAKER HAS BECOME A...A CANE!

AS I SAID, AN ENCHANTMENT THAT HAD OUTLIVED ITS PURPOSE. NOW, WHENEVER YOU NEED TO, STRIKE THE CANE UPON THE GROUND AND BETA RAY THOR WILL LIVE AGAIN.

MY LORD...

MY LORD...

STAND UP, NOBLE WARRIOR. YOU HAVE EARNED THE RIGHT.

WHAT SAY YOU, BILL, TO A JOUST NOW, EH?

BUT WAIT, IF ODIN'S ENCHANTMENT NOW RESTS WITHIN STORM BREAKER, WHAT OF MJOLNIR?

WHAT OF DONALD BLAKE?

HEAR ME, HOSTS OF ASGARD!

PRAISE THESE HEROES! BILL, WHO HAS BECOME THE SECOND SON I NEVER HAD!

AND THOR, WHO IS NOW AND FOR-EVER, INDIVISIBLY, THE FIRST SON OF ODIN, THE GOD OF THUNDER AND HEIR TO THE THRONE OF ASGARD!

THE CHEERING LASTS A LONG, LONG TIME.

BUT THOUGH THE FEAST RENEWS ITSELF AND LASTS BEYOND THE COCK'S CROW, AT LENGTH THE THRONGS DISPERSE AND GOODBYES ARE SAID.

I **MUST** GO, THOR! AS A WARRIOR MAIDEN, I HAVE BECOME BLUNT AND DULLED. I HAVE EVEN BE-LIEVED THINGS THAT I AM SURE NOW WERE BUT BE-TRAYALS OF MY EYES.

ON BILL'S QUEST, I MAY REGAIN MY TEMPER AS I NEVER COULD ON MIDGARD.*

DO NOT FORGET ME.

LADY, SOONER COULD I FORGET MY OWN NAME.

*EARTH

MAY YOU AND YOURS BE GRANTED SAFE HAVEN, BILL.

STAND TOGETHER AND I WILL SEND YOU TO YOUR SHIP THAT WAITS BEYOND THE RAINBOW BRIDGE.

FARE THEE WELL!

AND NOW, MY SON. TO BED. IT HAS BEEN A LONG DAY.

FATHER, BEFORE WE RETIRE, I MUST KNOW SOMETHING. DID YOU SEND US TO SKARTHEIM KNOWING BILL WOULD BEAT ME?

AND COULD I HAVE BEATEN HIM ELSE-WHERE?

THOR, HUMILITY IS A LESSON EVEN GODS CAN LEARN. SUCH WAS THE MEANING OF MJOLNIR'S SPELL WROUGHT LONG AGO.

THOUGH THY HAMMER STILL RETAINS SOME LITTLE ENCHANTMENT, YOU WILL CARRY THE MEMORY OF YOUR COMBAT WITH BILL FOREVER. WE MAY **ALL** PROFIT FROM THAT, NO?

AS FOR ANOTHER FIGHT WITH BILL...

...NOT EVEN THE ALL-WISE KNOWS EVERY-THING, MY SON.

98

AS NIGHT FALLS IN ASGARD, SO TOO IT BLANKETS EARTH BUT THE LARGE TANKER ASTRAGLIA, OFF CAPE COD AND BOUND FOR THE ST. LAWRENCE MOVES STEADILY ON UNDER THE STARRY SKY...

CALM NIGHT TONIGHT, EH, SKIPPER?

JUST A MILK RUN. DO YOU FEEL A SWELL?

NOT LIKELY ON A SHIP THIS SIZE. MAYBE YOU--

GOOD LORD! LOOK OUT, HANSON! LOOK OUT!

THE SKIPPER'S WARNING IS FUTILE AND THE ASTRAGLIA SHUDDERS AS SHE BEGINS TO BREAK APART UNDER A FURIOUS ASSAULT...

...BUT ONLY THE EARS OF THE DYING SEAMEN HEAR THE ROARING CRY THAT ECHOES ABOVE THE SOUND OF THE SHATTERED TANKER.

ODIN! HEAR ME! I HAVE RETURNED AND NO ONE SHALL STAY MY VENGEANCE!

THE LIFE OF YOUR SON IS FORFEIT!

THOR IS MINE!

NEXT ISSUE: **THE PAST IS A BUCKET OF ASHES!**

STICK AROUND, FOLKS! THINGS ARE ABOUT TO GET WORSE AGAIN!

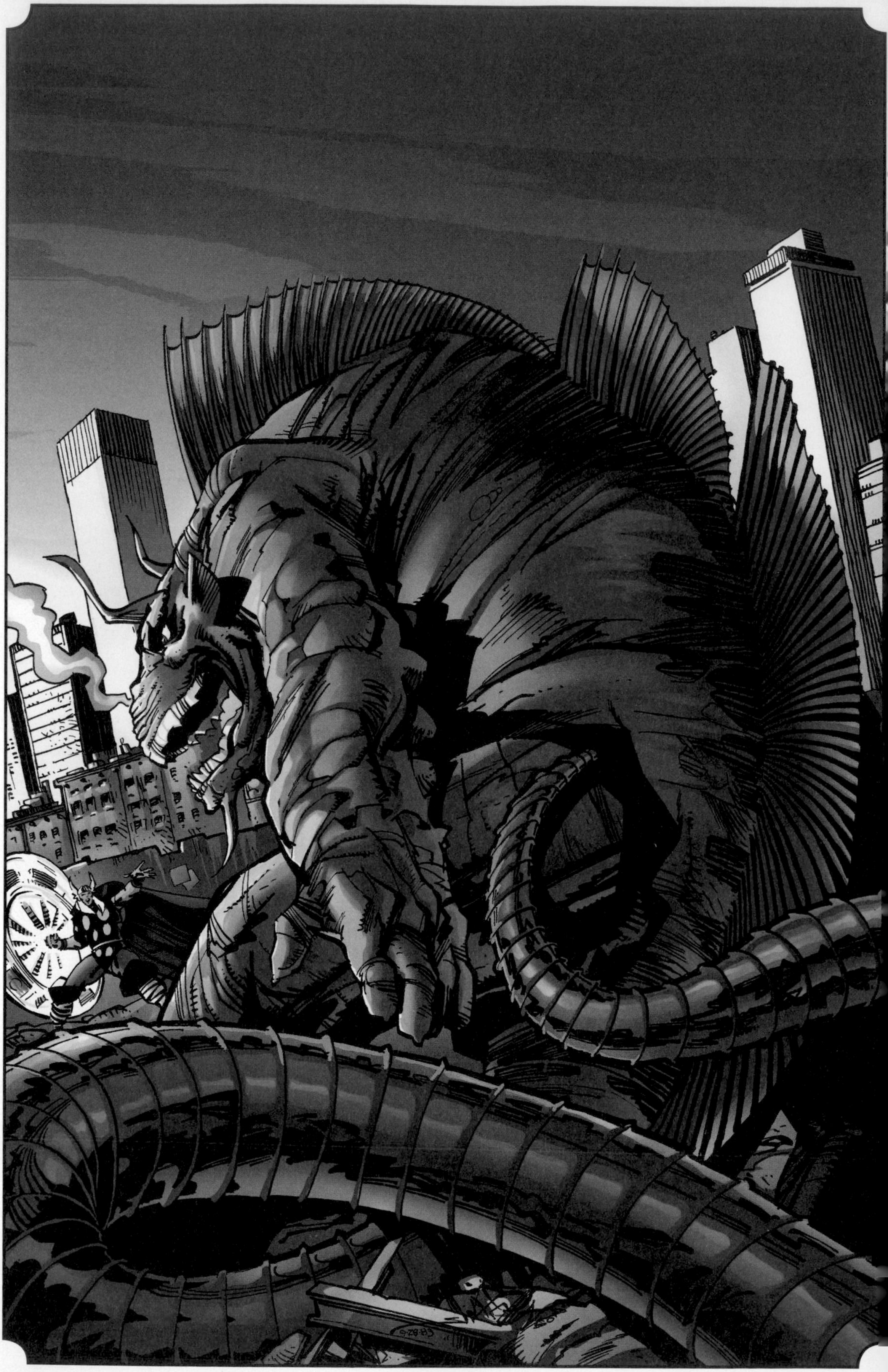

THE PAST IS A BUCKET OF ASHES

NEW YORK CITY, ON A CRISP, BLUE MORNING, WATCHES AS A POWERFUL FIGURE, LONG ABSENT FROM THE BUSY METROPOLIS, SOARS OVERHEAD...

AH, NOW MY HEART SINGS. THOUGH IT HAS BEEN MONTHS SINCE I LAST SAW HER, STILL THE GREAT CITY BUSTLES WITH THE FURIOUS ENERGY OF YOUTH. STILL I FEEL AT HOME HERE AS NOWHERE ELSE.

YET NOW THAT I AM NO LONGER THE MORTAL PHYSICIAN, DONALD BLAKE, I HAVE NO HOME IN ALL OF EARTH'S MANY REALMS.*

AND EVEN THE GOD OF THUNDER NEEDS A PLACE TO HANG HIS HAMMER ON A COLD WINTRY NIGHT.

BEEP! HONK! HONK! BEEEP! HONK!

QUICK, MILDRED! MY CAMERA! IT'S THE MIGHTY THOR!

OH, RONALD! I CAN'T BELIEVE IT. HE'S SO HANDSOME! OHHHHHHH!

MILDRED? MILDRED!!

*LAST ISSUE'S CLASSIC TALE. IF YOU MISSED IT, FOR SHAME!

ART AND STORY: WALTER SIMONSON · LETTERING: JOHN WORKMAN, JR.· COLORS: GEORGE ROUSSOS · EDITING: MARK GRUENWALD · EDITOR-IN-CHIEF: JIM SHOOTER

PERHAPS THE AVENGERS CAN HELP ME. WITHOUT THE MORTAL IDENTITY I HAVE HELD SO LONG, I SHALL HAVE TO BEGIN ANEW TO ESTABLISH A DWELLING PLACE HERE ON EARTH.

YET, STILL, I--

HEY, CHECK THIS OUT!

THOR! WE KNEW YOU'D COME BACK TO MANHATTAN.

LISTEN, MAN, HAVEN'T YOU HEARD? LONG HAIR IS DEFINITELY OUT. WHY NOT COME OVER TO OUR PLACE FOR A MOHAWK?

YOU'D LOOK REALLY GREAT!

I THANK THEE, BUT WERE I TO CUT MY HAIR, MY HELMET WOULD FALL OFF.

WAS HE KIDDIN'?

BEATS ME. BUT WITH THOSE SHOULDERS AND BLUE EYES, WHO CARES?

AND THE MIGHTY THOR DISAPPEAR WITHIN AVENGERS MANSION...

...TO FIND HIMSELF ON THE MOST SURPRISING ADVENTURE OF HIS CAREER.*

*SO SURPRISING, IN FACT, THAT WE CAN'T EVEN TELL YOU ABOUT IT UNTIL NEXT MONTH! WATCH THIS SPACE.

MEANWHILE, LET'S LOOK IN ON LORELEI, WHO HAS JUST GOTTEN OFF THE N.Y. SUBWAY AT A STATION WHERE EVEN THE COPS DON'T GO ALONE.

ACCORDING TO LOKI'S DIRECTIONS, I MUST BE NEARING THE PLACE. AND I CAN ALREADY SENSE THE PRESENCE OF THE ONE I SEEK.

I SHOULD BE ABLE TO PERSUADE HIM TO ASSIST ME WITH THOR. AFTER ALL, I CAN PERSUADE ANY MAN TO DO ANYTHING I WANT.

ALL IT TAKES IS A LITTLE--!

YO, MAMA! OVER HERE!

YOU FINE! YOU SO FINE, DARLIN'!

YOU SHOULDN'T BE RIDIN' NO SUBWAY THIS LATE. IT AIN'T SAFE.

YOU LIVE AROUND HERE, MAMA? MEBBE WE CAN WALK YOU HOME, HUH?

HEY, YOU LOOK LIKE BLONDIE. ANYONE EVER TELL YOU YOU LOOK LIKE BLONDIE?

SOME OTHER TIME, I MIGHT BE TEMPTED TO OBLIGE TWO BIG STRONG MEN LIKE YOU, BUT YOU DON'T WANT TO WALK ME HOME.

UH, WE DON'T?

LOOK AT ME. INTO MY EYES. WOULDN'T YOU RATHER BE... FIGHTING EACH OTHER. I MIGHT EVEN GO HOME...WITH THE WINNER.

I CAN SYMPATHIZE A LITTLE MORE WITH SIF'S ANTIPATHY TOWARD MIDGARD* IF THESE ARE TYPICAL INHABITANTS.

BIF! SOCK! KAPOW! OWW! SWAK!

THOUGH I MUST SAY THAT I DO FIND IT ALL RATHER EXCITING.

ASGARD HAS GOTTEN SO DULL OF LATE.

*EARTH

103

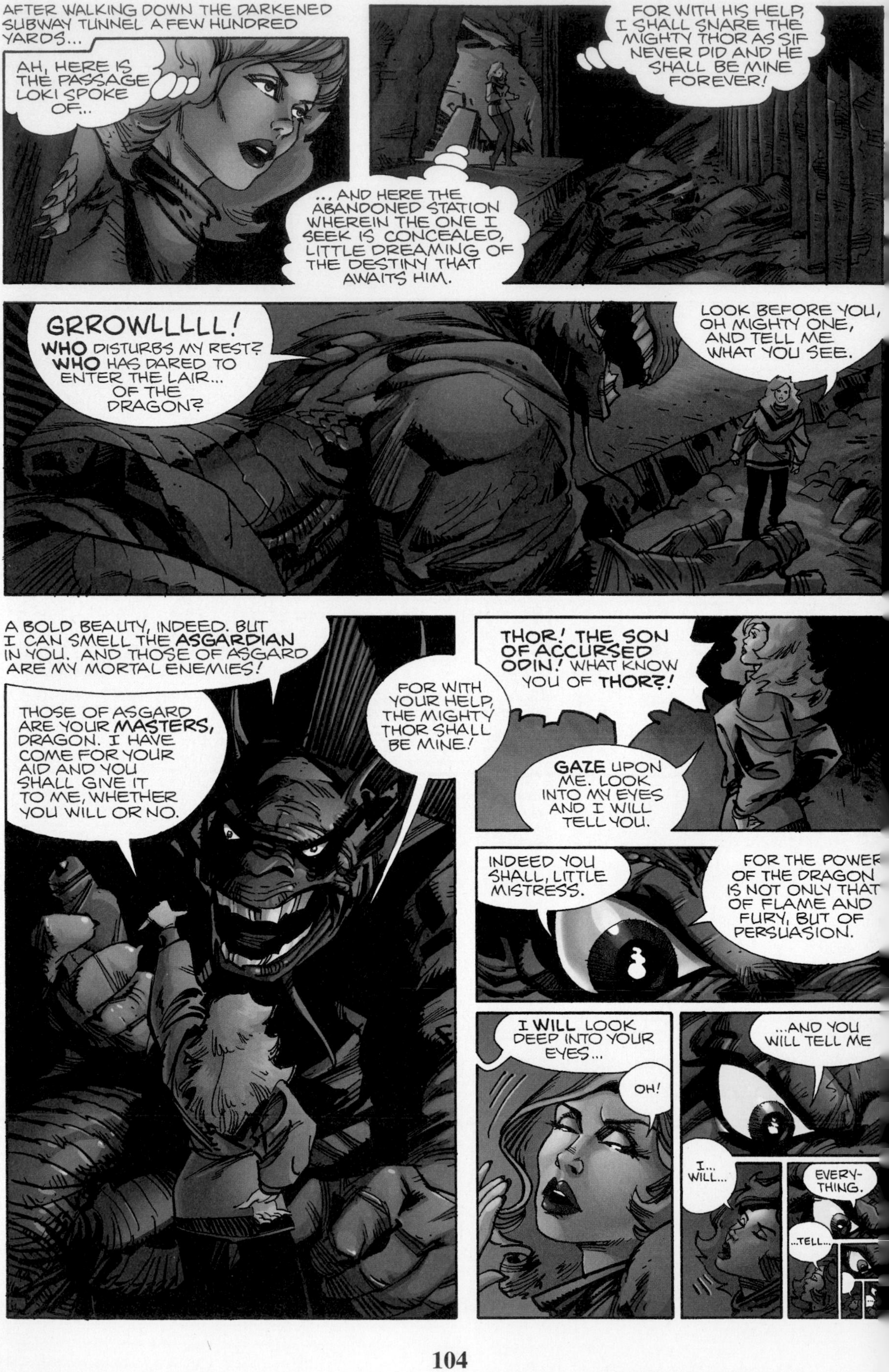

AFTER WALKING DOWN THE DARKENED SUBWAY TUNNEL A FEW HUNDRED YARDS...
AH, HERE IS THE PASSAGE LOKI SPOKE OF...
...AND HERE THE ABANDONED STATION WHEREIN THE ONE I SEEK IS CONCEALED, LITTLE DREAMING OF THE DESTINY THAT AWAITS HIM.
FOR WITH HIS HELP, I SHALL SNARE THE MIGHTY THOR AS SIF NEVER DID AND HE SHALL BE MINE FOREVER!
GRROWLLLLL! WHO DISTURBS MY REST? WHO HAS DARED TO ENTER THE LAIR... OF THE DRAGON?
LOOK BEFORE YOU, OH MIGHTY ONE, AND TELL ME WHAT YOU SEE.
A BOLD BEAUTY, INDEED. BUT I CAN SMELL THE ASGARDIAN IN YOU. AND THOSE OF ASGARD ARE MY MORTAL ENEMIES!
THOSE OF ASGARD ARE YOUR MASTERS, DRAGON. I HAVE COME FOR YOUR AID AND YOU SHALL GIVE IT TO ME, WHETHER YOU WILL OR NO.
FOR WITH YOUR HELP, THE MIGHTY THOR SHALL BE MINE!
THOR! THE SON OF ACCURSED ODIN! WHAT KNOW YOU OF THOR?!
GAZE UPON ME. LOOK INTO MY EYES AND I WILL TELL YOU.
INDEED YOU SHALL, LITTLE MISTRESS.
FOR THE POWER OF THE DRAGON IS NOT ONLY THAT OF FLAME AND FURY, BUT OF PERSUASION.
I WILL LOOK DEEP INTO YOUR EYES...
OH!
...AND YOU WILL TELL ME
I... WILL...
EVERY-THING.
...TELL...

GOT A VISITOR, NICK. AND I DON'T BE-LIEVE IT.

I THOUGHT MAYBE HE WUZ GONE FOR GOOD.

NOT A CHANCE. YOU JUST CAN'T STOP A JOE LIKE HIM.

HI, THOR. NICE OF YOU TO DROP IN. GLAD TO SEE YA MADE IT BACK IN ONE PIECE.

THIS A SOCIAL CALL?

I NEED AID, COLONEL. I THOUGHT PERHAPS **SHIELD** MIGHT BEST BE EQUIPPED TO ASSIST ME. IT'S--

STRANGE. FOR A MOMENT, I FELT AS THOUGH I HEARD SOMEONE CALL MY NAME, AS I HAVE NOT HEARD IT CALLED IN A THOUSAND YEARS.

THOR? YOU ALL RIGHT, FELLA?

NE, NICHOLAS. M FINE. MAY E TALK SOME-HERE, PRI-VATELY?

SURE. RANK HATH ITS PRIVIL-EGES.

NOT ONLY DO I GET TO RAMROD THE JOINT, I GET A PRIVATE SUITE. COURTESY OF THE TAXPAYERS.

AFTER YOU.

AND,
SHORTLY...

SUCH IS MY STORY, NICHOLAS. DONALD BLAKE IS NO MORE. THE ENCHANTMENT OF THE HAMMER WHICH ALLOWED ME TO ASSUME MORTAL GUISE HAS BEEN ALTERED BY MY FATHER.*

I COULD STAY AT THE AVENGERS MANSION...

*ALL LAST ISSUE.

...BUT MY YEARS OF LIVING AS DON BLAKE HAVE TAUGHT ME MUCH. I WOULD PREFER TO BE CLOSER TO THOSE I PROTECT.

SO WHAT YER SAYIN' IS THAT YA NEED TO BE SET UP IN A NEW CIVILIAN I.D.

AND YA WANT **SHIELD** TA HELP?

IF IT COULD BE ARRANGED. ALONG WITH A PLACE TO STAY.

BROTHER, YOU ASK THE TOUGH QUESTIONS.

AN I.D. WE CAN GET YA. BUT AN APARTMENT? WELL, WE'LL SEE WHAT WE CAN DO.

NINA, SEND THE COSTUMER UP. I GOTTA CUSTOMER FOR HIM.

FIRST THING WE GOTTA DO IS DUMP THAT OUTFIT. SEE IF WE CAN MAKE YA A LITTLE LESS CONSPICUOUS.

YOU GO WITH MARCO HERE. HE'LL SEE IF WE GOT ANYTHING THAT'LL FIT YOU. BUT DON'T HOLD YER BREATH.

I'LL SEE WHAT I CAN DO ABOUT FINDING YOU A PLACE TO STAY.

A HALF HOUR LATER...

KNOCK KNOCK

COME IN.

HOLY COW!

IS ANYTHING WRONG?

NAW, YOU LOOK GREAT.

I GOT AN APARTMENT FOR YA, BUT YA HAVETA SETTLE FER BROOKLYN. EVEN **SHIELD** CAN'T FIND NOTHIN' IN MANHATTAN.

IT'S YOU I'M WORRIED ABOUT. YOU MAY BE IN CIVVIES, BUT EVERYBODY'S STILL GONNA RECOGNIZE YA.

I KNEW THOSE SHOULDERS WERE GONNA BE TROUBLE.

HEY! HOLD THE PHONE A SEC. I JUST GOT THE GREATEST IDEA SINCE PIZZA.

WHERE'D I DUMP THOSE THINGS? AH, GOT 'EM!

HERE! PUT THESE CHEATERS ON! THEY ALWAYS WORKED FOR THAT OTHER GUY!

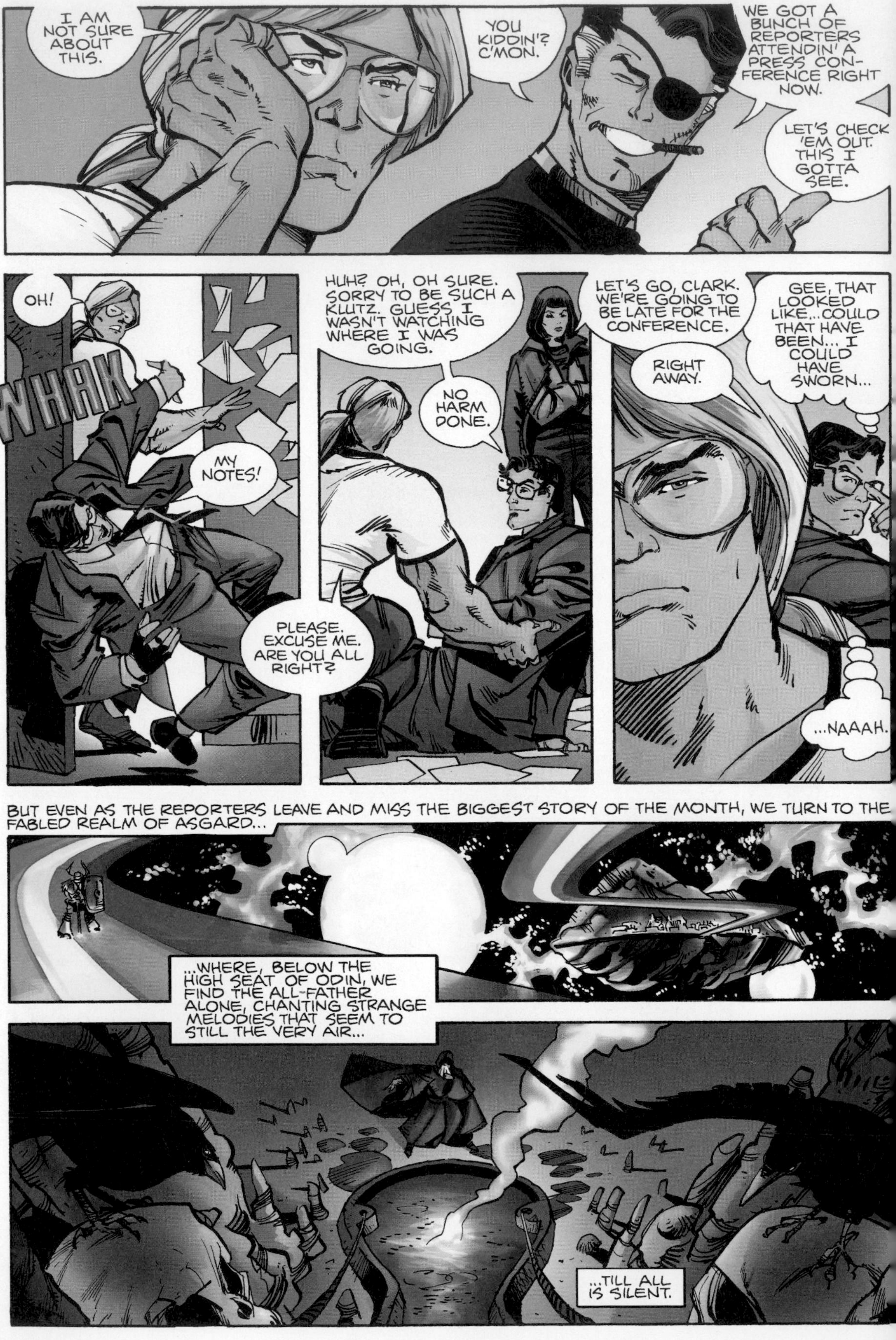
I AM NOT SURE ABOUT THIS.
YOU KIDDIN'? C'MON.
WE GOT A BUNCH OF REPORTERS ATTENDIN' A PRESS CONFERENCE RIGHT NOW.
LET'S CHECK 'EM OUT. THIS I GOTTA SEE.
OH!
WHAK
MY NOTES!
PLEASE. EXCUSE ME. ARE YOU ALL RIGHT?
HUH? OH, OH SURE. SORRY TO BE SUCH A KLUTZ. GUESS I WASN'T WATCHING WHERE I WAS GOING.
NO HARM DONE.
LET'S GO, CLARK. WE'RE GOING TO BE LATE FOR THE CONFERENCE.
RIGHT AWAY.
GEE, THAT LOOKED LIKE... COULD THAT HAVE BEEN... I COULD HAVE SWORN...
...NAAAH.
BUT EVEN AS THE REPORTERS LEAVE AND MISS THE BIGGEST STORY OF THE MONTH, WE TURN TO THE FABLED REALM OF ASGARD...
...WHERE, BELOW THE HIGH SEAT OF ODIN, WE FIND THE ALL-FATHER ALONE, CHANTING STRANGE MELODIES THAT SEEM TO STILL THE VERY AIR...
...TILL ALL IS SILENT.

WHEN I HUNG UPON **YGGDRA-SIL**, THE WORLD ASH, I LEARNED THE NINE SONGS AND THE SECRET OF THE RUNES.

COME, MY RAVENS. COME, HUGINN AND MUNINN. THERE IS MUCH THAT I WOULD KNOW AND LITTLE TIME TO LEARN IT.

FOR AS I HAVE HALLOWED THIS BLADE WITH THE SONGS OF THE DEAD...

...SO SHALL THE RUNES THAT I CUT INTO YOUR CLAWS ENABLE YOU TO TRAVEL EVERYWHERE.

NO BARRIER WILL STOP YOU, NO SPELL SHALL KEEP YOU OUT...

..., AND YOU WILL BE ABLE TO PENETRATE THE DEMONS' DOMAIN AS THOR AND BILL WERE NOT,* AND DISCOVER THE SECRET OF THEIR ORIGIN.

SOME TERRIBLE AGENCY IS AT WORK IN THE WORLD AND WE MUST UNCOVER IT.

GROW TALL AND STRONG, UNTIL YOU HAVE THE STRENGTH TO FLY ACROSS THE COSMOS TO THE BURNING GALAXY AND SEEK OUT THE DEMONS' SOURCE.

WHEN YOU HAVE LEARNED THE ANSWER TO THIS RIDDLE, RETURN AND I SHALL BE WAITING.

NOW, FLY! FLY!

*LAST ISSUE AGAIN!

109

LISSEN, JACK, YOU WANT A JOB, I WANT A JOB, EVERYBODY WANTS A JOB.

JUST 'CAUSE COUSIN NICK SEZ YOU CAN CUT IT DON'T MEAN NOTHIN' TO ME, MR...MR...

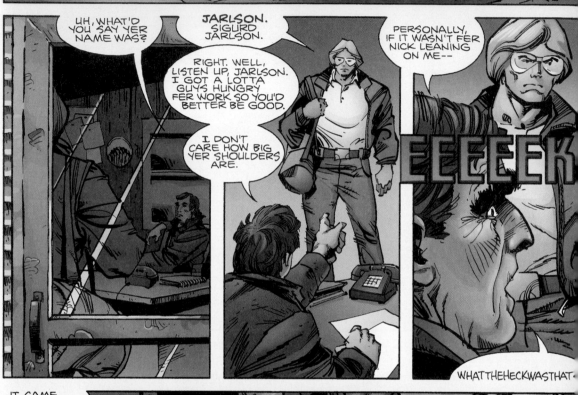

UH, WHAT'D YOU SAY YER NAME WAS?

JARLSON. SIGURD JARLSON.

RIGHT. WELL, LISTEN UP, JARLSON. I GOT A LOTTA GUYS HUNGRY FER WORK SO YOU'D BETTER BE GOOD.

I DON'T CARE HOW BIG YER SHOULDERS ARE.

PERSONALLY, IF IT WASN'T FER NICK LEANING ON ME--

EEEEEK

WHATTHEHECKWASTHAT.

IT CAME FROM THE CONSTRUCTION SITE.

BETTER GRAB A HARD HAT, JARLSON. **JARLSON!**

JARLSON! JARLSON, WHERE ARE YOU GOING?

SHE WILL BE KILLED UNLESS I CAN REACH HER IN TIME.

MJOLNIR IS IN MY KNAPSACK, BUT TO USE IT WOULD BE TO DESTROY THE IDENTITY NICHOLAS HAS SO CAREFULLY CONSTRUCTED.

I SHOULD BE ABLE TO REACH HER WITHOUT IT.

I DON'T BELIEVE IT! JARLSON'S HALFWAY UP THE BUILDING!

WHAT TH--? THE GROUND'S SHAKIN'! FEELS LIKE AN EARTHQUAKE! BUT THIS IS NEW YORK!

GOOD LORD! THERE'S SOMEBODY HANGING FROM THE CRANE!

SHE'LL BE KILLED!

IT'S A GIRL!

OH, NO! THE CRANE'S PLATFORM IS BEGINNING TO GIVE!

CLEAR THE SITE! SHE'S GOING OVER!

THE CRANE IS INDEED BEGINNING TO TILT!

BUT THIS CABLE SHOULD GIVE ME THE SPEED I NEED!

THE ROPE THAT SECURED HER TO THE CRANE HAS SLIPPED LOOSE! SHE'S FALLING!

EEEEEEEEEEK!

I SHALL HAVE BUT ONE CHANCE TO CATCH HER.

JUST IN TIME! ANOTHER MOMENT AND IT WOULD HAVE BEEN TOO LATE.

THE LADY SEEMS TO HAVE FAINTED FROM THE SHOCK.

YET HOW CAME SHE TO DANGLE ABOVE THE CITY SO?

THOUGH SHE IS SAFE FOR THE MOMENT, THERE IS MORE HERE THAN MEETS THE EYE.

AGAIN THE GROUND SHAKES! BUT 'TIS NO EARTHQUAKE!

AY?

AT LAST I HAVE FOUND THEE!

AND I WILL BE THY DEATH!

NAY, IT CANNOT BE! WHAT VISION OF EVIL IS THIS RISING OUT OF THE RIVER?

BEFORE ME STANDS THE LIKENESS OF ONE I DEFEATED AGES AGO, LARGER AND SEEMINGLY MORE DEADLY THAN EVER!

THOUGH THY GARB IS FOREIGN, YET DO I RECOGNIZE MY GREATEST ENEMY.

THE WENCH HAS SERVED ME WELL! THE TRAP IS SPRUNG!

REMEMBER, SON OF ODIN, THAT NOTHING COULD DEFEAT FAFNIR OF NASTROND FOREVER!

SHLORTTER!

AND CARRY THAT THOUGHT TO YOUR GRAVE!

THE VERY BUILDING COLLAPSES AROUND US.

MY HAMMER! I MUST REACH MY HAMMER!

ELSEWHERE, BE-YOND THE FIELDS WE KNOW, A HOST PAST COUNTING LISTENS TO A VOICE AS OLD AS TIME SPEAK...

"FROM THE STARLESS VOID...

"FROM THE REALMS OF ENDLESS NIGHT...

"BY THE POWER OF THE UNFIN-ISHED SWORD BEFORE ME...

"I SUMMON-- THE **DARK ELF!**

"HEED MY CALL! SEEK OUT THE SECOND SON OF ODIN!"

DOOM!

AND IN THE LIGHTLESS DEPTHS OF SPACE, A VOICE ANSWERS...

"I WILL."

MEANWHILE, ON EARTH...

ONLY A WHIRLING VORTEX CREATED BY MY ENCHANTED MALLET CAN SAVE US NOW.

IT WILL PREVENT THE DEBRIS FROM CRUSHING US AS WE LIGHT UPON THE GROUND.

AND WHILE THE RUBBLE SETTLES ABOVE US, I CAN FORM A CAVITY HERE TO HOLD HER SAFELY TILL I DEAL WITH FAFNIR.

BUT WAIT, AGAIN I HEAR MY NAME, AS THOUGH SOME-ONE WERE CALLING TO ME FROM A GREAT DISTANCE.

CALLING IN THE TONGUE OF THE NORSEMEN...

...YET SO SOFTLY THAT IT FADES AWAY TO NOTHING.

THIS RIDDLE CAN WAIT. NOW, **FAFNIR** THE DRAGON, WHOM I ONCE FOUGHT IN BATTLE,* HAS RETURNED.

HE HAS TRIED TO DESTROY BOTH THIS INNOCENT AND MYSELF...

...AND HE SHALL HAVE CAUSE TO **REGRET** THAT.

'TIS WELL THAT I AM NO LONGER DONALD BLAKE, FOR HE WOULD NOT HAVE SUR-VIVED THAT FALL.

STILL, SOME LITTLE ENCHANTMENT IS LEFT WITHIN MJOL-NIR, AND WHEN I STRIKE THE HAM-MER UPON THE GROUND, IT WILL COME TO MY AID.

*NO POINTS OR PRIZES IF YOU CAN REMEM-BER BACK THAT FAR, BUT WE'LL BE IMPRESSED.

SO **DIES** THE MIGHTY THOR, A VICTIM OF AN EVEN MIGHTIER--

KRACKE!

WHAT WAS **THAT?**

SURELY NOT EVEN THOR COULD HAVE SURVIVED THAT FALL, BUT I SHALL NOT UNDERESTIMATE HIM.

I SHALL FIND HIS BODY AND BURN IT TO A CINDER!

THEN WILL ODIN KNOW AND FEAR ME.

114

SCION OF EVIL! MY FATHER FEARS **NO** GOD OR DRAGON, WHATEVER HIS POWER!

UGGH!

UJHAROOM!

NOW SPEAK BEFORE I UNLEASH MY FURY! HOW CAME YOU HERE AND WHAT DO YOU SEEK?

TALK NOT TO ME OF FURY, SON OF AN AC-CURSED LINE! THE WRATH OF GODS COUNTS FOR **NOTHING** BESIDE THE TERRIBLE **ANGER** OF THE **DRAGON**!

AND YET I THANK BOTH YOU AND YOUR FATHER.

WHERE I WAS ONCE A MORTAL KING WHO DALLIED WITH PALTRY EVILS, NOW, BECAUSE OF **ODIN**, I AM AN INVINCIBLE CREATURE OF **HATE**!

FOR ODIN HIMSELF DESTROYED MY PEOPLE AND FORCED ME INTO THE WEARI-SOME EXILE...

...WHEREIN I DISCOVERED THE SECRET OF MY TRANSFORMATION!

I WISH TO REPAY ODIN'S GENEROSITY WITH THE **DEATH** OF HIS SON!

AND I **SHALL!**

EVIL YOU WERE, KING FAFNIR, AND EVIL YOU ARE STILL.

WELL DO I REMEMBER THE LAST TIME WE MET, THOUGH IT WAS AGES GONE BY.

"HOW YOU NURSED YOUR HATE AND VENGEANCE IN THE BLASTED LAND OF NASTROND, YOUR FORMER KINGDOM!"

"HOW YOU TRIED TO SLAY ME AND MY COMPANIONS WHEN WE JOURNEYED THERE AT NOBLE ODIN'S REQUEST...

"...AND HOW WITH THUNDER AND LIGHTNING I SPLIT THE VERY EARTH ASUNDER SO THAT YOU WERE SWALLOWED UP AND VANQUISHED."

TRUE! ALL TRUE! I WAS TRAPPED BENEATH THE EARTH FOR EONS, GROWING AND HATING...

...UNTIL RECENTLY THE GROUND SHOOK AGAIN AND BROKE, RELEASING ME FROM MY PRISON!

AND NOW, I SHALL HAVE MY LONG DELAYED VENGEANCE!

FAROOOOSHH!

116

MEANWHILE, IN GOLDEN ASGARD, VOLSTAGG THE ENORMOUS IS SEARCHING FOR HIS FRIEND, BALDER...

HARUUMPH! HERE IS BALDER'S SHINING HALL, BUT WHERE IS BALDER?

WHY, THE TABLE'S NOT EVEN LAID FOR DINNER. A FINE SHOW OF HOSPITALITY!

BALDER! FRIEND BALDER! 'TIS I, VOLSTAGG, THE VALIANT! PRESENT THYSELF!

STRANGE. HE SEEMS NOT TO BE HOME. PERHAPS HE'S GONE FOR A WALK.

IN WHICH CASE, I HAD BETTER EXAMINE THE LARDER CAREFULLY, TO BE SURE IT'S WELL STOCKED IN CASE SOME UNEXPECTED GUEST SHOULD CHANCE BY.

BUT BEYOND THE WALLS OF ASGARD, ON THE WILDERNESS ROAD...

METHINKS I HEARD THE MIGHTY BELLOW OF VOLSTAGG FOR A MOMENT.

HE ALONE OF THE ASGARDIANS MIGHT GUESS THAT I AM GONE, SO I HAVE LEFT THE PANTRY OF MY HALL WELL SUPPLIED.

BY THE TIME VOLSTAGG FINISHES EXAMINING IT AGAINST AN UNEXPECTED GUEST, I WILL BE FAR AWAY.

FOR HE MIGHT TRY TO PREVENT MY GOING, OR WORSE, INSIST ON ACCOMPANYING ME.

AND THOUGH HIS FRIENDSHIP IS A TREASURE TO ME, ALL COMPANY HAS NOW BECOME A BURDEN.

WHEN THE MERE MEMORY OF WHAT I WAS CAN PROVOKE AN ATTACK SUCH AS THE ONE VOLSTAGG STOPPED,* I CAN NO LONGER REMAIN IN ASGARD.

I MUST CLOSE MY HEART TILL ALL THAT I WAS IS LESS THAN THE SHADOW OF A MEMORY...

...AND ASGARD HERSELF REMEMBERS ME NO MORE.

*THOR 338.

117

AS NIGHT DRAWS ON...

PERHAPS IN THE WILDER-NESS OF THE OUTLANDS, I CAN LOSE MYSELF AND BE TORMENTED NO LONGER BY THE VISAGES OF THOSE I HAVE SLAIN.

BRAVE BALDER SEEMS A LITTLE PEAKED, MY MISTRESS, AND HE WANDERS DANGEROUSLY CLOSE TO YOUR OWN KINGDOM.

HE HAS BEEN STRANGELY CHANGED EVER SINCE HIS RETURN FROM HELA'S DOMAIN. MORE FEY, MORE... DANGEROUS.

I LIKE THAT.

PERHAPS I HAVE FINALLY TOUCHED HIS HEART.

WE WILL WATCH HIM, HAAG. BUT TAKE HEED AND SPREAD THE TIDINGS THROUGHOUT MY KINGDOM.

I'LL HAVE NO HARM DONE TO BALDER.

HIS WEAKENED STATE MAY PROVE TO BE HIS UNDOING AND MY TRIUMPH.

THIS TIME, KARNILLA SHALL WIN HIS SOUL.

ELSEWHERE, ON EARTH...

ONLY MY GREAT SPEED ENABLED ME TO DODGE FAFNIR'S FIERY BREATH!

YET THE FLAMES HAVE SET THE RUBBLE ALIGHT, AND THE FAIR LADY I DID SAVE MAY STILL PERISH IF I DO NOT ACT IMMEDIATELY.

COME, STORM! COME, LIGHTNING! RELEASE YOUR WRATH AND QUENCH THIS DEADLY BLAZE! YOUR MASTER COMMANDS!

BARROOM!
KRAASH!

THE THUNDER! THE BLAZING HEAVENS! THOR TRIES TO DESTROY ME AS HE DEFEATED ME ONCE BEFORE!

BUT NOT THIS TIME!

FOR I WILL CHOOSE ANOTHER BATTLE SITE AT SOME FUTURE DATE, AND THOR SHALL NOT TRAP ME BENEATH THE EARTH AGAIN!

THE FIRE IS NEARLY QUENCHED, BUT MY FOE HAS FLED THE FIELD!

COME BACK, BASE COWARD! TURN AND FACE MY HAMMER'S RIGHTEOUS ANGER!

NO REPLY. FAFNIR HAS TUNNELED INTO THE SUBWAY SYSTEM BENEATH MANHATTAN LIKE SOME GIANT MOLE AND VANISHED!

EVEN NOW, THE SOUND OF HIM IS DIMINISHING-- BUT WAIT, WHAT IS THIS NEW ROAR I HEAR?

'TIS LIKE THE SOUND OF MY OWN BELOVED THUNDER!

ODIN'S BLOOD! A WALL OF WATER!

FAFNIR HAS BROKEN THROUGH TO THE RIVER AND ESCAPED!

IF I CANNOT TURN THE WATER IN TIME, THOUSANDS OF INNOCENTS WILL PERISH MISERABLY IN THE FLOODING OF THE SUBWAY!

I SHALL WIELD MY MALLET AS NEVER BEFORE AND BRING DOWN THE ROOF OF THIS CAVERN!

SAKR...ASH!

KATHASSH!

NOW QUICKLY, BEFORE I MYSELF AM ENTOMBED BENEATH THE FALLING ROCK, I MUST ESCAPE BACK UP THE TUNNEL TO SAFETY!

BEHIND HIM, THE THUNDERING AVALANCHE MEETS THE RAGING WATER, AND THE CRASH SHAKES THE CITY TO ITS FOUNDATIONS!

BUT THE DAM HOLDS!

SAFE ENOUGH FOR THE MOMENT. BUT MY FOE HAS ESCAPED INTO THE RIVER!

HE IS BEYOND MY REACH FOR NOW, AND I MUST BE DOUBLY ON MY GUARD AGAINST HIS NEXT ATTACK.

STILL, HOW CAN I TRULY DEFEAT HIM?

IN HIS EAGERNESS TO FLEE, FAFNIR FAILED TO REALIZE THAT HIS ARMOR IS VIRTUALLY PROOF AGAINST MY HAMMER!

FOR WHEN I STRUCK HIM WITH IT WITH ALL MY STRENGTH, HE WAS BARELY LIFTED FROM THE GROUND.

WHAT WILL I DO WHEN HE RETURNS AS HE MUST? WHAT POWER ON EARTH WILL BE ABLE TO STOP HIM?

AND INDEED, THE SELFSAME THOUGHTS ARE CROSSING ANOTHER'S MIND AT THAT VERY MOMENT A LONG WAY AWAY...

...AS **LOKI, PRINCE OF ASGARD,** SITS IN HIS CASTLE AND MUSES.

AH, MY BROTHER, IT MAY HAVE BEEN WORTH MY LIFE JUST TO SEE YOU WEARING A PONY TAIL!

BUT IT IS *YOUR* LIFE THAT IS DRAWING TO A CLOSE.

WHEN FAFNIR RECOVERS WHAT LITTLE WITS HE HAS, HE MAY REALIZE THAT HE COULD HAVE MASTERED THE FIGHT AGAINST YOU.

WHAT A FOOL! BLESSED WITH POWER LIKE THAT AND NOT AN OUNCE OF BRAIN IN HIS ENTIRE BODY.

STILL, POWER IS WHAT COUNTS AGAINST THOR, AND FAFNIR HAS PLENTY TO SPARE.

PITY ABOUT LORELEI, BUT I SUPPOSE SHE'LL FIND SOME OTHER MALE TO PURSUE SHOULD THOR FINALLY HAVE MET HIS MATCH.

AND HOW RARE A TREAT TO WATCH HER HANG HERSELF FROM THE CRANE WHILE UNDER THE DRAGON'S SPELL.

FOOLISH GIRL! TO BELIEVE THAT HER SIMPLE WILES COULD SEDUCE A DRAGON TO HER WILL, WHEN EVERYONE KNOWS THAT THE DRAGON IS THE MOST IRRESISTIBLE SEDUCER OF ALL.

A MOST SATISFACTORY ENTERTAINMENT.

SHATTER!

I CAN HARDLY WAIT TO SEE HOW IT COMES OUT!

MEANWHILE, ON EARTH...

GOOD! THE CAVITY WAS UNTOUCHED BY THE FIRE. THE LADY SEEMS TO BE FINE.

HEY! HEY, JARLSON! YOU GUYS OKAY? WE ALL RAN LIKE RABBITS WHEN WE SAW THAT DRAGON!

HOLY COW! I THOUGHT YOU WERE DEAD FOR SURE!

WE'RE FINE, MR. SAPRISTI.

JUST A LITTLE SHAKEN UP.

JERRY. EVERYBODY WHO WORKS FOR ME CALLS ME JERRY. DON'T KNOW WHY, REALLY. MY NAME'S GUIDO!

MAN, I NEVER SAW NOTHIN' LIKE THE WAY YOU WENT UP THAT BUILDING. BUT I'LL TELL YOU THIS.

LOOKS LIKE WE'RE GONNA BE STARTIN' OVER HERE AND IF YOU WANT A JOB, YOU GOT IT!

OHHH. WHERE AM I? I REMEMBER SOME HORRIBLE DREAM, DOING THINGS AS THOUGH I COULDN'T HELP MYSELF. I... I THOUGHT...,

OOOH. WHO ARE YOU?

JUST RELAX, MISS. YOU HAVE HAD ENOUGH EXCITEMENT FOR ONE DAY.

I THINK YOU'RE RIGHT. BUT I... I FEEL MUCH SAFER NOW. MMMMM.

WHY, SHE'S ASLEEP! PROBABLY THE SHOCK. I'LL TAKE HER OVER TO THE FOREMAN'S SHACK. HOW BEAUTIFUL SHE IS.

HOLD! THERE IT IS AGAIN!

SOMEONE IS CALLING ME, IN THE LANGUAGE OF THE VIKING WARRIORS WHO SAILED UNDER MY PROTECTION ALL THOSE YEARS AGO.

I KNOW NOT WHO WOULD REMEMBER OR BELIEVE AFTER SO MUCH TIME, BUT AS SOON AS I PLACE MY CHARGE UNDER MEDICAL SUPERVISION, I SHALL SEEK OUT THE VOICE...

...AND LEARN WHO CALLS TO ME FROM A BYGONE AGE!

NEXT: THE LAST VIKING

122

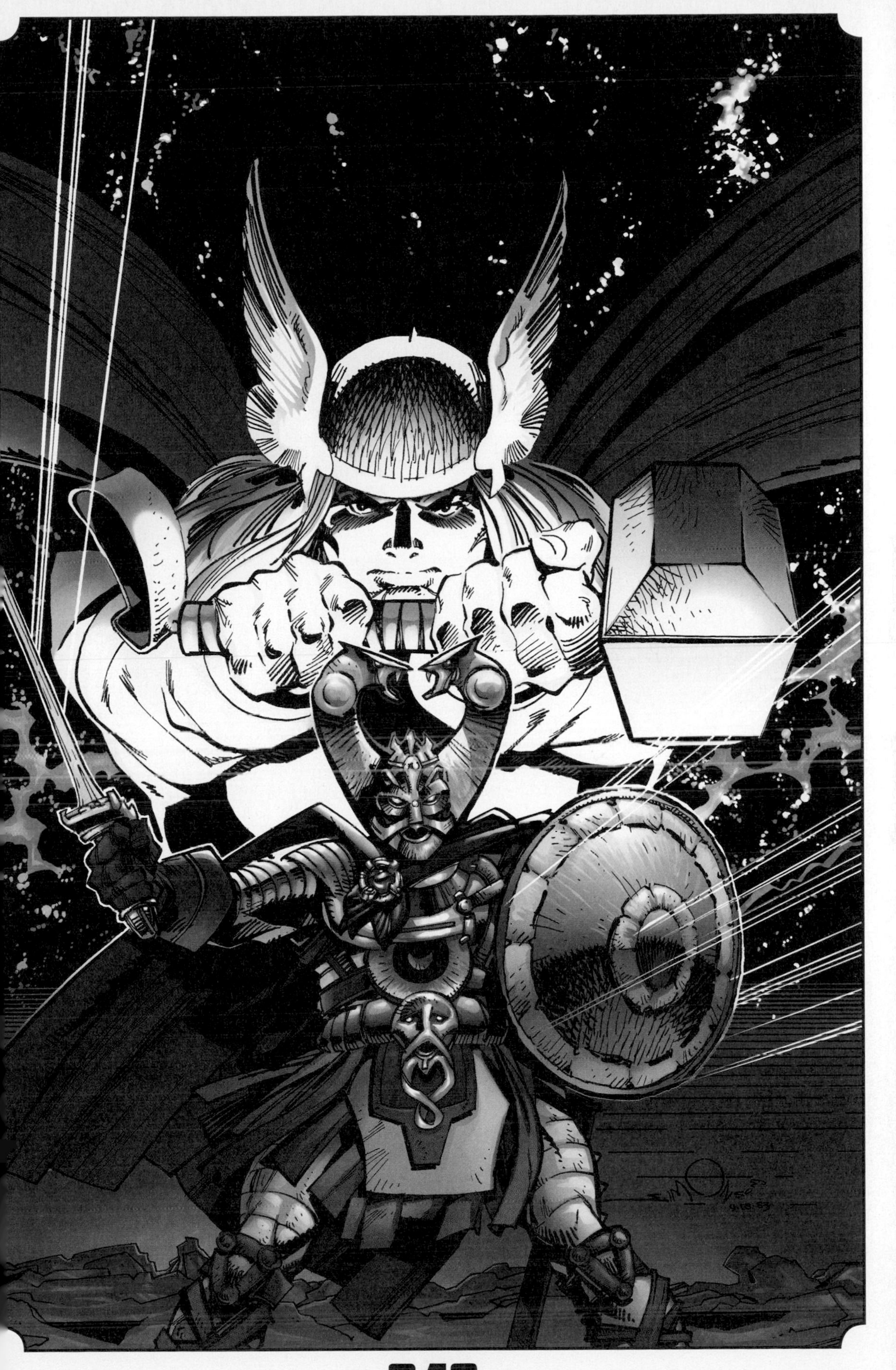

ASGARD! THE HOME OF THE MIGHTY NORSE GODS! AND AMONG ITS MOST HALLOWED HALLS IS VALHALLA...

...WHERE THE MORTAL HEROES CHOSEN BY THE VALKYRIES GATHER EACH SUNDOWN AFTER A DAY OF FIGHTING TO SIT BESIDE THE GODS AND REGALE EACH OTHER WITH TALES OF BRAVERY.

PRESIDING OVER THE GREAT HALL IS THE MOST POWERFUL GOD OF ALL, ODIN, THE ALL-FATHER, WHO SEES MORE WITH ONE EYE THAN MOST SEE WITH TWO.

ALL HAIL ODIN! MAY HIS HONOR AND MAJESTY ENDURE FOREVER!

PENCILS AND STORY: WALTER SIMONSON INKS: TERRY AUSTIN LETTERING: JOHN WORKMAN JR.
COLORS: CHRISTIE SCHEELE EDITING: MARK GRUENWALD EDITOR-IN-CHIEF: JIM SHOOTER

ODIN SALUTES HIS HEROES! MAY YOUR WEAPONS BE EVER SHARP! YOUR VIGILANCE ETERNAL! NOW THE FEAST IS READY. LET US BE SEATED.

THE TIME IS NEARLY FULL. WOULD THAT MY SON, THOR, HAD NOT RETURNED TO MIDGARD.* IF MY FOREBODINGS ARE CORRECT, WE MAY SOON HAVE NEED OF HIS GREAT STRENGTH.

WHAT WEIGHT OF TROUBLE FURROWS THE BROW OF NOBLE ODIN?

WE SHARE A DRINK EVERY EVENTIDE. PERHAPS OUR CUP TONIGHT WILL RELAX MY LORD.

THANK YOU, SAGA, BUT I THINK EVEN THE MEAD OF POETRY WOULD NOT SUFFICE TO BRING ME PLEASURE.

I SEE ACROSS THE HALL THE EMPTY CHAIR, HELD IN READINESS, LO THESE MANY YEARS, EVER WAITING FOR THE **LAST HERO** WHO WAS NEVER CHOSEN.

*EARTH

LONG HAVE WE WAITED IN VAIN TO CELEBRATE HIS ARRIVAL.

NOW THE WINDS TALK TO ME OF HIS COMING, AND THE NUMBER OF THE HALL SHALL BE COMPLETE.

SHOULD WE NOT THEN **REJOICE**, MY LORD?

WE WILL, SAGA. ODIN MOST OF ALL.

AND I WONDER, IF THE LAST HERO DOES INDEED APPEAR, WHAT HARBINGERS OF DOOM WILL HE BRING WITH HIM INTO ASGARD?

METHINKS I HEAR THEIR ECHOES ALREADY.

BUT WITH HIS COMING, I FEEL THE CLOSING OF THE CIRCLE, AND THE WEIGHT OF YEARS LIES UPON ME AS IT NEVER HAS BEFORE.

ELSEWHERE, ON MANHATTAN ISLAND, AT THE CONSTRUCTION SITE DECIMATED BY THE DRAGON FAFNIR*...

*ALL LAST ISSUE.

WELL, I SURE HOPE THE BUILDER HAS INSURANCE THAT'LL COVER AGAINST DESTRUCTION BY DRAGONS. WADDA MESS.

WE WERE LUCKY THOR WAS IN THE NEIGHBORHOOD AND SCARED HIM OFF.

I THOUGHT GOLDILOCKS WAS IN CHICAGO THESE DAYS.

PERHAPS HE IS REALLY A METS FAN AND RETURNED.

I DOUBT IT. GUYS LIKE HIM, THEY DON'T GET THE SAME WORRIES GUYS LIKE YOU 'N' ME DO. BE-SIDES, IT AIN'T BASEBALL SEASON!

HEY, MISTER! YOU WITH THE GLASSES!

JARLSON. SIGURD JARLSON.

WHATEVER.

WE'RE ABOUT TO TAKE THAT GIRL OFF TO THE HOSPITAL.

SAYS SHE WANTS TO THANK YOU FOR SAVING HER LIFE.

I'M PRETTY SURE SHE'S OKAY. JUST A LITTLE SHOCK, BUT YOU CAN'T BE TOO CAREFUL, YOU KNOW?

BROTHER, SHE SURE IS A **LOOKER!** YOU OUGHT TO GET HER PHONE NUMBER.

HELLO, MISS. GOOD TO SEE YOU'RE OKAY.

COULD YOU... COME A LITTLE CLOSER.

I'M GLAD YOU WERE STILL HERE. YOU SAVED ME FROM THE DRAGON AND I DON'T EVEN KNOW YOUR NAME.

SIGURD JARLSON, IF YOU CAN BELIEVE IT!

OH, I THINK THAT'S A WONDERFUL NAME. SO STRONG!

DO YOU LIVE IN THE CITY?

BROOKLYN, MISS. JUST MOVED IN LAST WEEK.

AS SOON AS I CAN, I'D LIKE TO BE ABLE TO THANK YOU PROPERLY FOR SAVING MY LIFE.

IF YOU'LL LET ME.

OH, AHEM... UH, CERTAINLY.

NO PROBLEM.

WONDERFUL. I'M LOOKING FORWARD TO IT.

LET'S GO, GUYS. WE'VE GOT TO GET ROLLING NOW IF YOU FOLKS DON'T MIND.

NO. NO, I DIDN'T, DID I?

YOU DOPE! YOU DIDN'T EVEN GET HER NAME!

127

BUT ENOUGH OF THIS. AGAIN I HEAR MY NAME AS IF SOMEONE WERE CALLING TO ME FROM A GREAT DISTANCE IN THE LANGUAGE OF THE VIKINGS*...

...AS ONCE THOSE SEA-FARERS CALLED FOR MY BLESSINGS IN THE PAST.

*WE HEARD IT LAST ISSUE, TOO.

'TIS TIME THIS MYSTERY WERE UNRAVELED!

I MUST GO, JERRY. I HAVE MUCH UNPACKING TO DO.

OKAY, SIG. REPORT IN MONDAY MORNING BRIGHT AND EARLY, AND WE'LL GET STARTED CLEANING UP THIS MESS.

Y'KNOW, I JUST THOUGHT OF SOMETHING.

AFTER WATCHING SIGURD SWING UP THAT CABLE TO SAVE THAT DAME FROM THE DRAGON, I WONDER IF HE COULD...D'YA SUPPOSE HE'S REALLY...

NAAH!

THIS DARKENED ALLEYWAY SHOULD SERVE MY PURPOSE.

I HAVE BUT TO RE-MOVE MY HAMMER, MJOLNIR, FROM MY KNAPSACK, AND STRIKE IT UPON THE GROUND.

SKRACKK!

...AND THE MIGHTY THOR LIVES AGAIN!

IN DAYS OF YORE, MY FOLLOWERS DID CALL MY NAME, AND EVEN IF I WERE WORLDS AWAY, I COULD HEAR THEM AND ANSWER IF IT PLEASED ME.

I THOUGHT SUCH DAYS WERE LONG FORGOTTEN, BUT THE VOICE THAT CALLS ME NOW SPEAKS WITH THE SAME PASSION, THE SAME BELIEF AS THOSE OF OLDEN TIMES.

SO I SHALL SEEK OUT THIS RE-MINDER OF THE PAST, AND LEARN WHO CALLS ME FROM OUT OF A BYGONE AGE.

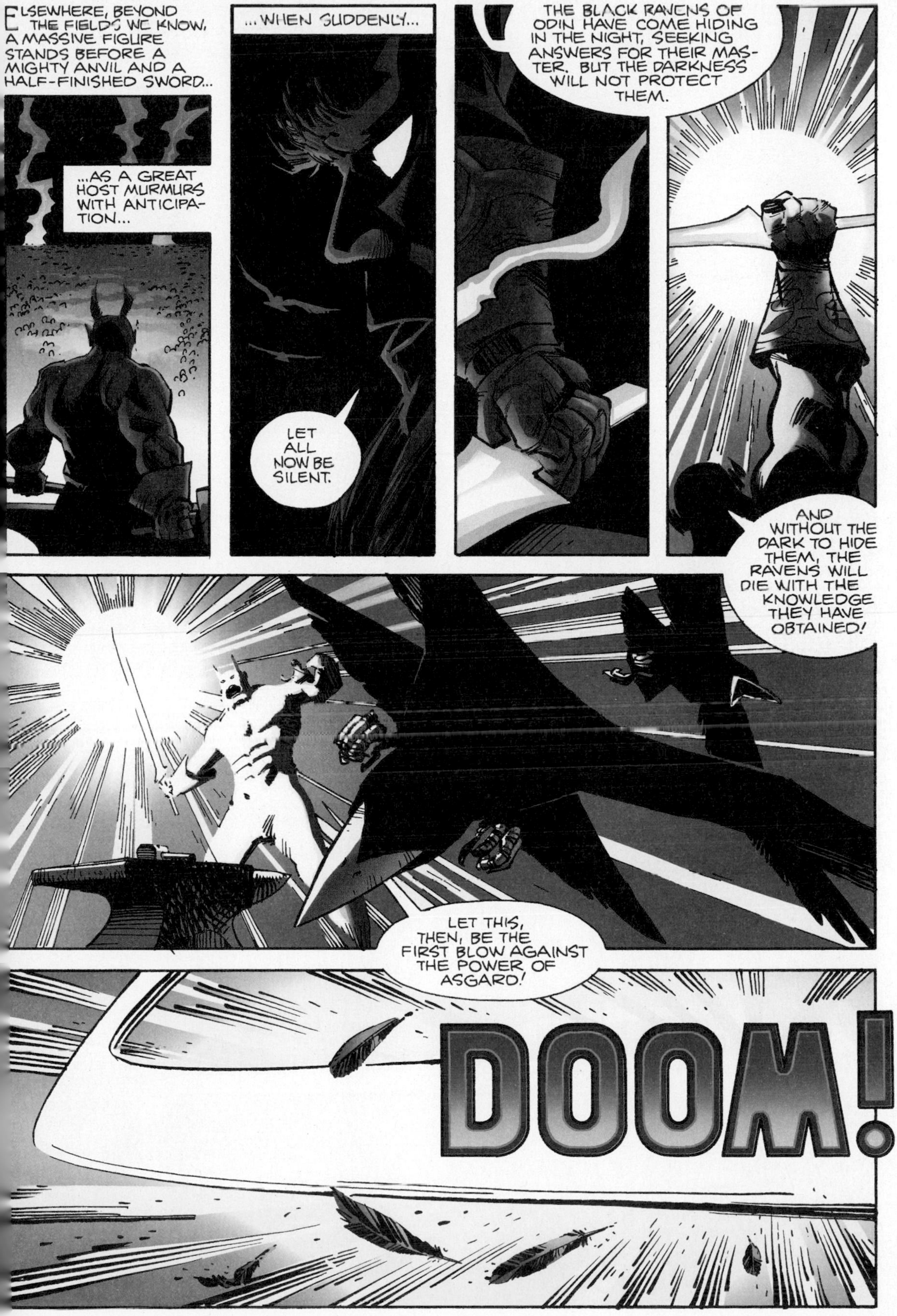
ELSEWHERE, BEYOND THE FIELDS WE KNOW, A MASSIVE FIGURE STANDS BEFORE A MIGHTY ANVIL AND A HALF-FINISHED SWORD...
...AS A GREAT HOST MURMURS WITH ANTICIPATION...
...WHEN SUDDENLY...
LET ALL NOW BE SILENT.
THE BLACK RAVENS OF ODIN HAVE COME HIDING IN THE NIGHT, SEEKING ANSWERS FOR THEIR MASTER. BUT THE DARKNESS WILL NOT PROTECT THEM.
AND WITHOUT THE DARK TO HIDE THEM, THE RAVENS WILL DIE WITH THE KNOWLEDGE THEY HAVE OBTAINED!
LET THIS, THEN, BE THE FIRST BLOW AGAINST THE POWER OF ASGARD!
DOOM!

MEANWHILE, ON EARTH...

ANTARCTICA! VAST CONTINENT OF ICE AND SNOW! MY SEARCH HAS BROUGHT ME TO THE END OF THE WORLD!

SOMEWHERE BELOW LIES THE ANSWER TO THE MYSTERY OF THE VOICE.

THOUGH I NO LONGER HEAR IT, I SENSE THAT ITS OWNER IS HIDDEN SOMEWHERE BEYOND THESE MISTS...

...WHICH HIDE A MIGHTY RANGE OF MOUNTAINS LOOMING BEFORE ME LIKE THE FORTRESS OF THE FROST GIANTS!

PERHAPS THE ANSWER LIES WITHIN THIS ANCIENT VOLCANIC CALDERA.

THE AIR! IT GROWS WARMER WITH EVERY FOOT I DESCEND!

INCREDIBLE! THE VALLEY BELOW ME TEEMS WITH LIFE!

THE VOLCANO'S HEAT RADIATES FROM THE VERY GROUND TO FILL THIS CRATER WITH LIFE-GIVING WARMTH.

AND THOUGH THE AIR IS STILL COOL, I FEEL AS THOUGH I HAD ARRIVED IN SOME TEMPERATE CLIME A THOUSAND MILES FROM HERE!

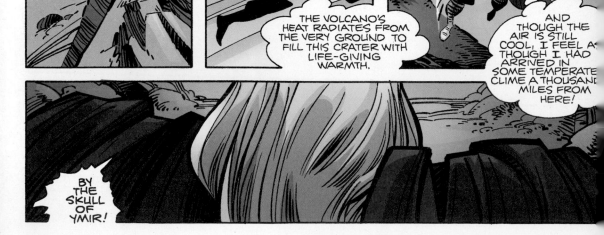

BY THE SKULL OF YMIR!

130

A VILLAGE! A VILLAGE LIKE UNTO THE TOWNS OF THE VIKINGS THEMSELVES! NESTLED IN THE VERY HEART OF THE VOLCANO'S THROAT!

HIDDEN BELOW THE MISTS OF THE ICY LAND FROM ANY WHO MIGHT SPY IT!

BUT NOT A SOUL CAN BE SEEN.

STAND FORTH! ARE THERE ANY ABOUT TO WELCOME A DISTANT TRAVELER?

NAUGHT BUT SILENCE.

AND YET, THE VOICE CAME FROM HERE, I AM SURE OF IT!

STAND A MOMENT. WHAT FRIENDLY SCENT IS THIS?

A COOKING POT, NEARLY FULL OF STEW.

AND FRESH, THOUGH COOL.

UM. NOT BAD.

THIS IS NO DESERTED VILLAGE, NO MATTER HOW IT MIGHT APPEAR!

PERHAPS THE VILLAGERS HAVE FLED FROM THE STRANGER AND HIDDEN.

AND YET, NOW THAT I AM CLOSER, I DO SEE THAT SOME OF THE HUTS HAVE BEEN LONG ABANDONED.

PERHAPS BEYOND THIS WALL, I MAY DISCOVER SOME ANSWER TO THESE RIDDLES.

I SHOULD HAVE GUESSED. A GRAVEYARD! A VIKING GRAVEYARD!

FILLED WITH THE STONE SHIPS THAT CARRIED THE VILLAGERS AWAY FROM THE LAND OF THE LIVING!

THESE **WERE** MY PEOPLE; THESE WERE TRUE VIKINGS!

BUT WHERE ARE THE VILLAGERS NOW? WHAT HAS BECOME OF THEM? AND WHERE IS THE OWNER OF THE VOICE THAT CALLED TO ME?

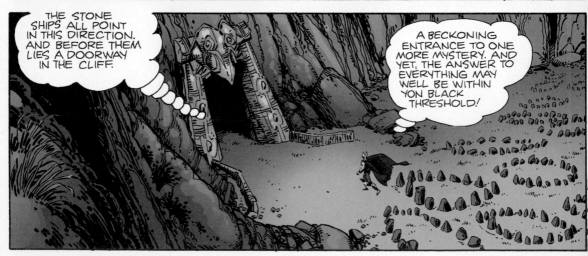

THE STONE SHIPS ALL POINT IN THIS DIRECTION. AND BEFORE THEM LIES A DOORWAY IN THE CLIFF.

A BECKONING ENTRANCE TO ONE MORE MYSTERY. AND YET, THE ANSWER TO EVERYTHING MAY WELL BE WITHIN YON BLACK THRESHOLD!

VERY WELL.

COME WHAT MAY, THE SON OF ODIN IS NO CHILD TO FEAR THE DARK.

WITH HAM-MER IN HAND, I WILL BOLDLY ENTER AND--!

W
H
R
A
M

HMMM. PERHAPS A MORE CAUTIOUS AP-PROACH WOULD HAVE BEEN BEST. THE PASSAGE IS MADE FAST BEHIND ME.

STILL, NO SUCH DOORWAY CAN LONG RESIST MJOLNIR'S KNOCK!

BRATH BRATH BRATH BRATH BRATH

ABOVE ME!

A THOUSAND DEADLY SPEARS!

ALL AIMED AT THE VERY SPOT UPON WHICH I STAND!

BUT WHILE THOR STANDS BENEATH A VERITABLE RAIN OF DEATH, WE FIND THE BRAVE BALDER, ALONE IN THE WILDERNESS FAR BEYOND THE WALLS OF ASGARD...

...OR PERHAPS NOT SO ALONE.

COME OUT OF THE SHADOWS, WAYFARER, AND REST BESIDE THE FIRE. THERE IS WARMTH ENOUGH HERE FOR TWO.

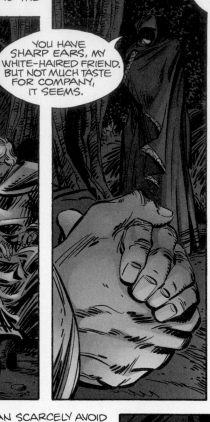

YOU HAVE SHARP EARS, MY WHITE-HAIRED FRIEND. BUT NOT MUCH TASTE FOR COMPANY, IT SEEMS.

YOU ARE FAR FROM ANYWHERE IN THESE WILDS.

PERHAPS MY PRESENCE IS AN UNWELCOME INTRUSION.

I HAVE SOUGHT SOLITUDE AND THE BEAUTY OF EMPTINESS. IT HAS ELUDED ME THUS FAR, EVEN HERE.

BUT I HAVE NOT FORSAKEN HOSPITALITY. AND PERHAPS I HAVE NOT LOST MY TASTE FOR COMPANY AS MUCH AS I HAD THOUGHT THESE LAST FEW WEEKS.

DO YOU SEEK COMPANIONSHIP NOW?

I CAN SCARCELY AVOID IT, IT SEEMS. I HEAR THE SOUND OF YOUR MEN AT ARMS IN THE WOODS. WILL THEY CARRY ME OFF IF YOUR BEAUTY FAILS TO MOVE ME?

YOU WERE ALWAYS LOVELY, KARNILLA. BUT I NEVER FOUND BEAUTY AND EVIL SEDUCTIVE.

WHAT DO YOU KNOW OF EVIL, BALDER? YOU WHOM THE VERY GODS ENVY FOR YOUR GOODNESS.

I HAVE PLUMBED THE DEPTHS OF HEL AS EVEN LOKI HAS NOT, MY LADY.

I HAVE SEEN FIRSTHAND THE DEATH THAT I HAVE DEALT, AND IT DOGS MY FOOTSTEPS, EVEN HERE IN THE WILDERNESS.

LET IT GO, BALDER!

EVERY LIVING CREATURE IS A PLAYTHING OF THE FATES, AND BOWS TO THE WILL OF TIME EVENTUALLY.

YOU CANNOT CARRY THE RESPONSIBILITY FOR EVERY DEATH, FOR EVERY CRY OF MERCY.

THAT IS A LESSON I HAVE YET TO LEARN, MY QUEEN.

THEN MAY YOU LEARN IT SOON, BRAVE BALDER, BEFORE YOU TEAR YOURSELF APART.

BUT SHOULD YOU TIRE OF THE OUTLAND AND NEED A DIFFERENT SANCTUARY, SEEK ME OUT. YOU'LL NOT BE DISTURBED, I PROMISE YOU.

I... I THOUGHT YOU MIGHT NEED PROVISIONS. MY MEN HAVE LEFT A PLENTIFUL SUPPLY BEYOND THE ROCKS, BUT REMEMBER ME, SHOULD YOU NEED A FRIEND.

I'LL BE WAITING.

AND BALDER SITS QUIETLY IN THE FLICKERING LIGHT, STARING IN THE DANCING FLAME...

MY WHIRLING HAMMER IS SUFFICIENT TO DESTROY THE DEAD... SPEAR!

YET NOW I AM ANGRY! I WOULD LEARN WHAT LIES AT THE END OF THIS DANGEROUS TUNNEL! AND LEARN IT, I SHALL!

RUMMBLE!

A DEADFALL! THERE ARE SOME WHO APPARENTLY WISH TO KEEP THE TUNNEL'S SECRET HIDDEN.

THAT SMALL SIDE CAVERN! QUICKLY! I'VE ONLY A MOMENT TO REACH IT!

SAFE! BARELY! I SEE I AM NOT THE FIRST TO ATTEMPT TO PENETRATE THE LABYRINTH'S SINISTER HEART!

BUT BY THE BURNING EYE OF MY FATHER, I SHALL BE THE FIRST TO SUCCEED!

SO SWEARS THOR!

AND THE SON OF ODIN BEGINS TO MAKE GOOD HIS OATH!

PAST THE DEADLY OBSTACLES HE GOES, EACH MORE DEADLY THAN THE LAST!

BUT NONE MORE DANGEROUS THAN THE MIGHTY THOR!

PAST THE NOXIOUS FUMES, THE FLAILS, THE VOLCANIC FLAMES, AND MORE UNTIL...

THESE BOULDERS SEALING THIS EXIT FROM THE LABYRINTH SHALL NOT STOP ME! ONE BLOW FROM MJOLNIR SHALL REDUCE THEM TO RUBBLE AND FREE THE PASSAGEWAY!

BRAKTHAUM!

BUT WAIT! WHAT MOVES IN THE SHADOWS BEFORE ME, GROWING LARGER AND LARGER? SURELY MY EYES DECEIVE ME!

LOOK WELL, LITTLE GOD, UPON THE VISAGE OF DEATH!

NONE HAVE EVER VENTURED SO FAR INTO THE LABYRINTH OF TERROR. NONE HAVE PROVEN WORTHY TO DIE BY MY OWN SPEAR.

SPEAK YOUR NAME, LITTLE ONE, AND WELCOME ME!

I AM THOR, GOD OF THUNDER, SON OF NOBLE ODIN, AND HEIR TO THE THRONE OF ASGARD!

IF I AM TO JOURNEY TODAY TO THE HALLS OF DEATH, THEN LET IT BE IN THE FIGHTING FURY OF MY WARRIOR'S WRATH.

HAVE AT YOU, VILLAIN. WERE YOU HELA'S OWN KIN, YOU WOULD NOT FIND ME SIMPLE PREY.

THRAKKSH!

WHA--! MY FOE'S HELMET! IT HAS COME LOOSE, FALLING AWAY TO REVEAL HIS FACE!

BY THE GODS... I CANNOT BELIEVE IT!

138

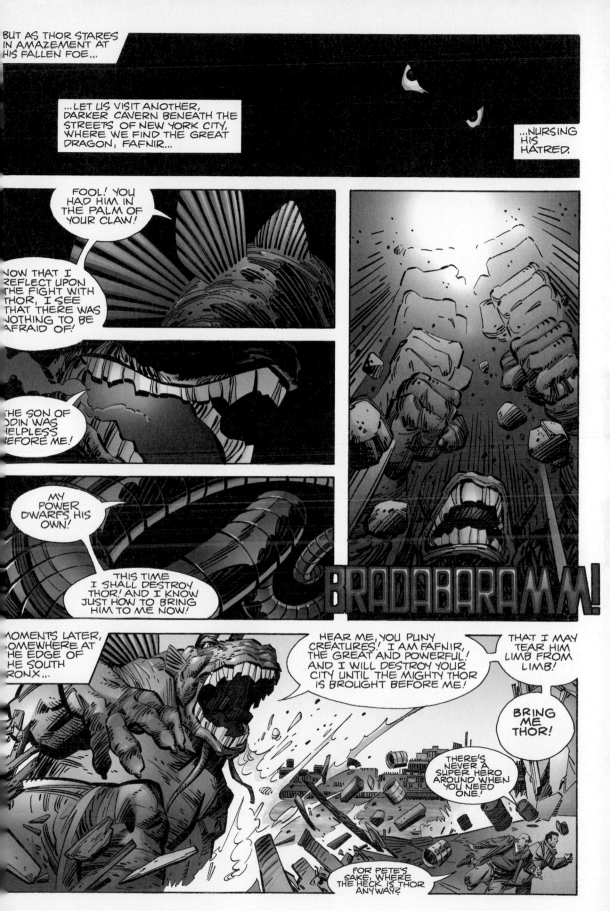

BUT AS THOR STARES IN AMAZEMENT AT HIS FALLEN FOE...

...LET US VISIT ANOTHER, DARKER CAVERN BENEATH THE STREETS OF NEW YORK CITY, WHERE WE FIND THE GREAT DRAGON, FAFNIR...

...NURSING HIS HATRED.

FOOL! YOU HAD HIM IN THE PALM OF YOUR CLAW!

NOW THAT I REFLECT UPON THE FIGHT WITH THOR, I SEE THAT THERE WAS NOTHING TO BE AFRAID OF!

THE SON OF ODIN WAS HELPLESS BEFORE ME!

MY POWER DWARFS HIS OWN!

THIS TIME I SHALL DESTROY THOR! AND I KNOW JUST HOW TO BRING HIM TO ME NOW!

BRADABARAMM!

MOMENTS LATER, SOMEWHERE AT THE EDGE OF THE SOUTH BRONX...

HEAR ME, YOU PUNY CREATURES! I AM FAFNIR, THE GREAT AND POWERFUL! AND I WILL DESTROY YOUR CITY UNTIL THE MIGHTY THOR IS BROUGHT BEFORE ME!

THAT I MAY TEAR HIM LIMB FROM LIMB!

BRING ME THOR!

THERE'S NEVER A SUPER HERO AROUND WHEN YOU NEED ONE!

FOR PETE'S SAKE, WHERE THE HECK IS THOR ANYWAY?

139

SHORTLY, ACROSS TOWN IN A PENTHOUSE OVERLOOKING CENTRAL PARK...

REPORTS CONTINUE TO COME IN SPORADICALLY FROM THE SOUTH BRONX ABOUT SOME SORT OF ATTACKING MONSTER.

THE HONORABLE SENATOR HAS ANNOUNCED THAT THE CREATURE IS UNDOUBTEDLY A TOOL OF THE RUSSIANS, ALTHOUGH STATE DEPARTMENT OFFICIALS ARE SKEPTICAL.

SO FAR, PALEONTOLOGISTS HAVE FAILED TO IDENTIFY THE CREATURE BUT ARE STILL TRYING.

AS YET, THERE IS NO CURRENT WHEREABOUTS OF THOR.

NO DOUBT FAFNIR HAS DECIDED TO TRY AGAIN. FOOLISH DRAGON.

BUT I DO OWE FAFNIR A DEBT OF GRATITUDE. WITH HIS UNWITTING HELP, I WAS ABLE TO MEET THOR IN HIS MORTAL IDENTITY.

WHEN THOR FINALLY DECIDES TO APPEAR, FAFNIR WILL WISH HE HAD NEVER BROKEN THROUGH TO MIDGARD. AND I SHALL BE AMPLY REVENGED FOR MY HUMILIATION AT HIS HANDS.

NOW I SHALL BE ABLE TO SEE THOR UNDER QUIETER, MORE INTIMATE CIRCUMSTANCES...

...TO THANK HIM FOR RESCUING ME...

...AND WHEN I DO, A LITTLE OF THIS GOLDEN MEAD WILL ENSURE THAT HE'LL NEVER THINK OF ANYONE ELSE AGAIN.

BUT UNAWARE OF THE VARIOUS DESIGNS UPON HIM, THE MIGHTY THOR STARES DOWN AT THE FIGURE BEFORE HIM...

...STUNNED TO DISCOVER THAT HIS ERSTWHILE FOE IS...

AN OLD MAN!

AT LAST, YOU HAVE COME! :GASP: NOW, MY LORD, DO NOT SPARE ME, FINISH THE JOB! :GASP:

NAY, I'LL NOT KILL AN ANCIENT, NO MATTER WHAT HE'S DONE.

BUT THE AIR IS FOUL AND STIFLING HERE WITHIN THE VOLCANO'S TUNNELS. LET ME CARRY YOU OUT OF THIS DEADLY PLACE.

THEN WE SHALL DISCOVER THE NATURE OF THIS BOLD WARRIOR WHO WOULD CHALLENGE THE GODS!

WHRIPPPAUM!

AT LAST WE'VE REACHED CLEAN AIR.

AS I THOUGHT. THE GREAT STATURE OF THE WARRIOR WAS MAINLY THE BULK OF THE ARMOR ITSELF.

NOW LET ME GENTLY REMOVE THE ARMOR THAT WEIGHS HIM DOWN.

THOUGH IN HI[S] YOUTH, THIS ANCIENT WAS N[O] DOUBT A LARGE AND DOUGHTY FIGHTER IN HIS OWN RIGHT.

BUT TIME AND AGE HAVE TAKEN THEIR TOLL AS WITH ALL MORTALS.

WHO ARE YOU, GRANDFATHER?

HOW CAME YOU HERE, GRANDFATHER, TO THIS PLACE FORGOTTEN EVEN BY THE GODS?

YOU HAVE LET ME LIVE, LORD THOR. DESERVEDLY SO, I EXPECT.

EILIF THE LOST.

MY FATHER'S FATHERS FOUND THI[S] VALLEY LONG AGO.

I SHOULD NEVER HAVE TRIED TO TRICK YOU INTO KILLING ME. THE GODS KNOW BEST, AND IF I MUST DIE THE STRAW DEATH, SUCH IS MY FATE.

"IT WAS AFTER THE DEFEAT OF KING HARALD HARDRADA IN THE YEAR 1066 BY CHRISTIAN RECKONING.

"WHEN KING HARALD WAS SLAIN IN THE INVASION OF ENGLAND, HIS WARRIORS WERE SCATTERED.

142

"SOME TOOK THEIR FAMILIES AND FLED FAR ALONG THE SOUTHERN COASTS, RAIDING WHERE THEY COULD, LIVING OFF THE LAND.

"THEY SAY THERE WERE SEVEN DRAGON SHIPS, BUT THAT STORMS AND FIGHTING CUT THEM DOWN...

"...UNTIL ONE SHIP WAS DRIVEN BY MONSTROUS WAVES TO A LAND OF PERPETUAL ICE, UNKNOWN TO THEM.

"THEY TOOK REFUGE IN A LARGE FJORD AND FOUND THAT IT DID NOT END, BUT BECAME A CAVERN OUT OF WHICH FLOWED WARM WATER.

"THEY FOLLOWED THE CAVERN THROUGH TO DAYLIGHT, THE SHIP STRUCK A HIDDEN ROCK AND WAS LOST.

THE SURVIVORS, MEN AND WOMEN, SALVAGED WHAT THEY COULD AND FOUND THAT THEY HAD EMERGED IN A LARGE VALLEY SURROUNDED BY IMPASSABLE WALLS.

"AND THERE THEY STAYED, AS DID THEIR CHILDREN. NOW I, WHO WAS THE LAST CHIEFTAIN, AM ALSO THE LAST SURVIVOR.

"AND MY DAYS ARE NUMBERED."

THE LABYRINTH?

PART OF THE ORIGINAL SERIES OF CAVERNS THAT LED MY ANCESTORS HERE.

WE HAD NO FOES, SO WE CREATED OUR OWN. WE BUILT THE MAZE TO TEST OUR PROWESS. TO BE-COME WARRIORS.

IN THE END, I HOPED TO USE THE LABYRINTH TO TRAP A GOD!

FOR THE TEMPER OF THOR IS LEGENDARY, AND I THOUGHT THAT I COULD PRO-VOKE HIM AND SO DIE IN BATTLE...

...AVOIDING THE "STRAW DEATH" IN BED THAT SENDS MEN DOWN TO HEL...

...AND PERHAPS WINNING THROUGH TO VALHALLA.

I SEE NOW THAT I ASKED TOO MUCH. WERE I FATED TO DIE IN BATTLE, I WOULD HAVE DIED LONG AGO...

...FIGHTING AGAINST DEATH WITH THE FEARLESS-NESS OF YOUTH...

...NOT BETRAYED TO IT BY AGE.

I HAVE LIVED TO SEE THE MIGHTY THOR HIMSELF. I WILL DIE IN BED AND BE CONTENT.

NO, GRANDFATHER! YOU SHALL NOT! DO YOU STILL THINK THAT YOUR FATE RESTS WITHIN YOURSELF?

THAT I HAVE COME ALL THIS WAY TO DISCOVER A DOTARD SEEKING VALHALLA THROUGH DECEPTION?

YOU HAVE CALLED UPON THE GODS OF THE ICY NORTH, AND THEY HAVE ANSWERED YOU!

NOW, YOUR LIFE IS MINE!

NEXT: IF I SHOULD DIE BEFORE I WAKE...

THOR! EILIF! LORELEI! FAFNIR! ODIN! DOOM! RAVENS? AND EVERYTHING ELSE WE CAN FIT INTO A SINGLE ISSUE! (OF COURSE, IT WILL ALL BE VERY, VERY TIN'

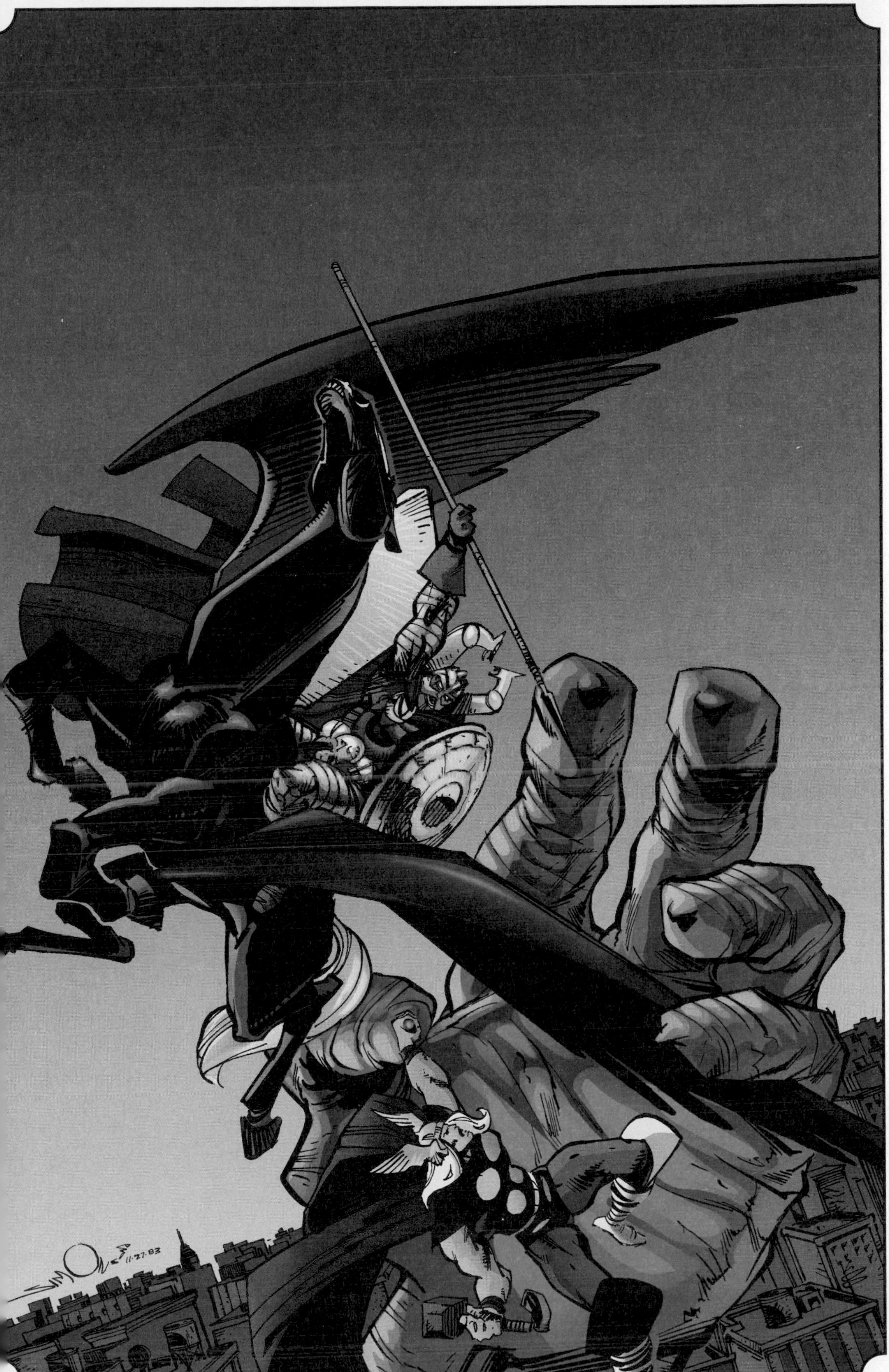

ART AND STORY: WALTER SIMONSON • LETTERING: JOHN WORKMAN, JR. • COLORS: CHRISTIE SCHEELE
EDITING: MARK GRUENWALD • EDITOR-IN-CHIEF: JIM SHOOTER

HEAR ME, THOR! COME OUT AND PLAY OR I WILL SLAUGHTER EVERY LAST MORTAL!

ARE YOU TOO MUCH A COWARD TO FACE ME?

BEWARE! NOTHING THESE PUNY HUMANS CAN DO CAN STOP ME!

THIS IS GREG GLENN, REPORTING FOR EYEWITNESS NEWS!

SO FAR, ALL EFFORTS TO STOP THE GREAT JUGGERNAUT HAVE FAILED.

HE HAS DESTROYED DOZENS OF OLD BUILDINGS NORTH OF THE HARLEM RIVER!

BUT HE'S BEGINNING TO MOVE SOUTH...TOWARD MANHATTAN!

AND THE QUESTION ON EVERYONE'S LIPS IS...WHERE *IS* THE MIGHTY THOR?

SO FAR, NOBODY SEEMS TO HAVE THE ANSWER.

AND EVEN THE NATIONAL GUARD IS HELPLESS BEFORE THE RAMPAGING BEHEMOTH!

I WONDER WHERE THOR IS. SURELY HE WOULD NEVER ABANDON THE MORTALS TO THE LIKES OF FAFNIR.

THE PENTHOUSE OF THE SORCERESS LORELEI, OVERLOOKING CENTRAL PARK...

PERHAPS HE IS BIDING HIS TIME, WAITING FOR THE MOST DRAMATIC MOMENT TO MAKE HIS ENTRANCE.

NO MATTER. SOONER OR LATER HE'LL DEAL WITH FAFNIR. AND THEN I SHALL DEAL WITH HIM! I CAN HARDLY WAIT.

147

...FOR HE IS DEEP INSIDE ANTARCTICA IN A LOST VALLEY...

...WHERE HE FOUND EILIF THE LOST, LAST SURVIVOR OF A VIKING COMMUNITY THAT HAS BEEN HIDDEN HERE FOR CENTURIES.*

*LAST ISSUE.

I HEARD YOUR CALL, EILIF. I ANSWERED IT. YOU SAY YOU WISHED TO DIE IN BATTLE AND PERHAPS REACH THE GOLDEN HALLS OF VALHALLA.

YET YOU WOULD HAVE TRICKED ME IN-TO KILLING YOU IF YOU COULD HAVE.

I WOULD HAVE FOUGHT A GOD, MY LORD. WHAT VIKING COULD HAVE ASKED FOR A MORE GLORIOUS DEATH?

BUT I AM TOO OLD TO DIE A PROPER WARRIOR NOW. I CAN BUT AWAIT HELA'S COLD ARMS, AND FOLLOW HER DOWN TO DARK-NESS.

FOR ALL YOUR YEARS, YOU ARE BOLD! TO CALL UPON THE GODS TO SLAY YOU RE-LESS COURAGE, EVEN ARRO-GANCE!

THERE MAY YET BE ANOTHER WAY, EILIF.

THE BLOOD OF THE VIKINGS RUNS TRUE IN YOU. I AM PLEASED.

AND WERE I AS HEADSTRONG AS THE STORIES ABOUT ME SAY, YOU MIGHT EVEN NOW BE DEAD.

BUT THE GRANTING OF VALHALLA IS BEYOND EVEN ME, EILIF.

ONLY MY FATHER AND HIS VALKYRIES CAN DECIDE WHO SHALL SIT WITHIN THAT CHERISHED REALM.

YET FOR OLD TIMES' SAKE, I WILL TAKE YOUR FATE INTO MY HANDS.

EILIF, A POWER-FUL FOE AWAITS ME FAR FROM HERE. EVEN NOW, HE SEEKS ME OUT, I AM SURE OF IT.

I MUST RETURN TO DO BATTLE WITH HIM AS SURELY AS I STAND BEFORE YOU.

PUT ON YOUR ARMOR. AND FOLLOW ME!

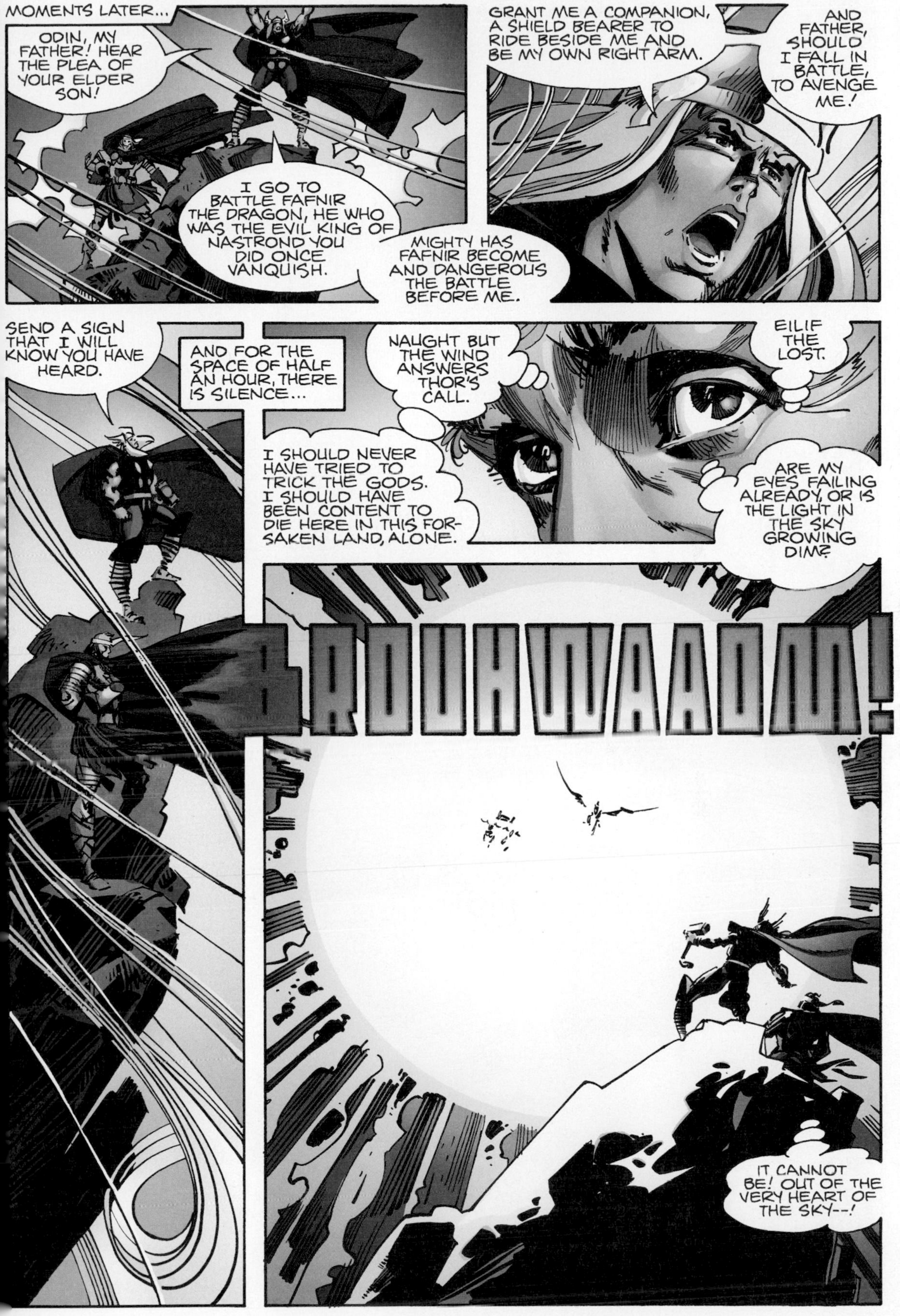
MOMENTS LATER...
ODIN, MY FATHER! HEAR THE PLEA OF YOUR ELDER SON!
I GO TO BATTLE FAFNIR THE DRAGON, HE WHO WAS THE EVIL KING OF NASTROND YOU DID ONCE VANQUISH.
MIGHTY HAS FAFNIR BECOME AND DANGEROUS THE BATTLE BEFORE ME.
GRANT ME A COMPANION, A SHIELD BEARER TO RIDE BESIDE ME AND BE MY OWN RIGHT ARM.
AND FATHER, SHOULD I FALL IN BATTLE, TO AVENGE ME!
SEND A SIGN THAT I WILL KNOW YOU HAVE HEARD.
AND FOR THE SPACE OF HALF AN HOUR, THERE IS SILENCE...
NAUGHT BUT THE WIND ANSWERS THOR'S CALL.
EILIF THE LOST.
I SHOULD NEVER HAVE TRIED TO TRICK THE GODS. I SHOULD HAVE BEEN CONTENT TO DIE HERE IN THIS FOR-SAKEN LAND, ALONE.
ARE MY EYES FAILING ALREADY, OR IS THE LIGHT IN THE SKY GROWING DIM?
BROUHWAAOM!
IT CANNOT BE! OUT OF THE VERY HEART OF THE SKY--!

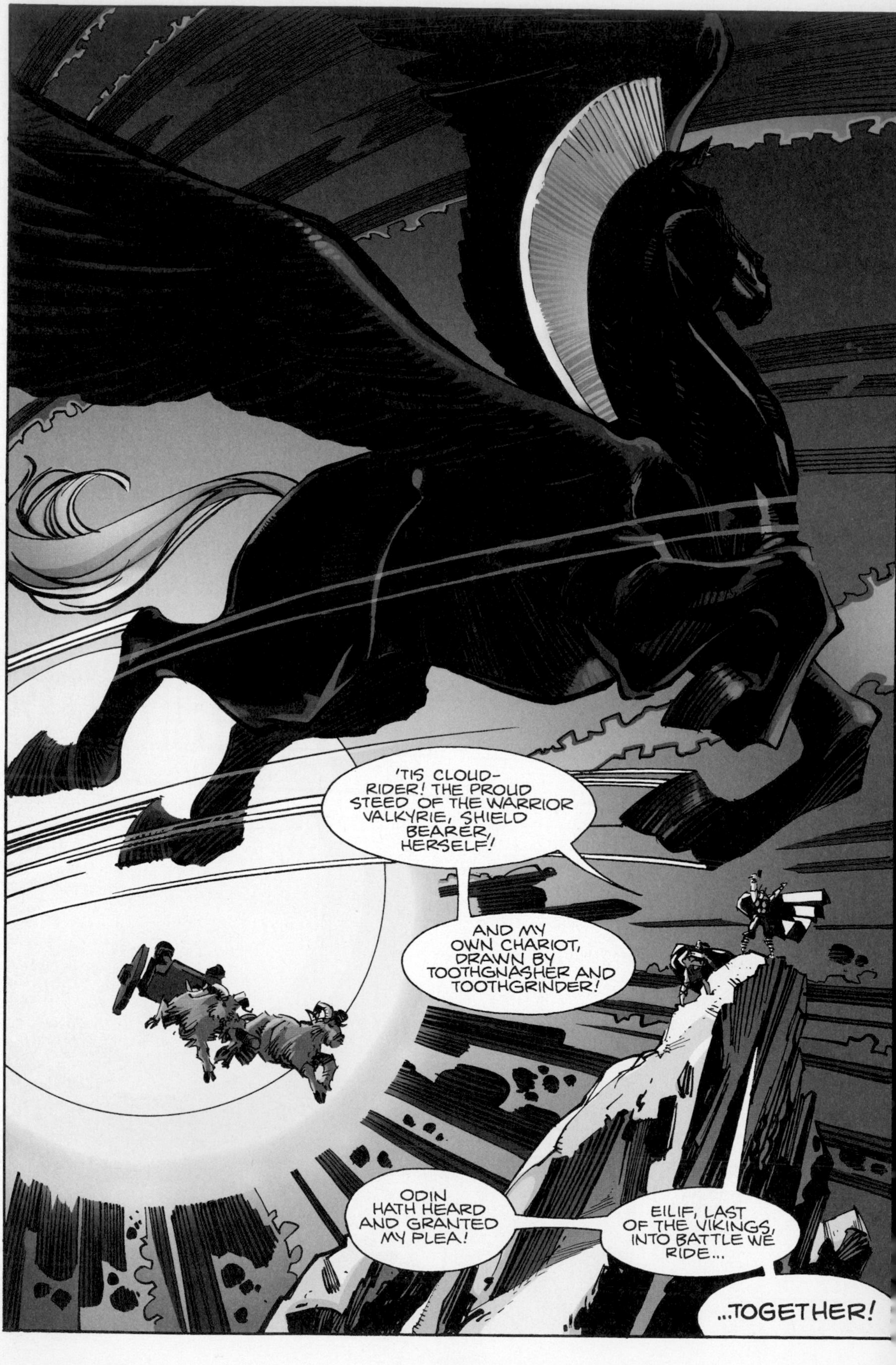
'TIS CLOUD-RIDER! THE PROUD STEED OF THE WARRIOR VALKYRIE, SHIELD BEARER, HERSELF!
AND MY OWN CHARIOT, DRAWN BY TOOTHGNASHER AND TOOTHGRINDER!
ODIN HATH HEARD AND GRANTED MY PLEA!
EILIF, LAST OF THE VIKINGS, INTO BATTLE WE RIDE...
...TOGETHER!

BUT AS THE MIGHTY STEEDS OF THE GODS DESCEND TO EARTH...

...WE FIND UNREST IN THE MYSTIC LAND OF KARNILLA, QUEEN OF THE NORNS...

MY MISTRESS IS UNUSUALLY QUIET THIS EVENING. PERHAPS OUR GUEST TROUBLES HER THOUGHTS AS SHE WOULD LIKE TO TROUBLE HIS.

HE BARELY ACKNOWLEDGES MY PRESENCE, HAAG. HE LOOKS ABOUT HIM AND SEES ONLY DEATH.

I HAVE PUT HIM IN THE CHAMBER NEXT TO YOUR OWN AS YOU ORDERED, MILADY.

LOKI DID THIS TO HIM, AND WHEN THE TIME IS RIGHT, HE WILL PAY FOR EVERY SMILE BALDER NO LONGER WEARS.

HOW HE SHALL PAY!

MY LADY WOULD FORGET HER OLD FRIENDS, ALL FOR THE SAKE OF A RUINED WARRIOR.

TSK! TSK! WHATEVER BECAME OF THE PROUD QUEEN OF THE NORNS?

VENOMOUS OLD FOOL! I CARE NOT A FIG FOR ASGARD, BUT KNOW THIS.

THOSE WHO WORK MISCHIEF WITH BALDER DO SO AT THEIR PERIL!

PERHAPS WE'LL BE IN- VITING ODIN HIMSELF TO DINNER NEXT!

NOW LEAVE ME.

I WANTED BALDER BECAUSE HE WAS SO PERFECT, SO FULL OF LIFE UNSPOILED BY UGLINESS.

CAN KARNILLA SOOTHE HIS TROUBLED BROW WITH GENTLENESS?

IS THE PRIZE STILL WORTH THE EFFORT?

BUT TO SEE HIM NOW. WOULD EVEN THE HEALING HAND OF A MOTHER CURE HIS ILLS?

LOKI, IF YOU HAVE COST ME THIS ONE TREASURE, MY VENGEANCE WILL BE TERRIBLE!

151

HE'S BEAUTIFUL.

YES, THE STEEDS OF THE VALKYRIES ARE THE FINEST ANIMALS IN ASGARD.

LET US MOUNT AND BE AWAY. WE HAVE LITTLE TIME.

VERY WELL. I...I...

SNORT!

EILIF?

IT'S NO USE, MY LORD. YOU HAD BEST LEAVE ME BEHIND.

HOW SAY YOU?

NOW THAT THE MOMENT IS UPON ME, I SEE THAT I AM NOT WORTHY OF THIS HONOR. AND I DOUBT IF I CAN DISCHARGE SUCH A TRUST.

DO YOU NOT SEE, LORD THOR? I AM OLD! TOO OLD TO BE OF SERVICE ANY LONGER!

I CAN BARELY LIFT MY SPEAR, MUCH LESS FIGHT IN REAL COMBAT.

I FEAR NO TOWERING FOE, BUT I CAN ONLY DISHONOR MYSELF IN BATTLE. AND BE NO AID TO YOU.

WHAT WORDS ARE THESE I HEAR? WHERE IS THE WARRIOR WHO DARED TO CALL THE GODS OUT OF THE SKY?

WHO LIFTED HIS WEAPON AGAINST THE MIGHTIEST FIGHTER OF ASGARD?

WHOSE PEOPLE DARED THE FURIOUS ELEMENTS OF THE OCEAN IN OPEN BOATS AND LAUGHED AT THE FEAR?

DOES HE SEEK AN EASY DEATH? A CHEAP SEAT IN THE HALLS OF VALHALLA?

I DO NOT SPEAK TO THE OLD MAN CRINGING BEFORE ME. I SPEAK TO THE WARRIOR WHO DARED TO TEST THE METTLE OF THE MIGHTY THOR.

LET HIM ANSWER ME!

152

HE IS **HERE,** MY LORD.

ANU HE IS **READY.**

THEN TOUCH MY EN-CHANTED MALLET, MJOLNIR, AND BE THOU NOT AFRAID.

OUR **FATES,** EILIF, WERE WRITTEN LONG BEFORE WE WERE BORN.

SCHRAKKLE!

NOW, **RISE UP** AND **MOUNT** THE **STEED** THAT **AWAITS** YOU!

MY **LIMBS!** MY **SINEWS!**

I FEEL THE VERY FIRE OF **YOUTH** COURSING THROUGH ME!

MY LORD THOR, LET US **RIDE.** AND LET THE BARDS LOOK TO THEIR **BALLADS!**

FOR OUR DEEDS SHALL RESOUND ACROSS MIDGARD TO THE VERY ROOTS OF THE WORLD ASH ITSELF!

WELL SAID, WARRIOR. LEAD ON.

BUT **WAIT!** WHO IS **THIS** I **SEE?**

ANOTHER IN THE VALLEY OF THE **LOST?**

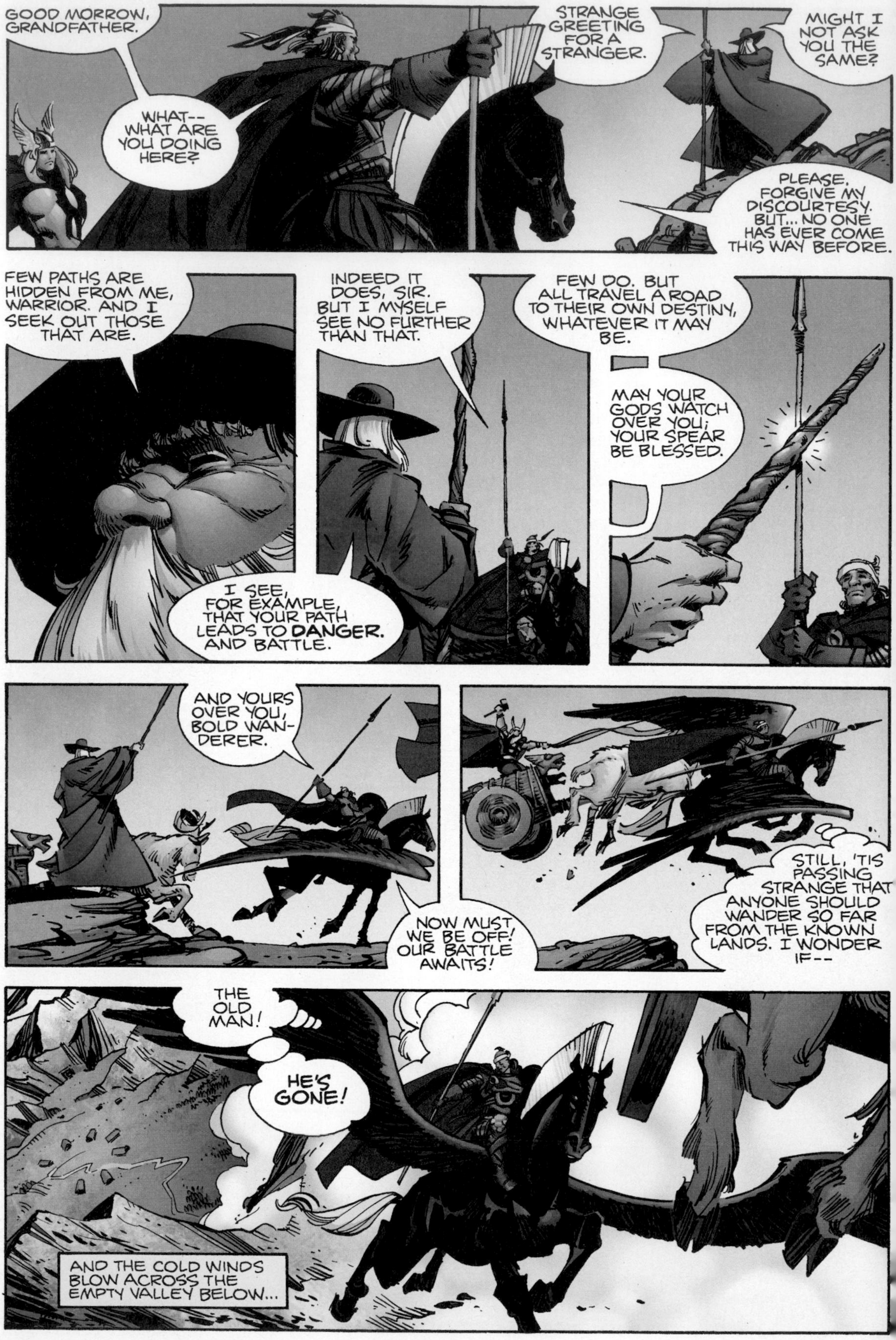
GOOD MORROW, GRANDFATHER.
STRANGE GREETING FOR A STRANGER.
MIGHT I NOT ASK YOU THE SAME?
WHAT-- WHAT ARE YOU DOING HERE?
PLEASE. FORGIVE MY DISCOURTESY. BUT... NO ONE HAS EVER COME THIS WAY BEFORE.
FEW PATHS ARE HIDDEN FROM ME, WARRIOR. AND I SEEK OUT THOSE THAT ARE.
INDEED IT DOES, SIR. BUT I MYSELF SEE NO FURTHER THAN THAT.
I SEE, FOR EXAMPLE, THAT YOUR PATH LEADS TO DANGER. AND BATTLE.
FEW DO. BUT ALL TRAVEL A ROAD TO THEIR OWN DESTINY, WHATEVER IT MAY BE.
MAY YOUR GODS WATCH OVER YOU; YOUR SPEAR BE BLESSED.
AND YOURS OVER YOU, BOLD WANDERER.
NOW MUST WE BE OFF! OUR BATTLE AWAITS!
STILL, 'TIS PASSING STRANGE THAT ANYONE SHOULD WANDER SO FAR FROM THE KNOWN LANDS. I WONDER IF--
THE OLD MAN!
HE'S GONE!
AND THE COLD WINDS BLOW ACROSS THE EMPTY VALLEY BELOW...

ELSEWHERE, BEYOND THE FIELDS WE KNOW...

AN ENDLESS HOST CHANTS...

THE NAME...

THE NAME...

THE NAME...

THE NAME...

AND A VOICE AS OLD AS TIME REPLIES...

DOOM!

THE SWORD IS NAMED...

...AND THE NAME IS-- TWILIGHT!

...AT LEAST IF YOU'RE IN THE NATIONAL GUARD.

WATCH OUT!

WATCH OUT!

WAY JUM

HERE HE COMES! HIT THE DIRT!

VERY WELL, THOR.

SINCE YOU CHOOSE TO REMAIN IN COWARDLY HIDING, I SHALL COMMENCE WITH THE **SERIOUS** DESTRUCTION OF THIS CITY!

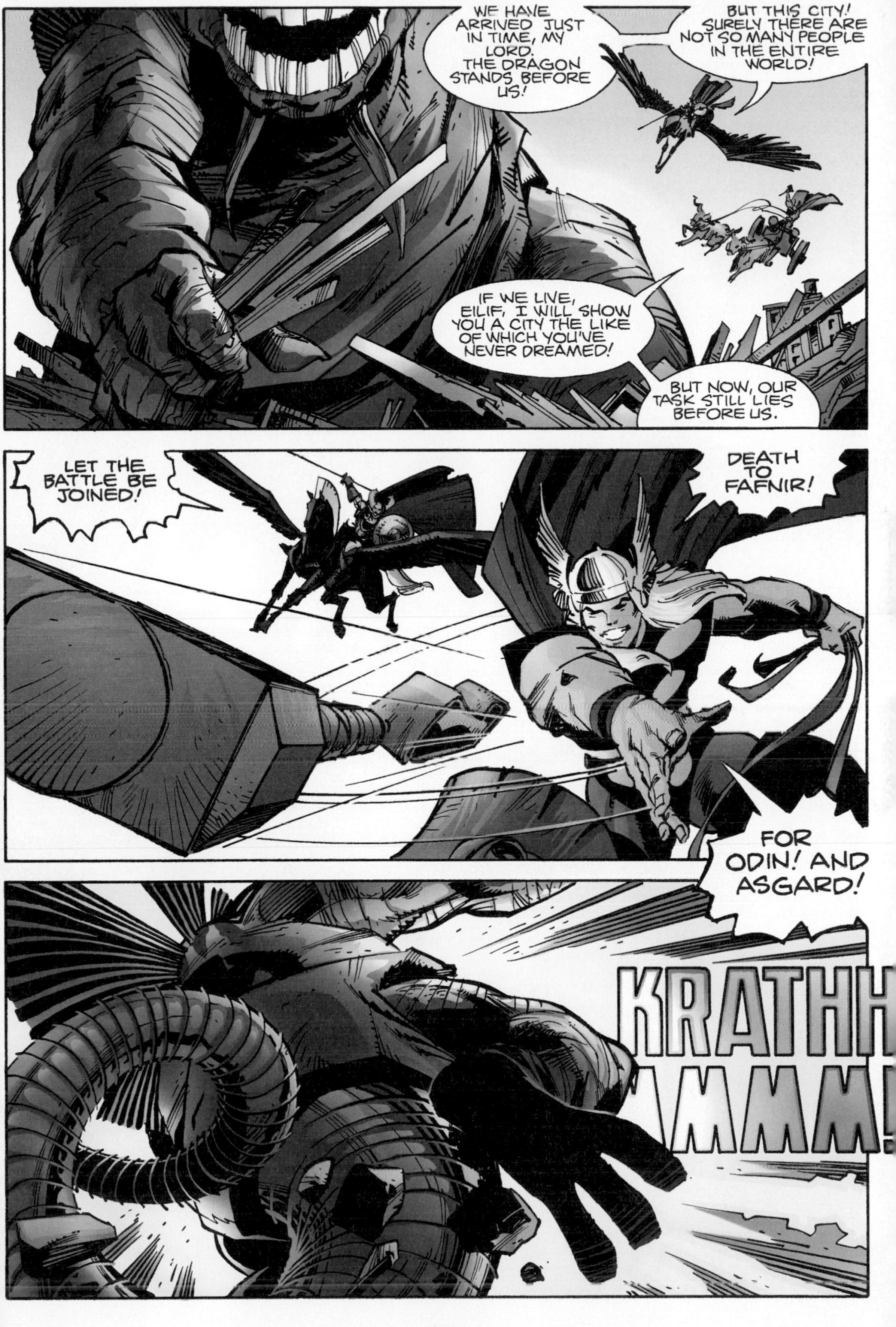
WE HAVE ARRIVED JUST IN TIME, MY LORD. THE DRAGON STANDS BEFORE US!
BUT THIS CITY! SURELY THERE ARE NOT SO MANY PEOPLE IN THE ENTIRE WORLD!
IF WE LIVE, EILIF, I WILL SHOW YOU A CITY THE LIKE OF WHICH YOU'VE NEVER DREAMED!
BUT NOW, OUR TASK STILL LIES BEFORE US.
LET THE BATTLE BE JOINED!
DEATH TO FAFNIR!
FOR ODIN! AND ASGARD!
KRATHH AMMM!

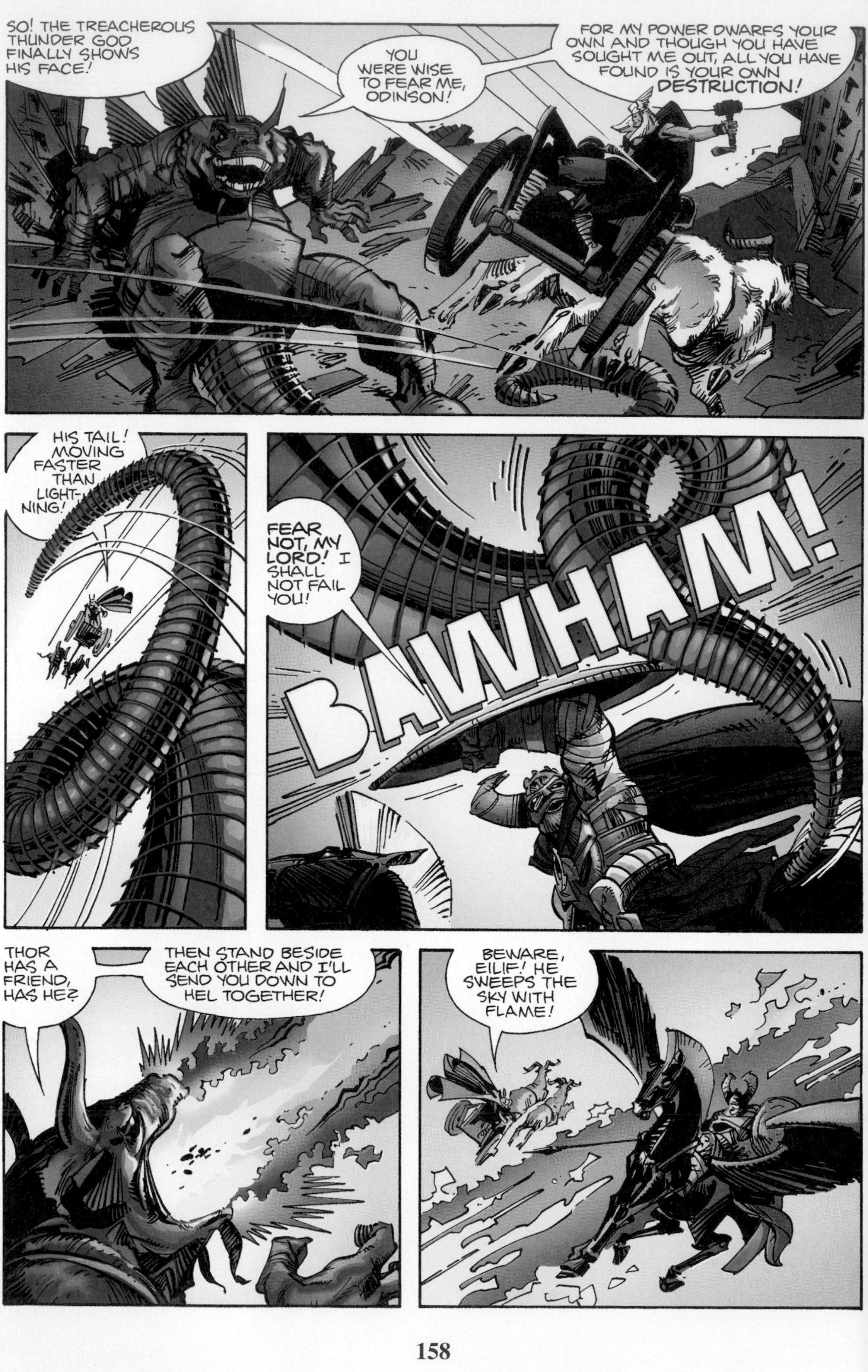
SO! THE TREACHEROUS THUNDER GOD FINALLY SHOWS HIS FACE!
YOU WERE WISE TO FEAR ME, ODINSON!
FOR MY POWER DWARFS YOUR OWN AND THOUGH YOU HAVE SOUGHT ME OUT, ALL YOU HAVE FOUND IS YOUR OWN DESTRUCTION!
HIS TAIL! MOVING FASTER THAN LIGHT-NING!
FEAR NOT, MY LORD! I SHALL NOT FAIL YOU!
BAWHAM!
THOR HAS A FRIEND, HAS HE?
THEN STAND BESIDE EACH OTHER AND I'LL SEND YOU DOWN TO HEL TOGETHER!
BEWARE, EILIF! HE SWEEPS THE SKY WITH FLAME!

BUT AS THINGS GO BADLY FOR OUR HEROES, WE LOOK IN ON HEIMDALL OF ASGARD, GUARDIAN OF THE RAINBOW BRIDGE...

...AND KEEN-EYED WATCHER OF THE GODS.

NEVER HAVE I SEEN THE LIKE.

THE STARS THEMSELVES ARE BLOTTED OUT BEFORE ME, AND EVEN I CANNOT PIERCE THE INKY VEIL.

CLOSER AND CLOSER COMES THE DARK, AND YET I DO SEE SOMETHING DEEP WITHIN THE BLACKNESS...

...RACING THIS WAY AS THOUGH ITS VERY LIFE WERE AT STAKE.

BY MY SWORD. 'TIS ODIN'S RAVEN MUNINN, SORELY HURT AND SPENT PAST ESCAPING.

EVEN NOW, HE FLUTTERS TO THE BRIDGE BESIDE ME.

AND THE BLACKNESS DRAWS NIGH!

BEGONE, SHADOW! THERE IS NO PLACE FOR YOU HERE IN THE GOLDEN REALM, AND I AM PLEDGED TO DEFEND THIS BRIDGE WITH MY LIFE!

THE DARKNESS SLIDES PAST ME LIKE A RIVER OF NIGHT AND IS GONE, NO MAN CAN SAY WHERE.

AND MUNINN YET LIVES! BUT WHERE IS HUGINN, ODIN'S OTHER RAVEN?

AND WHAT COULD HAVE INJURED MUNINN SO GRIEVOUSLY?

THIS PORTENDS SOME TERRIBLE EVIL, AWAKE AT LAST.

AND ODIN IS NOT IN ASGARD!

WHILE ON EARTH...

CHUCK CHERKLE HERE FOR ON-THE-SPOT NEWS!

THE BATTLE ROYALE CONTINUES BETWEEN THOR AND THE MONSTER!

THE POLICE AND GUARDSMEN HAVE EVACUATED THIS PART OF THE CITY AND--

UH-OH! THOR STOOD IN ONE SPOT TOO LONG, AND THE MONSTER'S ABOUT TO GRAB HIM!

SO FAR, THE FIGHT HAS BEEN ABOUT EVEN, THE CREATURE'S POWER MATCHED BY THOR'S SPEED AND AGILITY!

BACK, CREATURE OF EVIL! SEEK NOT TO TAKE WHAT YOU CANNOT HOLD!

CHARGRAKK!

ARRRGH!

AND NOW, BEFORE YOU CAN RECOVER, I SHALL STRIKE WITH ALL THE POWER OF MY ENCHANTED HAMMER!

THE FORCE OF THE BLOW IS FELT AS FAR AWAY AS PENNSYLVANIA!

UNBELIEVABLE. FAFNIR DOTH SHRUG OFF MY MOST POWERFUL BLOWS AS THOUGH THEY WERE THE LIGHTEST OF SUMMER RAINS!

AGAIN, HE DISCHARGES HIS FIERY BREATH.

HIS ARMOR IS VIRTUALLY IMPERVIOUS TO ANYTHING!

STAY BACK, EILIF. YOU'VE COME TOO LOW!

NAY, MY LORD! CLOUDRIDER AND I SHALL EVADE HIS TAIL WITH EASE!

RASH LITTLE GNAT! THIS TIME, YOU ARE MINE!

UGGH!

I AM UNHORSED!

AND SO HIGH!

SO HIGH!

CRASSHH!

EILIF!!

WELL SAID, GODLING! I KNEW YOUR CONCERN FOR THE MORTAL WOULD UNDO YOU SOONER OR LATER!

SMMMSH

THIS COULD BE IT, FOLKS! THE DRAGON'S REALLY LAYING INTO THOR NOW!

AND WITH-OUT HIS CHARIOT, THOR CAN'T GET CLEAR!

KLATT WHADOOM!

UH, FOLKS, WE'RE GOING TO RETURN YOU TO THE STUDIO NOW SO THAT WE CAN...RELOCATE...OUR REMOTE FACILITIES AT A...A... BETTER VANTAGE POINT!

WE'LL BE BACK WITH YOU AS SOON AS WE CAN!

LET'S GET THE HECK OUT OF HERE, CLANCY!

162

I'M STILL ALIVE, BUT I'M GROWING WEAKER BY THE MOMENT.

THOR MUST BE BADLY HURT, FOR THE MAGIC IS FADING!

WHERE IS YOUR **COURAGE** NOW, EILIF? YOU WERE BRAVE ENOUGH WHEN YOU WERE IMBUED WITH **YOUTH!**

AND THE DRAGON IS SEARCHING AMONG THE RUINS TO SLAY HIM.

RECKLESS, TOO, ELSE THE DRAGON WOULD NEVER HAVE CAUGHT YOU.

THE SON...

...OF ÓDIN...

...MUST NOT...

...PERISH...

...BECAUSE EILIF...

...FAILED IN HIS DUTY!

WHAT LITTLE STRENGTH IS MINE BY BIRTH IS WANING RAPIDLY. I AM DYING!

BUT I AM ABOVE THE GREAT BEAST NOW...

...AND I STILL HAVE MY SPEAR!

BUT I WILL BE THE WEAPON...

NOT EVEN VOICE LEFT TO SHOUT WITH.

163

...FOR ODIN, FOR THOR, AND ASGARD!

ARRROOOO!

WHO HAS DARED TO WOUND ME?

ACCURSED MORTAL! THOR CAN WAIT! ONLY YOUR DEATH WILL SATISFY ME NOW!

WHILE UNDER THE RUBBLE...

EILIF'S SPEAR! IT HATH PIERCED FAFNIR'S IMPENETRABLE HIDE!

I MUST GATHER MY REMAINING ENERGIES AND FLY!

FOR EILIF HATH SHOWED ME THE WAY, AND WHAT I COULD NOT DO ALONE...

...MAY YET BE ACCOMPLISHED! EILIF'S WEAPON SHALL BE THE DRAGON'S BANE!

NOW, BY ALL THE STRENGTH OF MY HERITAGE, BY THE POWER OF MJOLNIR, LET EVIL PERISH!

AAAH...EEE!

'TIS DONE! THE SPEAR HATH BEEN DRIVEN INTO THE BEAST FULL FORCE!

AND HE BEGINS TO TOPPLE!

THE DRAGON'S FIRE...

BOOOOM!

...IS QUENCHED!

BUT WHAT OF VALIANT EILIF?

EILIF! EILIF!

HAS THE LIFE FLED YOUR SHATTERED BODY?

CAN YOU NO LONGER HEAR EVEN THE VOICES OF THE GODS?

A TRUER COMPANION HATH NO MORTAL BEEN TO ME!

OH, EILIF, MY SHIELD BEARER EILIF!

LOOKS LIKE THE ACTION'S OVER, SARGE. SHALL WE MOVE IN NOW?

WELL, CORPORAL--

A VIKING'S FUNERAL, EILIF! AS I AM GOD OF THUNDER, YOU SHALL HAVE A VIKING'S FUNERAL!

KAROSSSH!

I THINK WE'LL WAIT!

WHAT'S HE DOING, SARGE, PILING UP ALL THAT RUBBLE?

IT'S... IT'S A FUNERAL PYRE, FOR THE GUY THAT WAS WITH HIM!

I DON'T BELIEVE IT! HE'S LIFTING THE DRAGON!

IT'S A DOG!

HUH?

HE'S PUTTING A DOG AT THE VIKING'S FEET!

THAT'S HOW THEY BURNED THEIR DEAD, THEY SAY!

UH-OH! GET YOUR HEAD DOWN, CORPORAL, AND FAST!

HEAR ME, YOU ELEMENTS! HEAR ME, STORMS!

RISE UP IN YOUR WRATH!

A WARRIOR HATH DIED THIS DAY, AND YOU SHALL CARRY HIM TO HIS DESTINY!

NO LONGER EILIF THE LOST, BUT EILIF THE DRAGONSLAYER!

barooom!

STRIKE NOW! AND FIRE THIS HOLY MOUND!

SARGE, UP THERE! IN THE SKY!

I DON'T BELIEVE IT!

THEY'RE COMING FOR HIM! SOMEBODY'S COMING FOR THE DEAD MAN!

AND THE PYRE ERUPTS IN GLORY!

FOR A MOMENT, THE ENTIRE CITY LIES STUNNED BY THE BLINDING LIGHT!

BUT ONLY A FEW SEE MORE THAN THE PLAY OF LIGHTNING AND THE DANCING SHADOWS!

AND NONE SEE THE LOOMING FIGURE THAT TOWERS OVER ALL, AS FATHER ODIN AND HIS VALKYRIE MAIDENS WELCOME THE LAST VIKING...

KATHOOM!

...INTO VALHALLA!

AS THE WILD RIDERS DISAPPEAR INTO THE NIGHT...

LET'S GO HOME, CORPORAL. NOTHING MORE WE CAN DO HERE.

WHILE IN BROOKLYN, IN A SMALL APARTMENT IN BAY RIDGE...

FOR THOUGH THE VICTORY WAS OURS, EILIF IS GONE AND THIS ROOM, THIS VERY EARTH, SEEMS THE MEANER FOR IT.

PERHAPS I SHOULD HAVE STAYED IN THE AVENGERS' MANSION AFTER ALL, AMONG FAMILIAR SURROUNDINGS.

OR NOT GIVEN UP MY DONALD BLAKE IDENTITY, HE AT LEAST HAD A HOME AND FRIENDS.

AFTER LAST NIGHT, I SHOULD BE JOYFUL. AND YET, I FIND MYSELF WEARY OF SPIRIT.

AND SIF IS GONE AS WELL.

THOUGH SHE IS BETTER OFF QUESTING ACROSS THE UNIVERSE WITH BETA RAY BILL. NOW I FIND I MISS HER TOUCH.

NOK! NOK!

EH?

WHY, IT'S... I NEVER DID KNOW YOUR NAME.

MELODI. JERRY TOLD ME WHERE TO FIND YOU.

MOVING INTO NEW SURROUNDINGS IS ALWAYS SO DEPRESSING, DON'T YOU THINK?

AND I DID SAY I WANTED TO THANK YOU FOR SAVING MY LIFE.

SEE? I BROUGHT ALONG SOMETHING SPECIAL TO DRINK TO CELEBRATE.

ARE YOU ALL RIGHT?

WHAT? OH, I WAS JUST... IN A FIGHT. NOTHING SERIOUS.

I KNOW WHAT YOU NEED. A GOOD BACKRUB WILL TAKE ALL THOSE NASTY KINKS RIGHT OUT.

click

WHY DON'T YOU TAKE OFF YOUR SHIRT?

NEXT: *WHATEVER HAPPENED TO*

BALDER THE BRAVE?

ALONG WITH OTHER GREAT STUFF!

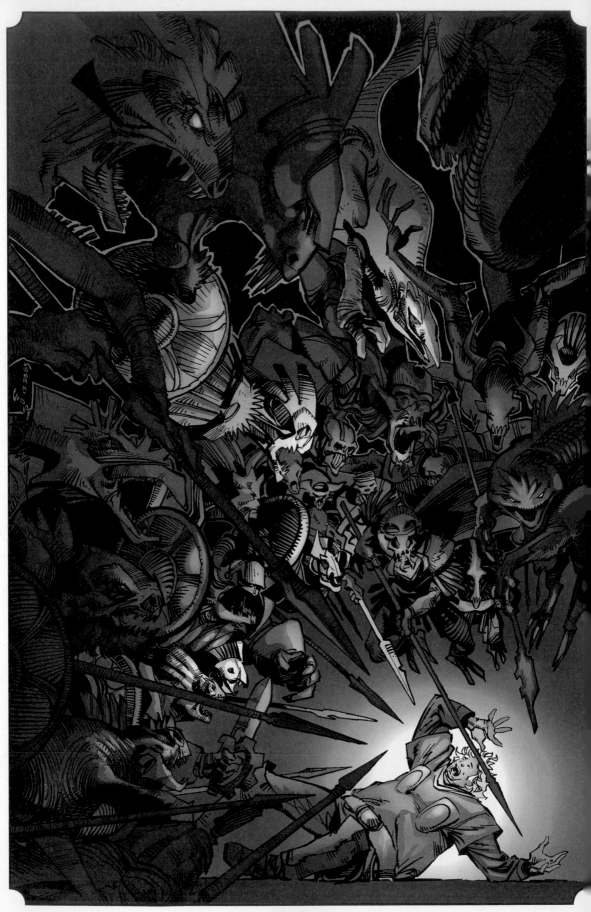

WHATEVER HAPPENED TO BALDER THE BRAVE?

NORNKEEP, THE FORTRESS CARVED FROM THE LIVING ROCK OF THE EARTH, HOME OF KARNILLA, THE NORN QUEEN.

HERE SHE KEEPS HER ANCIENT COURT AND HERE SHE GOVERNS HER DANGEROUS REALM.

AND IT IS TO THESE GATES WHERE NO LIVING MAN WOULD DARE TO VENTURE THAT THE WOLF HAS COME AT LAST.

FOR THOUGH DANGEROUS IS THE REALM, STILL MORE DANGEROUS IS THE **WOLF.**

RT AND STORY: WALTER SIMONSON · LETTERING: JOHN WORKMAN, JR. · COLORS: CHRISTIE SCHEELE
EDITING: MARK GRUENWALD · EDITOR-IN-CHIEF: JIM SHOOTER

GUARDSMAN! WHAT'S THIS? I GAVE NO ORDER THAT THE PORTCULLIS SHOULD BE RAISED!

CAPTAIN, I SWEAR TO YOU--!

WHAT? LOOK YONDER! A FELL BEAST! TO ARMS!

STAY BACK, YOU FOOLS! DO YOU NOT RECOGNIZE HIM? 'TIS GERI, ONE OF ODIN'S WOLVES.

HINDER HIM ON PERIL OF YOUR LIFE! HE COMES AS A MESSENGER FROM ASGARD!

MILADY! BEWARE! YOUR ENEMIES SEEK TO DESTROY US!

HOW DARE YOU ENTER THIS THRONE ROOM? DEPART LEST I SUMMON THE HOSTS OF HEL TO DRAG YOU DOWN TO DOOM!

SAVE YOUR SPELLS, O QUEEN, FOR THEY WOULD AVAIL YOU NAUGHT.

THE CHILDREN OF ODIN TRAVEL UNDER HIS PROTECTION AND ARE SENT TO SUMMON THOSE THE ALL-FATHER WISHES TO ASGARD.

AS GERI HAS BEEN SENT TO SUMMON ME.

AND THOUGH I HAD HOPED TO LOSE MYSELF FOREVER, I CANNOT DISOBEY MY LIEGE.

FAITHFUL GERI, I WILL COME WITH YOU.

UNTIL...

WHO STANDS BEFORE ME IN THE SHADOWS? COME FORTH, THAT I MAY SEE THEE PLAINLY.

LONG HAVE YOU SAT AND BROODED ON YOUR GREAT THRONE, MY LORD, ABOUT MATTERS I CAN ONLY GUESS AT.

YOUR WIFE **FRIGGA** IT IS WHO HAS COME TO GREET HER HUSBAND.

YOU CARRY A TERRIBLE BURDEN, ODIN. WILL YOU NOT LET ME SHARE IT WITH YOU?

AH, FRIGGA, MY DEAREST WIFE, YOU ARE AS LOVELY NOW AS WHEN WE FIRST MET.

TO SEE YOU ONLY DELIGHTS ME.

I WILL SHARE MY TROUBLES WITH YOU. THOUGH I FEAR RATHER THAN EASING MY BURDEN, IT WILL ONLY DARKEN YOUR RADIANT VISION.

FEAR NOT, HUSBAND. MY CANDLE IS NOT SO EASILY DIMMED.

VERY WELL.

I HAVE SUMMONED BALDER HOME TO ASGARD. FOR HE AND ONLY HE MAY ACCOMPLISH WHAT MUST BE DONE.

MY LORD--!

HEAR ME OUT, FRIGGA.

AND YET, WHEN ALL IS FINISHED, HE MAY NEVER FORGIVE ME FOR WHAT I AM ABOUT TO DO.

"WHEN I RETURNED FROM MIDGARD YESTER-EVE, I FOUND HEIMDALL, GUARDIAN OF THE RAINBOW BRIDGE, AWAITING ME ANXIOUSLY.

"QUICKLY, HE TOOK ME TO HIS HOME BESIDE THE BRIDGE.

"AND THERE I FOUND MUNINN, MY RAVEN, SORELY HURT. HEIMDALL HAD RESCUED HIM WHILE I WAS GONE AND KEPT HIM FOR MY RETURN.

"OF MY OTHER RAVEN, HUGINN, THERE WAS NO SIGN.

"I SENT HEIM-DALL BACK TO HIS POST AND SPOKE WITH MUNINN.

"FOR I HAD SENT MY RAVENS ON A MISSION TO PENETRATE THE BURNING GALAXY AND FERRET OUT ITS SECRET.

"I HAD GIVEN THEM GREAT SIZE AND STRENGTH TO DO SO.

"AND NOW ONLY MUNINN HAD RETURNED.

"HIS MAGIC WAS SPENT, HIS VOICE NEARLY GONE.

"WE SPOKE FOR A LONG TIME, HE AND I...

"...TILL FINALLY I LEARNED...

"...WHAT I MUST KNOW.

"THEN I BROUGHT MUNINN HOME.

NOW, FOR ALL OUR SAKES, I MUST SEND LOYAL BALDER INTO THE LION'S DEN FOR ONLY SO CAN THE FATES BE AVERTED AND ALL THAT WE HAVE DONE BE SAVED.

THE DANGER IS EVEN GREATER THAN I FEARED.

MY LIEGE, I HAVE RETURNED TO ASGARD AT YOUR BIDDING. HOW MAY I SERVE YOU?

NOT EASILY, BRAVE BALDER. FOR I WOULD MAKE YOU MY AMBASSADOR TO DELIVER A LETTER FOR ME...

MY LORD! YOU WOULD SEND ME TO THE GOD RESPONSIBLE FOR MY DEATH*? WHO TRAPPED ME IN HEL WITH THE LEGIONS OF THE DEAD TILL I ESCAPED? WHO DESPISES ME WITH A RANCOR MATCHED ONLY BY HIS HATRED OF THOR HIMSELF?!

HOW WELL I KNOW IT. AND YET, IN THIS MATTER, MY BRAVE, ONLY YOU WILL DO.

...AND THOUGH THE JOURNEY ITSELF IS DANGEROUS, IT IS THE ONE WHOM YOU SEEK THAT IS THE GREATEST DANGER.

I MUST SEND YOU TO LOKI.

*THOR #274.

FOR THE IMPORTANCE OF THIS MISSION IS BEYOND TELLING...

...AND THOUGH HE DESPISES YOU, EVEN LOKI KNOWS THAT THE WORD OF BALDER IS THE VERY MEASURE OF TRUTH.

MAYHAP HE WILL BELIEVE YOU AS HE WOULD BELIEVE NO OTHER.

VERY WELL, LORD ODIN, I WILL UNDERTAKE THIS AMBASSADORSHIP.

BUT ON ONE CONDITION. I NO LONGER HAVE THE STOMACH FOR KILLING AND HAVE FORSWORN ALL VIOLENCE. I WILL NOT RAISE A SWORD NOR KILL A SOUL, NOT EVEN FOR ASGARD.

[S]O BE IT. THESE [A]RE MATTERS, [B]RAVE BALDER, OF [IN]DIVIDUAL CONSCIENCE. YOU [M]UST DO AS [YO]U THINK BEST.

TAKE THIS LETTER. READ IT AND THEN CARRY IT TO MY STEPSON THAT HE MAY BE PERSUADED TO JOIN WITH US.

AND BALDER, NO ONE ELSE IS TO KNOW OF THIS BUSINESS!

IT SHALL BE DONE, MY LIEGE.

175

MEANWHILE, IN BAY RIDGE, BROOKLYN, IN A THIRD FLOOR APARTMENT, WE FIND THOR (IN HIS CIVILIAN IDENTITY) ENTERTAINING LORELEI (IN **HER** CIVILIAN IDENTITY).

HE DOESN'T KNOW WHO SHE IS; SHE KNOWS **EXACTLY** WHO HE IS!

UMMMMM. THAT DOES INDEED FEEL WONDERFUL. YOU WERE RIGHT, MELODI!

I DIDN'T REALIZE I WAS SO TIRED.

I KNEW IT WOULD BE.

A BACK-RUB WAS JUST WHAT I NEEDED.

OW. GENTLY, PLEASE.

OW.

CRYBABY.

DON'T WORRY. I KNOW JUST WHAT I'M DOING.

THIS IS GOING TO RELAX YOU LIKE NOTHING ELSE EVER HAS.

WHY, WHEN I'M THROUGH, YOU'LL WONDER WHERE I'VE BEEN ALL YOUR LIFE.

HOW ABOUT SOME GOLDEN MEAD TO HELP YOU ENJOY YOURSELF?

HUMMMM?

SIGURD?

SIGURD!

176

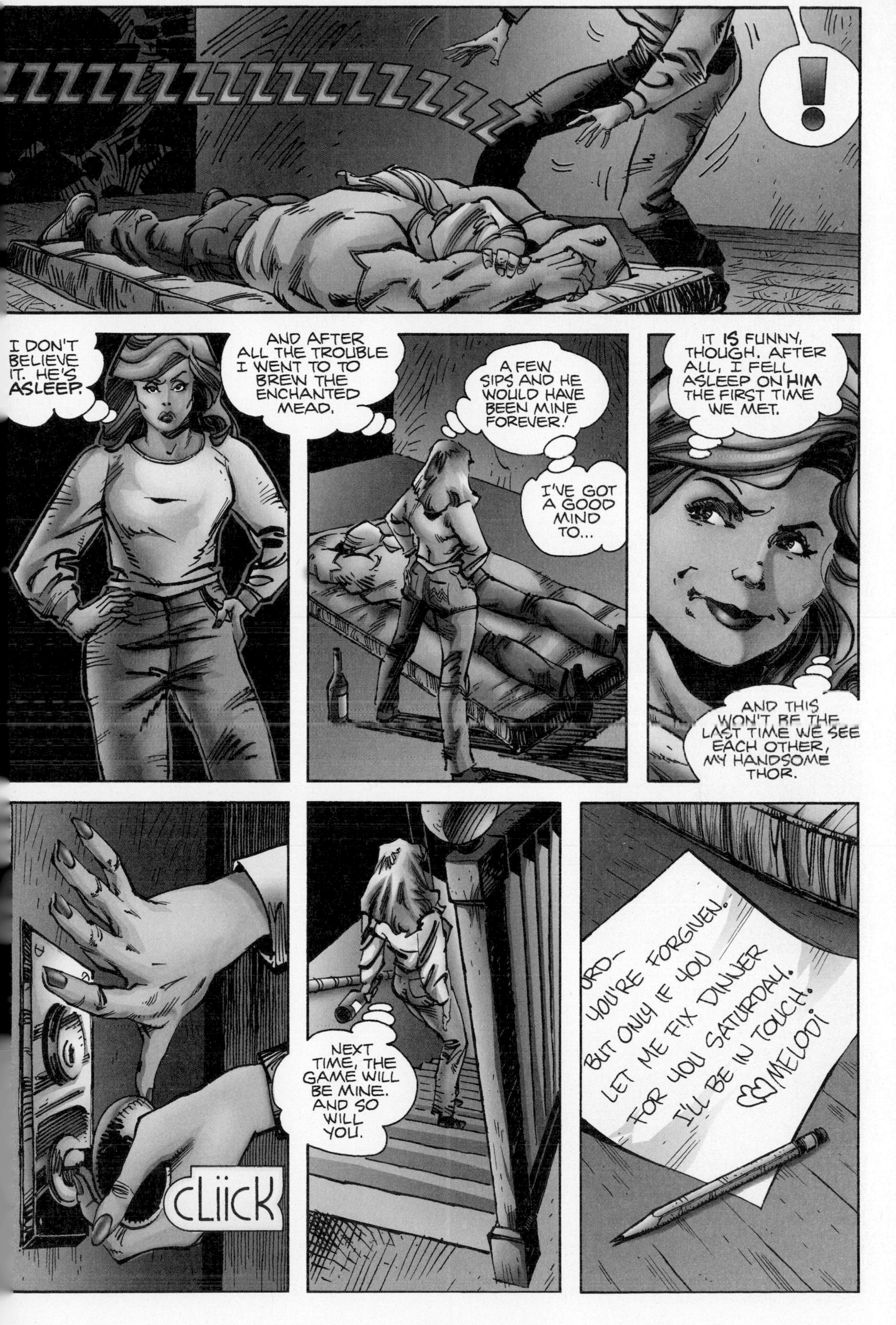
ZZZZZZZZZZZZZZZZZZ
!
I DON'T BELIEVE IT. HE'S ASLEEP.
AND AFTER ALL THE TROUBLE I WENT TO TO BREW THE ENCHANTED MEAD.
A FEW SIPS AND HE WOULD HAVE BEEN MINE FOREVER!
I'VE GOT A GOOD MIND TO...
IT IS FUNNY, THOUGH. AFTER ALL, I FELL ASLEEP ON HIM THE FIRST TIME WE MET.
AND THIS WON'T BE THE LAST TIME WE SEE EACH OTHER, MY HANDSOME THOR.
CLiiCK
NEXT TIME, THE GAME WILL BE MINE. AND SO WILL YOU.
YOU'RE FORGIVEN. BUT ONLY IF YOU LET ME FIX DINNER FOR YOU SATURDAY. I'LL BE IN TOUCH.
MELODI

MEANWHILE, FAR BEYOND THE GREEN FIELDS OF ASGARD...

MY FAITHFUL STEED, OUR JOURNEY IS NEARLY AT AN END. BEYOND THE FAR MOUNTAINS LIES THE LONELY DWELLING OF LOKI.

FORWARD, NOBLE SILVER-HOOF, AND GALLOP AS THE WIND!

STILL, THE GREATEST DANGERS ARE YET TO COME.

FOR IF THE LEGENDS ARE TRUE, NOW THE CHASE BEGINS!

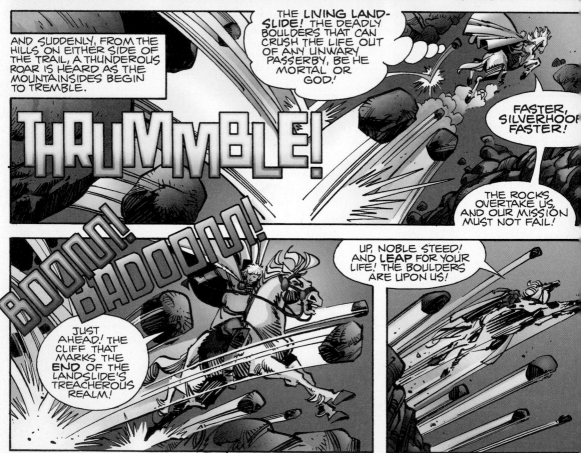

AND SUDDENLY, FROM THE HILLS ON EITHER SIDE OF THE TRAIL, A THUNDEROUS ROAR IS HEARD AS THE MOUNTAINSIDES BEGIN TO TREMBLE.

THE LIVING LANDSLIDE! THE DEADLY BOULDERS THAT CAN CRUSH THE LIFE OUT OF ANY UNWARY PASSERBY, BE HE MORTAL OR GOD!

THRUMMBLE!

FASTER, SILVERHOOF, FASTER!

THE ROCKS OVERTAKE US, AND OUR MISSION MUST NOT FAIL!

BOONNN! BADOOOM!

UP, NOBLE STEED! AND LEAP FOR YOUR LIFE! THE BOULDERS ARE UPON US!

JUST AHEAD! THE CLIFF THAT MARKS THE END OF THE LANDSLIDE'S TREACHEROUS REALM!

WELL DONE, SILVER-HOOF! ONCE BEYOND THIS TALUS SLOPE, THE POWER OF THE LIVING LANDSLIDE CEASES!

SCREEE!

YET SLACK NOT YOUR PACE. FOR EVEN NOW WE MUST PLUNGE FULL FORCE INTO THE PERILOUS FORBIDDEN FOREST!

WHERE THE TREES AND VINES LURE THE UNWARY WITH THEIR PLEASANT SCENT AND THEN ENFOLD THEM IN DEADLY EMBRACE!

ON, SILVERHOOF, ON!

OUR MISSION FOR LORD ODIN IS TOO VITAL TO LET SUCH ANCIENT EVIL PREVENT OUR PASSAGE.

RIP!

SHRIPP!

THOUGH I AM BUT A SHADOW OF MY FORMER SELF, STILL I AM A SON OF ASGARD AND WILL NOT BE DENIED!

STILL, WE WILL WIN THROUGH!

UNTIL THE VINES ARE GROWN AGAIN, THERE WILL BE SAFE PASSAGE THROUGH THAT DANGEROUS PLACE.

BUT NOW, THE MOST HAZARDOUS PERIL OF ALL AWAITS US. FOR BEFORE US LIE THE LEAGUES OF THE DEADLY DESERT...

...WHERE THE SANDSTORMS RAGE CONSTANTLY AND PRECIOUS WATER CANNOT BE FOUND.

I WILL COVER THY HEAD WITH MY OWN CLOAK AND BE THINE EYES, SILVERHOOF.

ODIN WATCH OVER US THAT WE MAY NOT FALL INTO THE DEADLY PITFALLS OF THE REGION.

THE HOURS DRAG BY AS BALDER AND HIS MOUNT SLOWLY FIGHT THEIR WAY INCH BY INCH ACROSS THE TREACHEROUS SANDS UNTIL AT LAST...

THERE! BEFORE ME IN THE RAGING STORM! IS THAT A SHADOW THAT I SEE OR ONLY ANOTHER ILLUSION OF THE DUST AND WIND?

PRAISE ODIN! THE WIND ABATES AND I SEE THAT WE HAVE AT LAST REACHED THE END OF THE DEADLY DESERT.

FOR THESE DRAGON HEADS MARK THE BEGINNING OF THE TRAIL THAT LEADS TO THE END OF OUR JOURNEY.

THEY POINT THE WAY TO THE CASTLE OF LOKI!

THE SILENCE OF THAT DESOLATE REGION IS ENDLESS, SAVE ONLY THE CAWING OF SOME WINGED CREATURE TOO HIGH FOR THE NAKED EYE TO SEE...

...AND THE SOUND OF SILVERHOOF'S HOOVES UPON THE STONES.

CLOP CLOP CLOP

WHEN SUDDENLY...

NOW, BROTHERS! TAKE HIM!

BUT SLAY HIM NOT! THE MASTER WANTS HIM ALIVE!

TROLLS! BUT HOW COME THEY HERE, EVEN AT THE EDGE OF ASGARD!

WAIT! THESE ARE NO TROLLS! THESE ARE--!

ELSEWHERE, FAR BEYOND THE FIELDS WE KNOW...

...A GREAT FIGURE TURNS FROM THE ANVIL BEFORE HIM AND STRETCHES FORTH HIS HAND.

LAKES OF BRIMSTONE SPRING UP ON EVERY SIDE...

...AND THEN...

DOOM!

THE SWORD IS **TEMPERED!**

MEANWHILE, INSIDE THE CASTLE OF...

LOKI! I MIGHT HAVE KNOWN THESE WERE YOUR CREATURES.

ONLY YOU WOULD BE BOLD ENOUGH TO HARBOR DEMONS OF THE FIRE WITHIN THE BOUNDARIES OF ASGARD!

RELEASE ME! I COME AS AN AMBASSADOR FROM ODIN HIMSELF!

ODIN DOES **NOT** RULE HERE. NOR IN FACT ARE THE DEMONS MINE.

BUT I HAVE A MESSAGE OF THE VERY HIGHEST IMPORTANCE.

YOU ARE **NOT** THE FIRST SUCH AMBASSADOR TO REACH ME. STRANGE THAT LOKI'S AID SHOULD SUDDENLY BE SOUGHT BY SO MANY.

PERHAPS YOU REMEMBER THE ONE WHO STANDS BESIDE ME. HE WHOM ODIN DID BANISH TO THE LIMBO OF ENDLESS NIGHT SO MANY AGES AGONE.

MAY I PRESENT MALEKITH, THE DARK ELF.

THE GENTLEMEN HOLDING YOU ARE PART OF HIS ENTOURAGE.

MALEKITH! BUT 'TIS HE AND HIS MASTER WHO WOULD DESTROY US ALL!

LOKI, YOU MUST LISTEN TO ME!

THIS UNSEEMLY OUTBURST DISPLEASES US, MY DEMONS. GAG HIM!

LOK-- MMMMPH!

AH, BALDER, EVER THE TOOTHLESS UNDERSTRAPPER OF THE NOBILITY OF ASGARD.

THE YEARS HAVE NOT BEEN KIND TO YOU, BRAVE BALDER. YOU WERE HANDSOME ONCE.

IS THIS THE BEST THAT ODIN CAN DO?

SEND A SPINELESS, OVERWEIGHT FLUNKY TO CURRY THE FAVOR OF HIS STEP SON...

...WHEN ALL KNOW THAT ODIN REGRETS EVER HAVING ADOPTED LOKI IN THE FIRST PLACE!

REMEMBER, LOKI, WHEN THE POWERS THAT BE HAVE BEEN DESTROYED, THERE WILL BE PLENTY LEFT OVER FOR THOSE **RUTHLESS** AND **BOLD** ENOUGH TO SEIZE IT!

AND AS A TOKEN OF MY GOOD FAITH, LET ME PRESENT YOU WITH A VERY SPECIAL GIFT...

...THE HEAD OF BALDER THE BRAVE.

KILL HIM!

UMMMPH!

UGGKKH!

HOLD HIM! HE'S BREAKING LOOSE!

OWWW!

CATCH HIM, YOU FOOLS! HE MUST BE SLAIN!

LOKI! STOP THEM! PLEASE!

HIS BONDS! HE'S SLIPPED FROM HIS BONDS!

AFTER HIM! HE LEAPS INTO THE COURT-YARD!

HE CAN'T ESCAPE US ALL!

LOKI! HEAR ME OUT! YOU KNOW I CANNOT **FIGHT** THESE DEMONS!

LOKI! HEED MY PLEA!

SEEK NOT MY DESTRUCTION UNTIL YOU KNOW THE TRUTH! THEN GLADLY WILL I DIE!

UMMPH!

THE VERY FATE OF THE UNIVERSE DEPENDS UPON MY WORDS!

NOW WE HAVE HIM. CLOSE IN, BROTHERS, AND WE WILL SPLIT THE ASGARDIAN LIKE A RIPE FRUIT.

SO IT IS TRUE. BALDER THE BRAVE HAS BECOME A SPINELESS MILKSOP!

AFRAID TO KILL EVEN THE DEMONS OF HEL!

LOKI! PLEASE! MY MISSION MUST NOT FAIL!

COME, MALEKITH. YOU AND I HAVE MUCH TO DISCUSS.

I DON'T SUPPOSE WE'LL EVER LEARN WHAT ODIN'S MESSAGE WAS NOW.

PITY!

LOKI!

NOW BY MY HAND DIES BALDER THE BRAVE!

NO! DO NOT MAKE ME DO IT!

THWACKK!

KILL HIM!

KILL HIM!

184

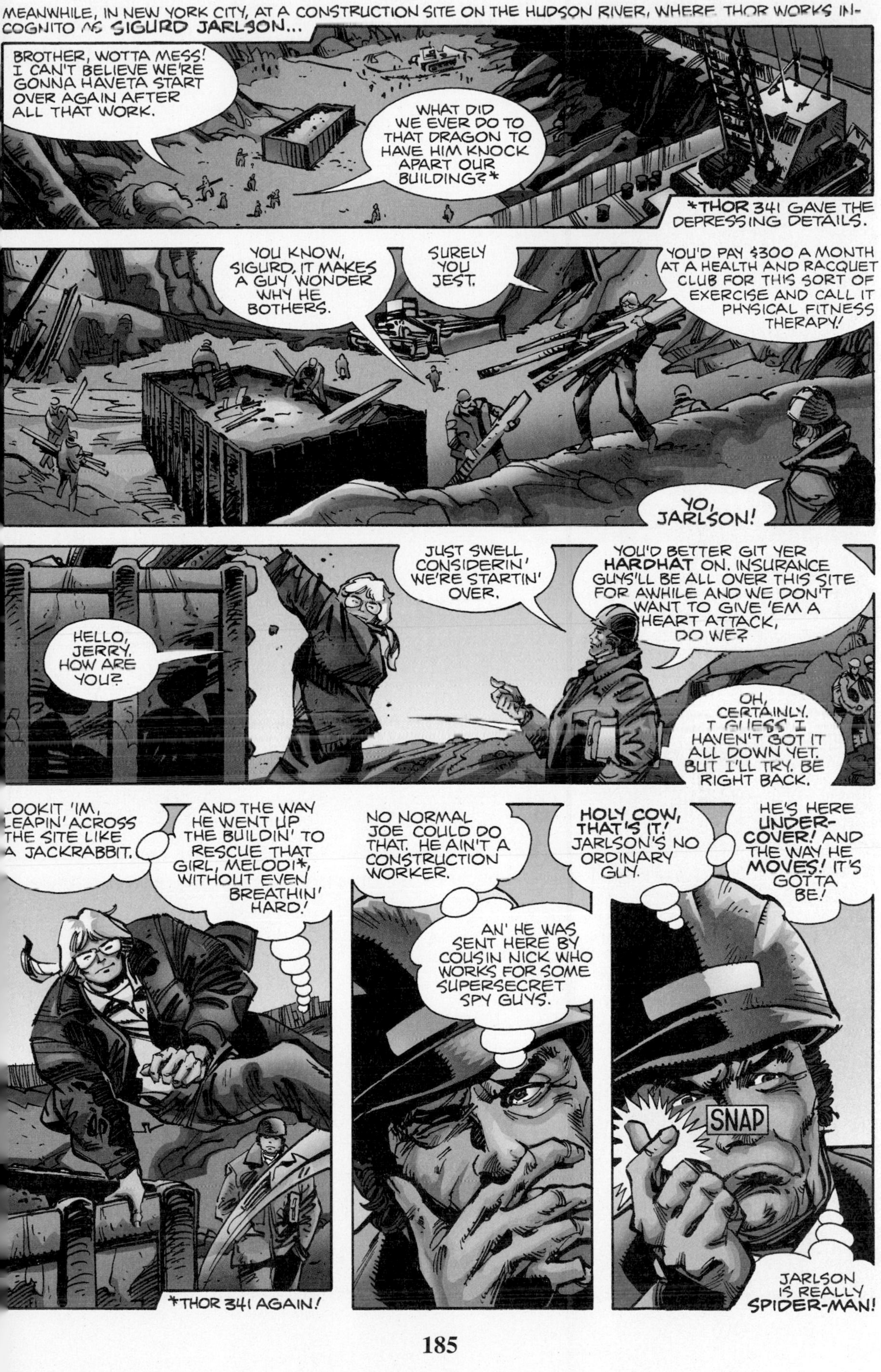

MEANWHILE, IN NEW YORK CITY, AT A CONSTRUCTION SITE ON THE HUDSON RIVER, WHERE THOR WORKS INCOGNITO AS SIGURD JARLSON...
BROTHER, WOTTA MESS! I CAN'T BELIEVE WE'RE GONNA HAVETA START OVER AGAIN AFTER ALL THAT WORK.
WHAT DID WE EVER DO TO THAT DRAGON TO HAVE HIM KNOCK APART OUR BUILDING?*
*THOR 341 GAVE THE DEPRESSING DETAILS.
YOU KNOW, SIGURD, IT MAKES A GUY WONDER WHY HE BOTHERS.
SURELY YOU JEST.
YOU'D PAY $300 A MONTH AT A HEALTH AND RACQUET CLUB FOR THIS SORT OF EXERCISE AND CALL IT PHYSICAL FITNESS THERAPY!
YO, JARLSON!
HELLO, JERRY. HOW ARE YOU?
JUST SWELL CONSIDERIN' WE'RE STARTIN' OVER.
YOU'D BETTER GIT YER HARDHAT ON. INSURANCE GUYS'LL BE ALL OVER THIS SITE FOR AWHILE AND WE DON'T WANT TO GIVE 'EM A HEART ATTACK, DO WE?
OH, CERTAINLY. I GUESS I HAVEN'T GOT IT ALL DOWN YET. BUT I'LL TRY. BE RIGHT BACK.
LOOKIT 'IM, LEAPIN' ACROSS THE SITE LIKE A JACKRABBIT.
AND THE WAY HE WENT UP THE BUILDIN' TO RESCUE THAT GIRL, MELODI*, WITHOUT EVEN BREATHIN' HARD!
*THOR 341 AGAIN!
NO NORMAL JOE COULD DO THAT. HE AIN'T A CONSTRUCTION WORKER.
AN' HE WAS SENT HERE BY COUSIN NICK WHO WORKS FOR SOME SUPERSECRET SPY GUYS.
HOLY COW, THAT'S IT! JARLSON'S NO ORDINARY GUY.
HE'S HERE UNDERCOVER! AND THE WAY HE MOVES! IT'S GOTTA BE!
SNAP
JARLSON IS REALLY SPIDER-MAN!

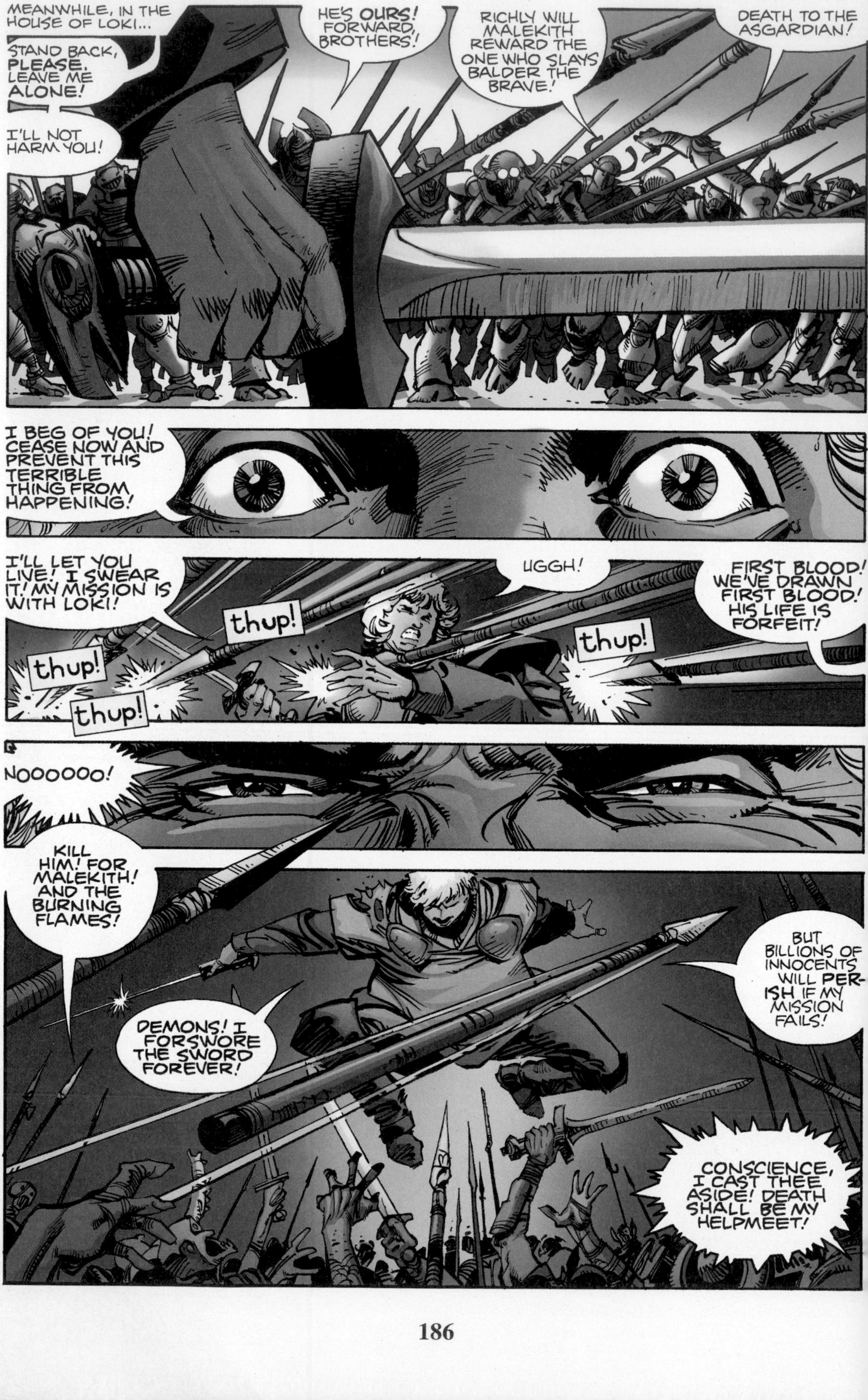
MEANWHILE, IN THE HOUSE OF LOKI...
STAND BACK, PLEASE. LEAVE ME ALONE!
I'LL NOT HARM YOU!
HE'S OURS! FORWARD, BROTHERS!
RICHLY WILL MALEKITH REWARD THE ONE WHO SLAYS BALDER THE BRAVE!
DEATH TO THE ASGARDIAN!
I BEG OF YOU! CEASE NOW AND PREVENT THIS TERRIBLE THING FROM HAPPENING!
I'LL LET YOU LIVE! I SWEAR IT! MY MISSION IS WITH LOKI!
UGGH!
FIRST BLOOD! WE'VE DRAWN FIRST BLOOD! HIS LIFE IS FORFEIT!
thup!
thup!
thup!
thup!
NOOOOOO!
KILL HIM! FOR MALEKITH! AND THE BURNING FLAMES!
DEMONS! I FORSWORE THE SWORD FOREVER!
BUT BILLIONS OF INNOCENTS WILL PERISH IF MY MISSION FAILS!
CONSCIENCE, I CAST THEE ASIDE! DEATH SHALL BE MY HELPMEET!

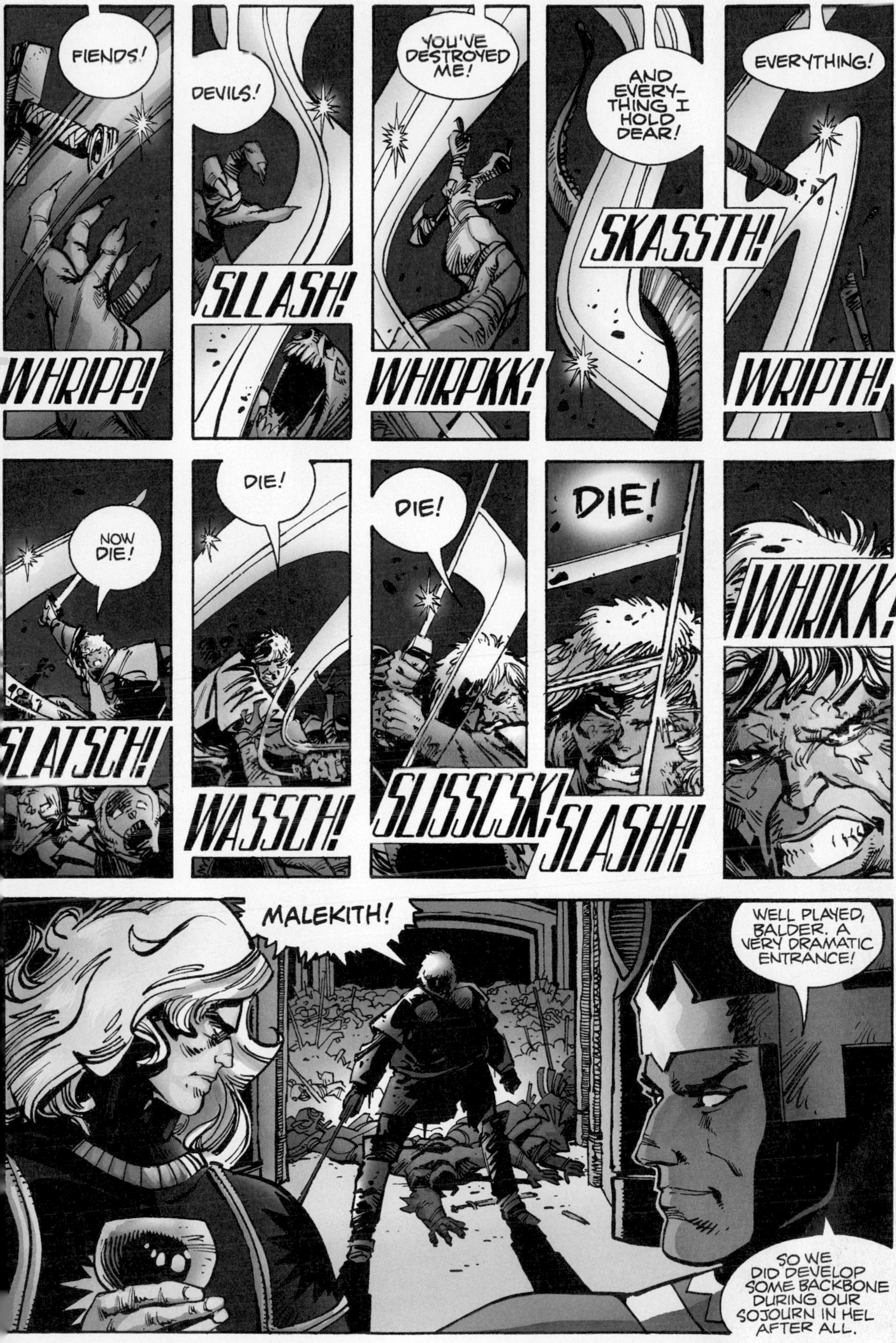
FIENDS!
WHRIPP!
DEVILS!
SLLASH!
YOU'VE DESTROYED ME!
WHIRPKK!
AND EVERY-THING I HOLD DEAR!
SKASSTH!
EVERYTHING!
WRIPTH!
NOW DIE!
SLATSCH!
DIE!
WASSCH!
DIE!
SLISSCSK!
DIE!
SLASHH!
WHRKK!
MALEKITH!
WELL PLAYED, BALDER. A VERY DRAMATIC ENTRANCE!
SO WE DID DEVELOP SOME BACKBONE DURING OUR SOJOURN IN HEL AFTER ALL.

MALEKITH, FOUL CREATURE! FOR WHAT YOU HAVE DONE TO ME THIS DAY, YOU WILL LIE WITH YOUR DEMONS TONIGHT IN HEL!

SLASSTH!

WHA--!

HE'S GONE, AND ONLY HIS CLOAK REMAINS.

FOOLISH BALDER. DO YOU NOT REMEMBER THE POWER OF THE DARK ELF, TO ENTER THE SHADOWS AND VANISH...

...TO TRAVEL WHERE HE WILL, AND EMERGE EVEN ON THE OTHER SIDE OF THE UNIVERSE?

HE HAS ESCAPED YOU.

BUT NOT PREVENTED ME FROM FULFILLING MY DUTY.

HERE IS THE LETTER, LOKI. THOUGH IT COST ME MY SOUL, I HAVE COMPLETED MY MISSION FOR MY LORD ODIN.

THE FATE OF THE UNIVERSE HANGS IN THE BALANCE.

YOU ARE A FOOL, BALDER, TO THINK THAT A MESSAGE FROM MY STEP FATHER COULD POSSIBLY BE OF CONCERN TO ME.

WHAT?!

I HAVE ALREADY DECIDED TO ACCEPT MALEKITH'S OFFER.

AFTER ALL, I HAVE THE BLOOD OF GIANTS IN MY VEINS, AS MY STEP-FATHER NEVER TIRES OF REMINDING ME.

BUT IT WAS SO DELIGHTFUL TO WATCH A PACIFIST SLAY HIS THOUSANDS THAT I SIMPLY COULDN'T BRING MYSELF TO MENTION IT BEFORE THIS.

WHY, IT WOULD HAVE SPOILED THE FUN.

DEVILSPAWN! WAS IT NOT ENOUGH THAT YOU *KILL* ME AND SEND ME DOWN TO HEL?

NOW YOU DESTROY WHAT *LITTLE* LIFE I HAD LEFT!

ASGARD MAY YET PERISH BY THE SWORD BUT NOT BEFORE I RID THE WORLD OF THE DEADLIEST SERPENT IN HER HALLS!

THREATEN ME NOT, THOU SAPLESS WEAKLING.

THOU HAST NOT THE METTLE FOR THE DEED!

LIAR!

SHLIKKK!

THUD

I CANNOT DO IT!

EVEN HERE, IN THE CHAMBERS OF MY GREATEST SORCERY, MY MAGICKS CANNOT PIERCE THE MYSTIC SCREENS SURROUNDING LOKI'S DOMAIN.

AND BALDER'S FATE REMAINS UNKNOWN TO ME.

SURELY, MISTRESS, LOKI WOULD NOT DARE TO HARM BALDER WHEN HE IS ON A MISSION FOR ODIN.

I DO NOT TRUST THE SLY ONE. HE WOULD BETRAY ANYONE IF IT SUITED HIS PURPOSE.

HE IS SO UNPREDICTABLE, HIS GAMES SO TWISTED THAT--

WEEEO

THE ALARM! SOMEONE HAS EMERGED FROM THE MISTS SURROUNDING LOKI'S CASTLE!

OH NO!

'TIS BALDER, MY LADY. BUT HIS FACE! LOOK AT HIS FACE!

HE HAS THE LOOK OF THE DAMNED ABOUT HIM!

ARRRGGGH!

RIDE ON! RIDE ON, SILVER-HOOF!

BETTER THAT I HAD **DIED** AND STAYED IN HEL THAN RETURN TO THIS EXISTENCE WHICH TORTURES ME BEYOND ENDURANCE!

...THAT I MIGHT END THIS AGONY OF LIVING AND REJOIN THE SERRIED RANKS OF THE DEAD!

NOW SHALL I LOSE MYSELF IN THE TRACKLESS WASTES BEYOND KARNILLA'S LAND AND SEEK OUT DEATH, MY ONLY FRIEND AND COMPANION...

MAY IT BE SOON!

RIDE ON, SILVER-HOOF! **RIDE ON!**

"TILL ONLY THE WHISPERS OF THE WIND ARE LEFT TO DISTURB THE SILENCE OF THE ANCIENT AND ILLIMITABLE DESERT...

"...AND BALDER THE BRAVE IS NO MORE."

191

NEXT: **DINNER FOR TWO** or **THAT WAS NO LADY!**

RETURN WITH US NOW TO MIDGARD... IN WHICH ONE MAN'S JOURNEY ENDS IN DEADLY ECSTASY, AND THE THUNDER GOD ENJOYS A FREE MEAL!

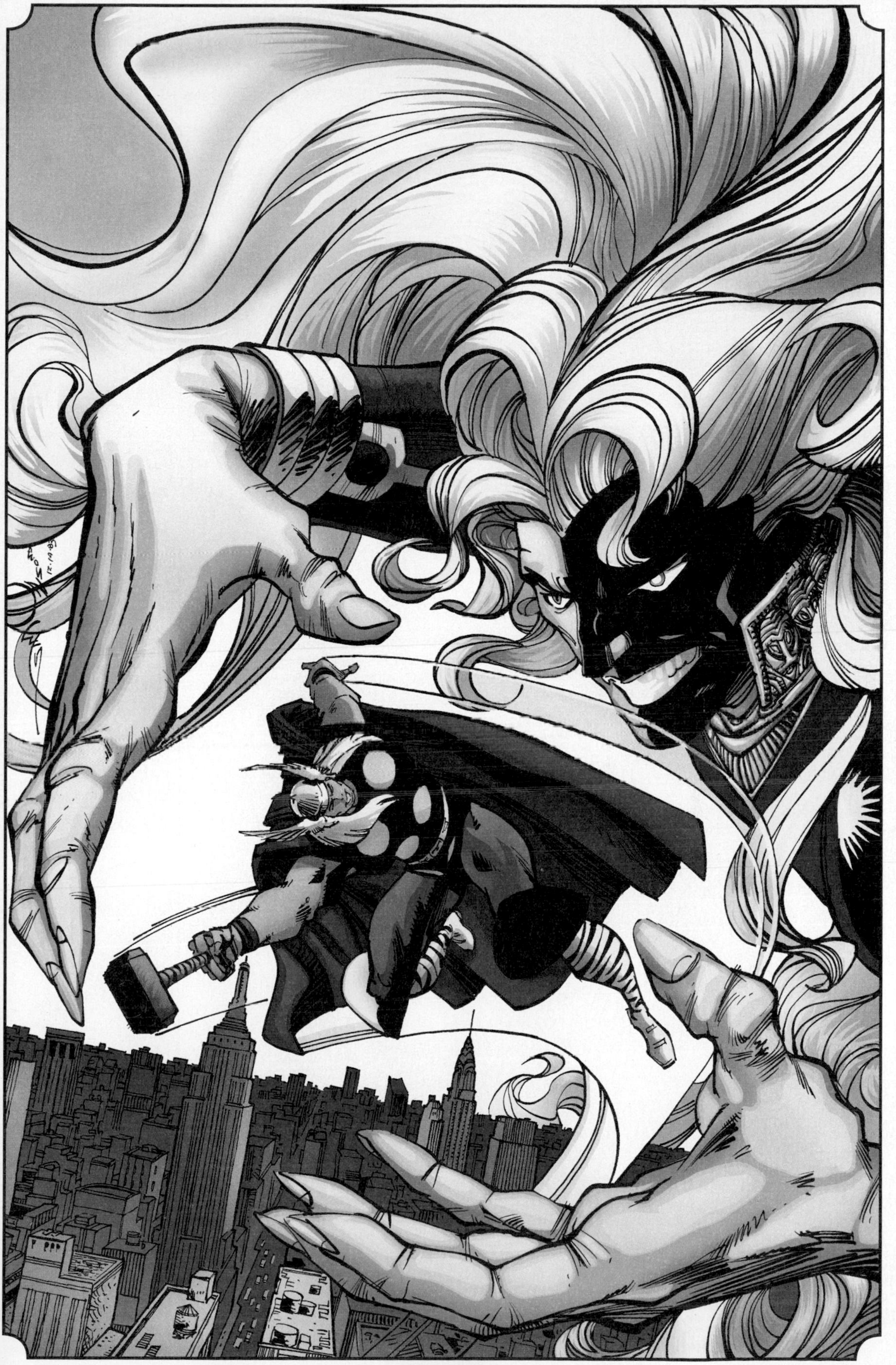

STAN LEE PRESENTS: the MIGHTY THOR®

MANHATTAN: 9:16 AM.

MISS ORDWAY, WOULD YOU COME IN HERE A MOMENT, PLEASE?

CERTAINLY, DOCTOR WILLIS.

DR. E. WILLI... M.D.

YES-SIR?

OHH-- UMMPH!

ART AND STORY: WALTER SIMONSON · LETTERING: JOHN WORKMAN, JR. · COLORS: CHRISTIE SCHEELE
EDITING: MARK GRUENWALD · EDITOR-IN-CHIEF: JIM SHOOTER

I HOPE YOU'RE COMFORTABLE, MISS ORDWAY? YOU ARE ABOUT TO JOIN ME IN AN EXPERIMENT ON THE NATURE OF MORTALS.

I'VE TAKEN THE LIBERTY OF ORDERING IN LUNCH, YOU SEE. THE BEST McBURGER MONEY CAN BUY.

FRIES, TOO, WHICH I PERSONALLY PREFER. ⊰CHOMP CHOMP.⊱

OOPS. DROPPED ONE. WHERE DID THAT LITTLE BEGGAR GET TO?

MMMPH!

OH, LET'S NOT BE TOO IMPATIENT. AFTER, ALL, I'VE SAVED THE PIECE DE RESISTANCE JUST FOR YOU.

YOU DO LIKE McBURGERS, DON'T YOU?

NOW, NOW. IF YOU REFUSE TO TAKE A BITE, I SHALL JUST HAVE TO HOLD YOUR NOSE UNTIL LACK OF OXYGEN FORCES YOU TO OPEN YOUR MOUTH.

GASP!

THAT'S A GOOD GIRL. OPEN WIDE ...AND SAY AHH.

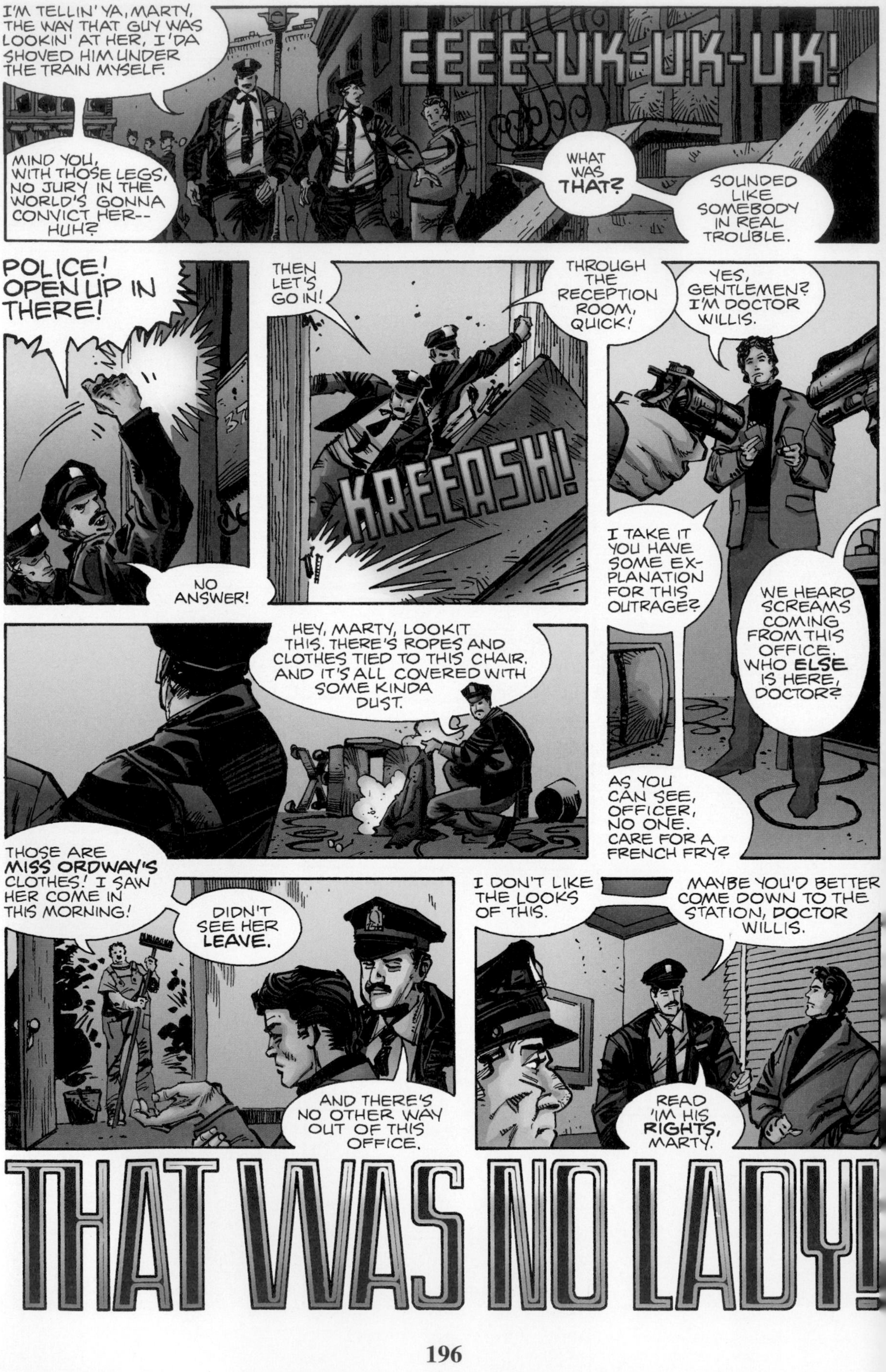
I'M TELLIN' YA, MARTY, THE WAY THAT GUY WAS LOOKIN' AT HER, I'DA SHOVED HIM UNDER THE TRAIN MYSELF.
EEEE-UK-UK-UK!
MIND YOU, WITH THOSE LEGS, NO JURY IN THE WORLD'S GONNA CONVICT HER-- HUH?
WHAT WAS THAT?
SOUNDED LIKE SOMEBODY IN REAL TROUBLE.
POLICE! OPEN UP IN THERE!
NO ANSWER!
THEN LET'S GO IN!
KREEASH!
THROUGH THE RECEPTION ROOM, QUICK!
YES, GENTLEMEN? I'M DOCTOR WILLIS.
I TAKE IT YOU HAVE SOME EXPLANATION FOR THIS OUTRAGE?
WE HEARD SCREAMS COMING FROM THIS OFFICE. WHO ELSE IS HERE, DOCTOR?
HEY, MARTY, LOOKIT THIS. THERE'S ROPES AND CLOTHES TIED TO THIS CHAIR. AND IT'S ALL COVERED WITH SOME KINDA DUST.
AS YOU CAN SEE, OFFICER, NO ONE. CARE FOR A FRENCH FRY?
THOSE ARE MISS ORDWAY'S CLOTHES! I SAW HER COME IN THIS MORNING!
DIDN'T SEE HER LEAVE.
AND THERE'S NO OTHER WAY OUT OF THIS OFFICE.
I DON'T LIKE THE LOOKS OF THIS.
MAYBE YOU'D BETTER COME DOWN TO THE STATION, DOCTOR WILLIS.
READ 'IM HIS RIGHTS, MARTY.
THAT WAS NO LADY!

...AND IN EACH OTHER.

AND WHETHER HE WILLS IT OR NOT, HE WOULD FOLLOW ME THROUGH THE GATES OF HEL ITSELF.

WHAT SAY YOU TO A RIDE THROUGH CENTRAL PARK, MELODI?

LITTLE DOES THOR SUSPECT THAT I KNOW HIS TRUE IDENTITY OR THAT TONIGHT WHEN WE DINE AT MY APARTMENT, I SHALL GIVE HIM A GLASS OF THE GOLDEN MEAD.

THEN SHALL THE THOUGHTS OF ODIN'S SON TURN TO LORELEI WITH A CONSUMING PASSION THAT WILL MAKE HIM MINE FOREVER.

I'D LOVE IT.

YOU ARE STRANGELY QUIET NOW. WHERE DO YOUR THOUGHTS FLY?

I WAS JUST THINKING HOW PERFECTLY THE BRISK MARCH WIND BECOMES YOU. WE ALL SHIVER AND YOU WALK AROUND WITH AN OPEN JACKET!

NO DOUBT THE LEGACY OF MY VIKING BLOOD! WITH A NAME LIKE SIGURD JARLSON, I SHOULD PROBABLY HAVE SAILED A VIKING SHIP OF OLD.

OR MORE LIKELY LED A PARTY OF RED-BEARDED RAIDERS IN SEARCH OF SPOILS.

OKI WAS RIGHT. THIS WORLD OF MORTALS, SO FULL OF LIFE AND DEATH, IS MORE TO MY LIKING THAN THE PALE BEAUTY OF ASGARD.

AND AFTER TONIGHT, I SHALL HOLD THE BEST OF BOTH WORLDS IN MY HANDS.

MEANWHILE, IN A SMALL PRECINCT JAIL IN UPPER MANHATTAN...

WELL, I WAS RIGHT. SHEILA ORDWAY **WAS** TROUBLE. I SHOULD HAVE HANDLED THAT DIFFERENTLY.

BUT I HAD TO BE SURE. NOW I'M CAUGHT HERE LIKE A SITTING DUCK.

WHO--?

OFFICER GRIER, DR. WILLIS. WOULD YOU LIKE SOMETHING TO EAT?

NO, THANKS. BUT HOW ABOUT A PHONE CALL TO MY LAWYER? OR IS THAT BIT OF ROUTINE ONLY IN NOVELS?

I'LL SEE WHAT I CAN DO, DOCTOR.

SHORTLY...

YES, I'M **SURE** IT'S THE MAN. THE ONE SHEILA WAS SENT TO INVESTIGATE.

YOU WANT ME TO **WHAT?**

BUT THAT WILL BLOW MY COVER HERE AT THE STATION. THE AUTHORITIES ARE BOUND TO DISCOVER SOMETHING IN TIME.

YES, YES. I UNDERSTAND. THIS MATTER IS IMPORTANT ENOUGH TO DEMAND **ANY** SACRIFICE.

HE FOUND OUT SOMEHOW AND **DISPOSED** OF HER. WE WON'T BE ABLE TO HOLD HIM FOR MORE THAN ANOTHER DAY OR SO.

I'LL DO IT AT ONCE.

WHAT'S THIS, ROSIE?

GIRL SCOUTS BEEN SELLING YOU A BILL OF GOODS AGAIN?

JUST A LITTLE RECIPE OF MY OWN, FELLOWS. THOUGHT YOU MIGHT LIKE TO TRY SOMETHING A LITTLE DIFFERENT.

WHOA, THESE ARE **GREAT!**

198

IN THE CELL...

SOMETHING'S WRONG. NOBODY'S COME BACK HERE IN OVER AN HOUR.

IT'S THAT LADY COP. I SHOULD HAVE RECOGNIZED HER AURA.

THEY'VE FOUND ME AGAIN.

QUITE RIGHT, DOCTOR WILLIS. AND THIS TIME, YOU'LL NOT ESCAPE US.

I'VE MADE CERTAIN OF THAT!

AND NOW I'LL MAKE CERTAIN OF YOU.

WHO ARE YOU?

AN OBEDIENT SERVANT OF YOUR DEADLIEST ENEMY, DOCTOR.

AN ENEMY WHO HAS DECIDED TO BE MERCIFUL.

THERE IS NO HOPE OF ESCAPE.

EVERYONE IN THE STATION HAS ALREADY TASTED MY SPECIAL COOKIES. AND ENJOYED THEM IMMENSELY, I MIGHT ADD.

NOW THEY ARE OURS, AS SOULLESS AND OBEDIENT AS I AM MYSELF.

S YOU WILL E IF YOU ASTE THESE NMORTAL AFERS.

THERE IS NO PAIN, I PROMISE YOU. AND EVERYTHING WILL BE SO EASY.

DENY YOURSELF THIS PLEASURE, AND YOU WILL STILL TELL US EVERYTHING WE WISH TO KNOW.

AFTER WHICH, MY MASTER MAY AMUSE HIMSELF BY CALLING OUT THE WILD HUNT WITH YOU AS THE QUARRY!

I'LL BE BACK SHORTLY FOR YOUR ANSWER.

199

LATE AFTERNOON, THE LAW OFFICES OF STROTHER AND MARTIN...

THAT WAS THE FULL REPORT, MR. STROTHER. APPARENTLY DR. WILLIS WAS ARRESTED ON SUSPICION OF MURDER.

BUT WE HAVE BEEN UNABLE TO TRACE HIS CURRENT WHEREABOUTS. NOBODY SEEMS TO KNOW WHERE HE'S BEING HELD.

I THINK WE'RE BEING GIVEN THE RUNAROUND.

I SEE. THANK YOU, MISS BLUM.

I NEED A PACKAGE DELIVERED TO LONG ISLAND AS SOON AS POSSIBLE, TO DR. WILLIS'S FATHER.

HOLD ALL MY CALLS AND PHONE THE MESSENGER SERVICE IMMEDIATELY.

ERIC, MY OLD FRIEND, WE BOTH HOPED I WOULD NEVER NEED TO OPEN THE Q-FILE. BUT I THINK WE BOTH KNEW THE DAY MIGHT COME.

AND NOW IT HAS.

I WILL OBEY YOUR INSTRUCTIONS TO THE LETTER AND PRAY THAT I'M NOT TOO LATE.

200

MEANWHILE, IN A FAR DISTANT CORNER OF THE FABULOUS REALM OF **ASGARD**, DEEP IN THE VAST WASTES...

HOME, NOBLE SILVERHOOF, HOME! YOU HAVE SERVED ME WELL AND SHOULD NOT SHARE MY FATE.

SEEK AGAIN THE GREEN PASTURES OF ASGARD AND LIVE FREE...

...AS I NEVER SHALL.

I, WHO HAVE **BROKEN** ALL MY OATHS...

...WHO, AGAINST MY OWN WILL, TOOK THE LIVES OF COUNTLESS DEMONS...

...AND WHO, IN MY TRUST AS AN AMBASSADOR, **SLEW** THE ADOPTED SON OF ODIN, **LOKI**...

...WHEN I FAILED IN MY MISSION TO THAT WRETCHED GOD.*

*NOT THE WHOLE STORY, BUT A FAIR SUMMATION OF THOR #344!

...I HAVE COME TO THE VERY EDGE OF THE WORLD.

BEYOND THIS LAST MOUNTAINOUS BASTION OF THE NORN QUEEN'S KINGDOM LIE ONLY ENDLESS LEAGUES OF DESERT.

AND THERE SHALL THE FATE OF BALDER BE DECIDED.

DEATH! I, WHO HAVE ALREADY DIED BEFORE, WOULD GAZE UPON YOUR VISAGE ONCE MORE!

SO YOU SEEK **DEATH**, DO YOU, BALDER?

THEN LOOK NO FURTHER! MY **SWORD** WILL SEND YOU SWIFTLY INTO HELA'S WAITING ARMS!

HERE WE ARE, SIGURD.

JUST HANG YOUR JACKET IN THE CLOSET. DINNER WILL BE READY SHORTLY. WOULD YOU LIKE A DRINK?

NOT QUITE YET, MELODI, THANKS.

THEN COME AND SIT BESIDE ME. I NEVER THOUGHT I'D SEE ANYONE AS BRAVE AS YOU WERE WHEN YOU SAVED ME FROM THAT AWFUL DRAGON.*

*THOR #341.

IT...UH...IT WAS NOTHING. REALLY.

WELL, PERHAPS YOU SAVE GIRLS FROM DRAGONS EVERY DAY, BUT I NEVER MET ANYONE QUITE LIKE YOU BEFORE.

AND I WANT TO LET YOU KNOW JUST HOW MUCH I APPRECIATE IT.

I WANT TO MAKE THIS EVENING... PERFECT...

...FOR BOTH OF US.

...AND THE DOCUMENTS INSIDE A SEALED PACKET ARE PULLED INTO THE LIGHT FOR THE FIRST TIME.

"Dear Roger,

"If you are reading this now, it can only mean that I am at long last dead--or as good as dead.

"In which case, I can finally speak to you as I have never been able to and tell you who I am and what I have done.

"I know that things have never been well between us, that the barriers I have had to erect around my life prevented me from being there when you needed me...

"But I know, too, that you have become the kind of man who will see what must be done... and do it. And I am proud of you for it.

"The enclosed papers explain everything. Study them well, and destroy them.

"I am handing over to you the greatest trust the human race has ever known.

"I have guarded it with my life.

"Now you must guard it with your own.

LONG ISLAND RAILROAD NEW YORK CITY

"Your loving father."

203

ELSEWHERE, IN A CELL IN MANHATTAN...

ANYTIME NOW, THEY'LL COME FOR ME, AND WHEN THEY DO, I'LL TELL THEM EVERYTHING.

I'LL BE FORCED TO EVEN IF I DON'T EAT THE FOOD.

IF ONLY-- WHAT'S THIS?

A FRENCH FRY! THE ONE I DROPPED THIS MORNING! MAYBE I'VE GOT A CHANCE AFTER ALL.

FIRST, I'LL GET RID OF THESE COOKIES.

SHORTLY...

I SEE YOU'VE EATEN YOUR SNACK. EXCELLENT. STAND UP AND COME OVER HERE.

NOW THAT YOU'RE ONE OF US, PERHAPS YOU FEEL LIKE TALKING.

I...I DON'T KNOW WHERE TO BEGIN.

WHY NOT START WITH THE CASKET'S LOCATION.

I'D RATHER START WITH BREAKFAST! I HAD FRIES!

WHAT?!

HERE, TRY ONE! THEY'RE DELICIOUS!

MUMPH!

GONE! JUST LIKE ALL OF THEM! AND NOTHING LEFT BUT THE CLOTHES OFF HER BACK...

...ALONG WITH MY TICKET OUT OF HERE!

FAWHAAATHH!

SOON, ON A ROSLYN-BOUND BUS ON THE LONG ISLAND EXPRESSWAY...

NOBODY HOME AT EITHER STROTHER'S OR ROGER'S.

LUCKY OFFICER GRIER HAD ENOUGH MONEY ON HER TO COVER BUS FARE.

IF I CAN JUST REACH ROGER IN TIME, MAYBE TO-GETHER WE CAN ESCAPE THE PUR-SUIT THAT'S CERTAIN TO FOLLOW.

I'VE NO WHERE ELSE TO TURN.

IF THEY CALL OUT THE WILD HUNT WHEN THEY'RE THIS CLOSE, WE'RE BOTH DEAD!

THIS IS IT!

BUS STOP

IRONIC IF THE LONG CHASE ENDS HERE IN THE SUBURBS OF NEW YORK CITY.

I NEVER WANTED THIS FOR ANY OF MY CHILDREN. MAYBE I SHOULDN'T HAVE HAD ANY.

BUT WHERE ELSE COULD I TURN IF THE HUNT EVER GOT CLOSE? WHO ELSE COULD I DEPEND UPON TO BECOME THE GUARDIAN OF THE CASKET?

MAYBE, JUST MAYBE, THEY HAVEN'T FIGURED OUT WHERE I'VE GONE YET.

OR MAYBE THEY HAVE!

MEANWHILE, IN THAT MANHATTAN PENTHOUSE...

UMMM. THIS MUSIC MAKES ME FEEL VERY ROMANTIC.

LET ME SLIP INTO SOMETHING A LITTLE MORE COMFORTABLE.

AND THEN I HAVE A **SPECIAL** DRINK FOR YOU. IT SHOULD BRING OUT ALL THE FIRE IN YOUR VIKING BLOOD!

NOT AT ALL. THE PHONE'S ON THE TABLE BEHIND YOU. I WON'T BE LONG.

UMM... FINE.

WOULD YOU MIND... IF I MADE A BRIEF PHONE CALL?

THE AVENGERS' MANSION, ON THE EAST SIDE OF MANHATTAN...

RING! RING! RING! RING!

AVENGERS' RESIDENCE. JARVIS SPEAKING. WHO IS CALLING, MAY I ASK?

'TIS THOR, JARVIS. BE THERE ANY MESSAGES FOR ME?

AH, MASTER THOR. INDEED, A GENTLEMAN DID CALL ABOUT TWO HOURS AGO.

A MR. STROTHER, ESQUIRE, A LAWYER, SIR. IT DID SOUND RATHER URGENT.

SOMETHING CONCERN- ING A "CASKET OF ANCIENT WINTERS" AND AN IN- DIVIDUAL WHOSE NAME I AM AFRAID I DIDN'T QUITE CATCH.

MUMBLE MUMBLE

YESSIR, I BELIEVE THAT WAS THE NAME.

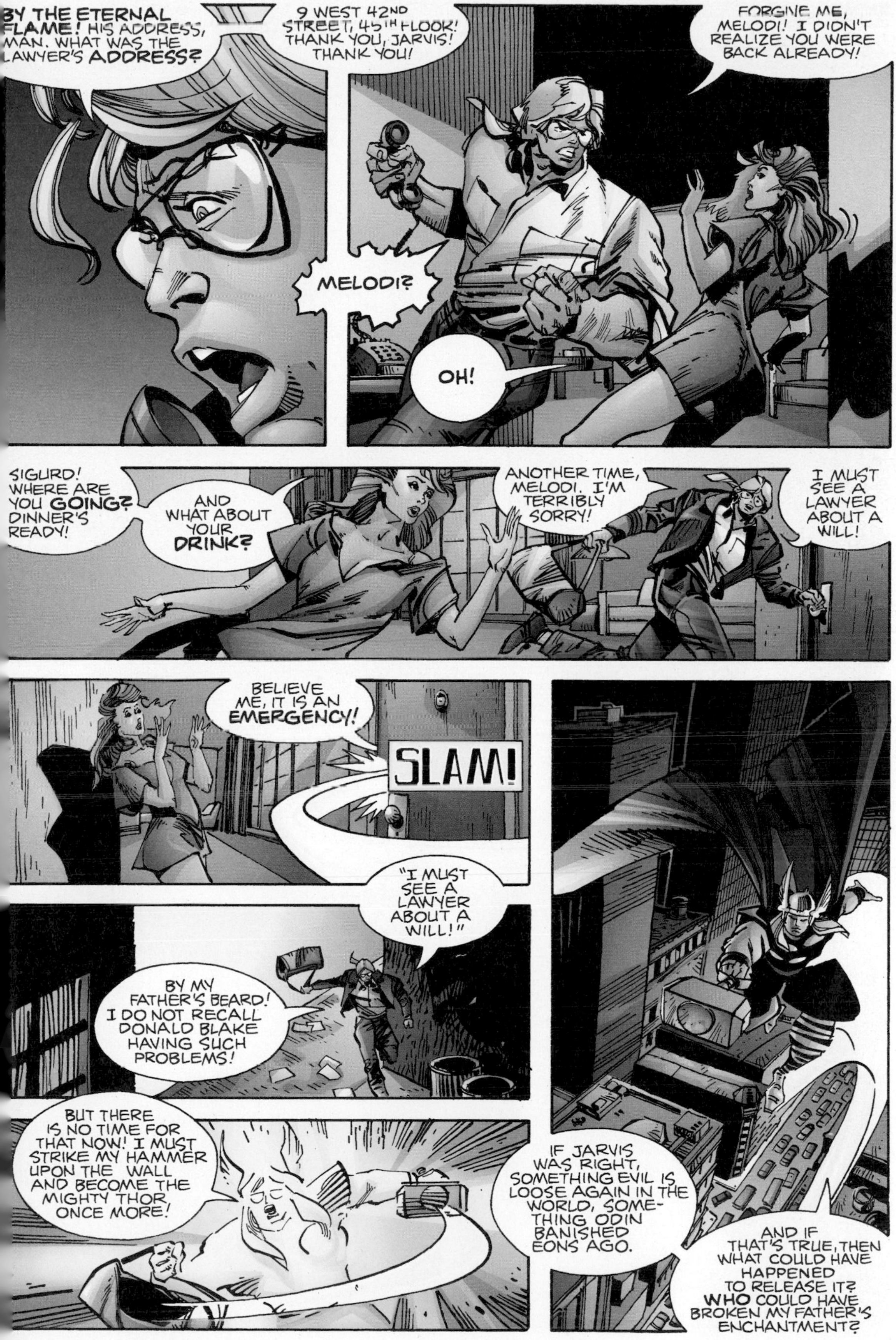
BY THE ETERNAL FLAME! HIS ADDRESS, MAN. WHAT WAS THE LAWYER'S ADDRESS?
9 WEST 42ND STREET, 45TH FLOOR! THANK YOU, JARVIS! THANK YOU!
FORGIVE ME, MELODI! I DIDN'T REALIZE YOU WERE BACK ALREADY!
MELODI?
OH!
SIGURD! WHERE ARE YOU GOING? DINNER'S READY!
AND WHAT ABOUT YOUR DRINK?
ANOTHER TIME, MELODI. I'M TERRIBLY SORRY!
I MUST SEE A LAWYER ABOUT A WILL!
BELIEVE ME, IT IS AN EMERGENCY!
SLAM!
"I MUST SEE A LAWYER ABOUT A WILL!"
BY MY FATHER'S BEARD! I DO NOT RECALL DONALD BLAKE HAVING SUCH PROBLEMS!
BUT THERE IS NO TIME FOR THAT NOW! I MUST STRIKE MY HAMMER UPON THE WALL AND BECOME THE MIGHTY THOR ONCE MORE!
IF JARVIS WAS RIGHT, SOMETHING EVIL IS LOOSE AGAIN IN THE WORLD, SOMETHING ODIN BANISHED EONS AGO.
AND IF THAT'S TRUE, THEN WHAT COULD HAVE HAPPENED TO RELEASE IT? WHO COULD HAVE BROKEN MY FATHER'S ENCHANTMENT?

ROSLYN...

I WAS RIGHT. THE CAR IS FOLLOWING ME. PLAYING CAT AND MOUSE RIGHT NOW TO SHAKE ME UP.

AND THERE'S NOT EVEN A DOG-WALKER OUT TONIGHT!

MAYBE IF I CUT DOWN THIS SIDE STREET, I'LL BE ABLE TO LOSE THEM.

ANOTHER ONE!

THAT TEARS IT!

I'LL HAVE TO CUT BETWEEN THESE HOUSES AND HOPE I CAN GIVE THEM THE SLIP BEFORE THEY GET ANY CLOSER!

DON'T LET HIM GET AWAY.

IT'LL BE THE **WILD HUNT** FOR US IF HE ESCAPES AGAIN!

SPLIT UP AND CUT HIM OFF!

208

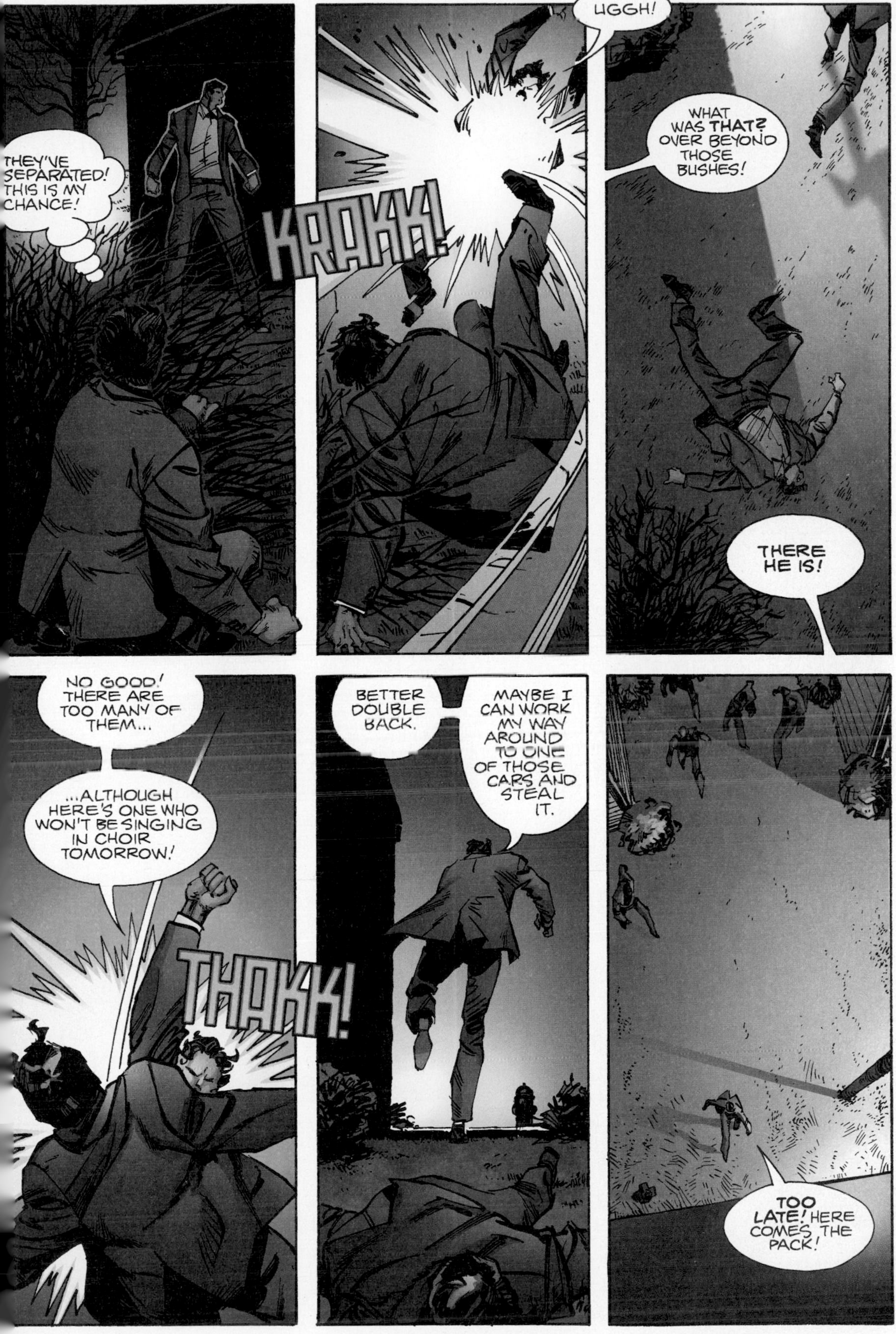
THEY'VE SEPARATED! THIS IS MY CHANCE!
UGGH!
KRAKK!
WHAT WAS THAT? OVER BEYOND THOSE BUSHES!
THERE HE IS!
NO GOOD! THERE ARE TOO MANY OF THEM...
...ALTHOUGH HERE'S ONE WHO WON'T BE SINGING IN CHOIR TOMORROW!
THAKK!
BETTER DOUBLE BACK.
MAYBE I CAN WORK MY WAY AROUND TO ONE OF THOSE CARS AND STEAL IT.
TOO LATE! HERE COMES THE PACK!

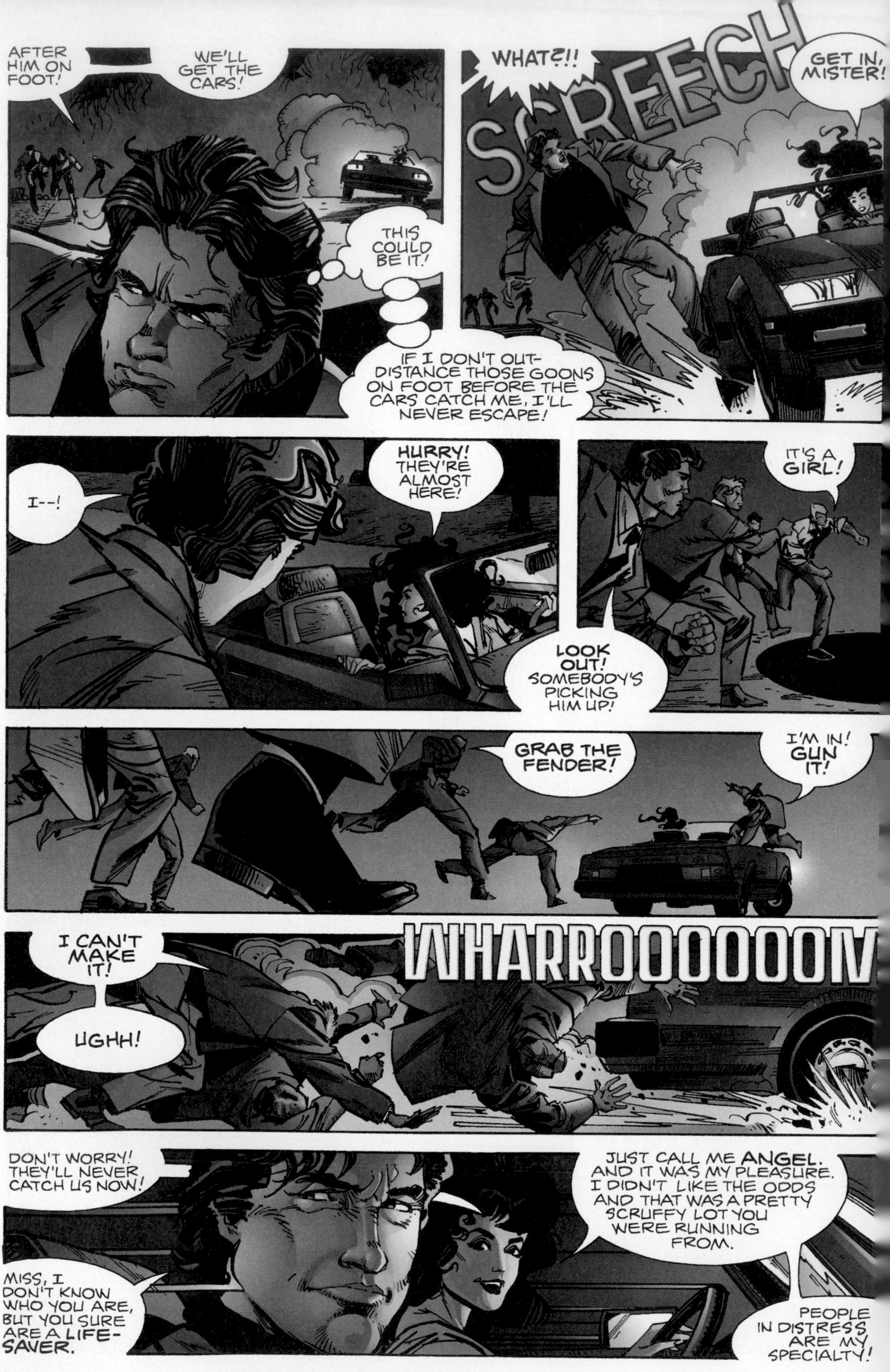
AFTER HIM ON FOOT!
WE'LL GET THE CARS!
THIS COULD BE IT!
IF I DON'T OUT-DISTANCE THOSE GOONS ON FOOT BEFORE THE CARS CATCH ME, I'LL NEVER ESCAPE!
WHAT?!!
SCREECH
GET IN, MISTER!
I--!
HURRY! THEY'RE ALMOST HERE!
IT'S A GIRL!
LOOK OUT! SOMEBODY'S PICKING HIM UP!
GRAB THE FENDER!
I'M IN! GUN IT!
I CAN'T MAKE IT!
UGHH!
WHARROOOOOOM
DON'T WORRY! THEY'LL NEVER CATCH US NOW!
MISS, I DON'T KNOW WHO YOU ARE, BUT YOU SURE ARE A LIFE-SAVER.
JUST CALL ME ANGEL. AND IT WAS MY PLEASURE. I DIDN'T LIKE THE ODDS AND THAT WAS A PRETTY SCRUFFY LOT YOU WERE RUNNING FROM.
PEOPLE IN DISTRESS ARE MY SPECIALTY!

YONDER IS THE LAWYER'S OFFICE. AND THE LIGHT IS STILL ON.

EXCELLENT.

THE **CASKET OF ANCIENT WINTERS** WAS THOUGHT LOST EONS AGO, EVEN BEFORE MY FATHER BANISHED ITS **KEEPER** BEYOND THE STARS.

IF IT HAS BEEN UNEARTHED AT LONG LAST, THEN SURELY SOME ANCIENT EVIL HAS COME TO MIDGARD.*

I FEEL AS THOUGH A **STORM** LONG IN THE MAKING IS ABOUT TO BREAK.

GOOD, THE WINDOW IS UNLOCKED.

*EARTH.

WHO--? AH, THOR, THEN YOU DID GET MY MESSAGE.

I HAVE COME ON THE WINGS OF THE WIND, MR STROTHER.

FOR THE WORD YOU SPOKE TO JARVIS IN YOUR CALL STILL ECHOES ACROSS THE CENTURIES, AND IF YOU HAVE TIDINGS TO TELL ME, THEY HAD BEST BE SAID QUICKLY.

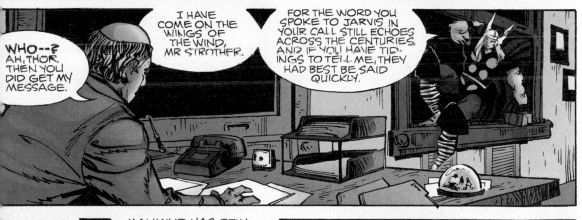

TIME IS OF THE ESSENCE.

MANKIND HAS FEW ENEMIES AS DEADLY AS THIS ONE, AND NONE THAT SURPASS THE **DARK ELF** IN VILLAINY.

YOU HAVE SPOKEN THE NAME OF **MALEKITH THE ACCURSED!**

MEANWHILE, IN ROSLYN...

IT IS MUSIC TO SOOTHE THE SOUL. TO HELP A PERSON GENTLY SAIL AWAY ON THE WINGS OF DREAMS.

I CAN'T BELIEVE HOW RELAXED I FEEL, ESPECIALLY AFTER SUCH A NARROW ESCAPE.

AND THAT MUSIC ON THE RADIO. IT SEEMS TO FLOW RIGHT THROUGH ME. WHAT STATION IS THAT?

IT'S STRANGE, ANGEL. I FEEL SO AT PEACE WITH YOU, AS IF I'VE KNOWN YOU ALL MY LIFE.

WE'VE... WE'VE NEVER MET BEFORE, HAVE WE?

PERHAPS WE **HAVE**, ERIC, IN DREAMS.

I HAVE BEEN WAITING TO MEET YOU FOR A LONG TIME.

AND YOU HAVE BEEN WAITING TO MEET ME.

I...I HAVE?

BUT NOW THAT I LOOK AT YOU, I...I THINK YOU'RE RIGHT.

THERE'S SOMETHING ABOUT YOU THAT'S FAMILIAR.

MAYBE IT'S THE MUSIC. IT'S WEAVING THROUGH MY BRAIN. I CAN'T SEEM TO HOLD ONTO MY THOUGHTS...

...BUT I'VE NEVER SEEN A WOMAN MORE BEAUTIFUL.

WHY ARE WE STOPPING, ANGEL?

BECAUSE I KNOW WHAT YOU WANT, ERIC.

YOU WANT TO KISS ME, DON'T YOU, ERIC?

THE BLOOD IN YOUR VEINS IS TURNING TO FIRE AND YOU MUST KISS ME NOW AS THOUGH YOU HAD NEVER KISSED A WOMAN BEFORE.

YES, YES, I DO. I MUST. ANGEL, I LOVE YOU.

YOU... YOU DO?

BUT FIRST, YOU WANT TO TELL ME WHERE YOU HAVE HIDDEN THE CASKET OF ANCIENT WINTERS.

YOU DO WANT TO NOW, DON'T YOU, ERIC?

YES. YES. I COULD NEVER HAVE ANY SECRETS FROM YOU.

AND WHEN YOU HAVE TOLD ME, DARLING, WE WILL KISS AND YOU WILL TASTE FORBIDDEN PLEASURES THAT FEW HAVE EVEN DREAMED OF.

AND YOU WILL BE MINE, FOREVER.

ELSEWHERE, FAR BEYOND THE FIELDS WE KNOW, A MIGHTY HOST SWAYS IN EC-STASY AND A GREAT VOICE FILLS THE BURNING VOID...

THE SHEATHLESS SWORD IS FINISHED!

THE ANVIL'S WORK IS DONE!

NOW SHALL I STRIKE THE SECOND BLOW AGAINST ASGARD AND ALL HER POWER!

DOOM!

214

AND, BACK IN ROSLYN...

ERIC, MY LOVE, THAT WAS BEAUTIFUL.

I RARELY MEET A SOUL SO DEVOTED TO DUTY.

WHICH IS PRECISELY WHY THEY ARE SO DELICIOUS.

BUT OF COURSE, IT COULD END NO OTHER WAY.

NOW MY EAGER SERVANT'S WILL SEEK OUT YOUR SON AND DESTROY THE LAST TRACES OF YOUR KNOWLEDGE.

I, WHO PURSUED ODIN'S RAVEN TO THE VERY GATES OF ASGARD COULD HARDLY BE DENIED BY ANY MORTAL, NO MATTER HOW DEVOTED.

AND THE ISLAND OF MANHATTAN WILL YIELD UP MY ANCIENT TREASURE...

...FOR THE TIME HAS COME TO OPEN AND RELEASE ITS CONTENTS, AS MY LORD COMMANDS.

TOO LONG HAS MY GREATEST POSSESSION BEEN DENIED ME. TONIGHT, THE CASKET WILL BE MINE AT LAST EVEN IF I MUST CALL THE WILD HUNT ITSELF!

AND WOE TO THOSE...

...WHO STAND BETWEEN MALEKITH AND HIS GOAL!

CONFUSED? BEWILDERED? AFRAID TO EAT A McBURGER AGAIN? DON'T BE! ALL WILL BE EXPLAINED NEXT ISSUE (IF WE CAN FIGURE IT OUT IN TIME)!

NEXT: THE WILD HUNT!

"This drawing was done on typewriter paper with Pentel and colored pencils. I did a whole series of full figures in front of logos in the flush of my early enthusiasm for Marvel Comics in 1966." — Walter Simonson

House ad by Walter Simonson

House ads by Walter Simonson

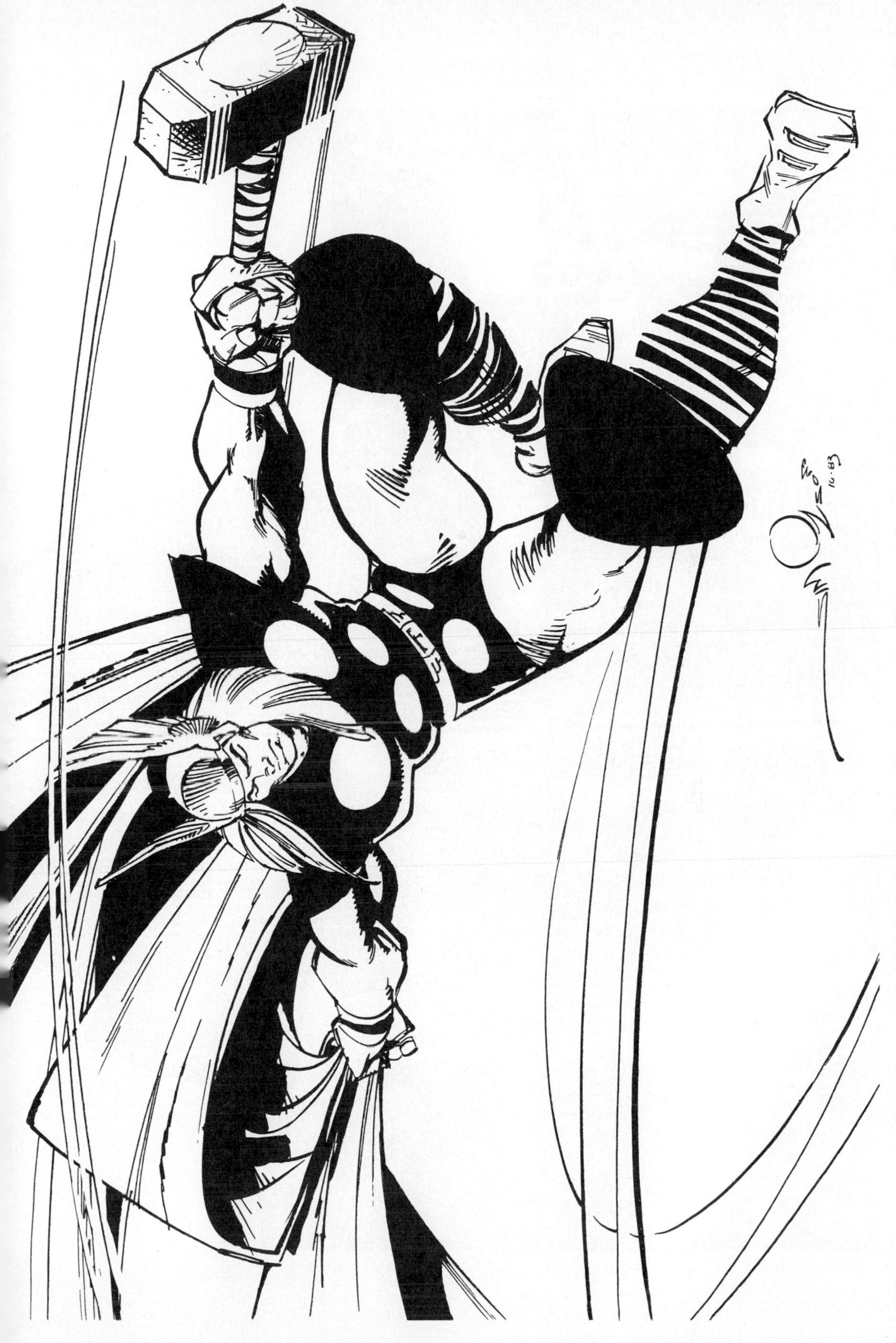

Beta Ray Bill house ad by Walter Simonson

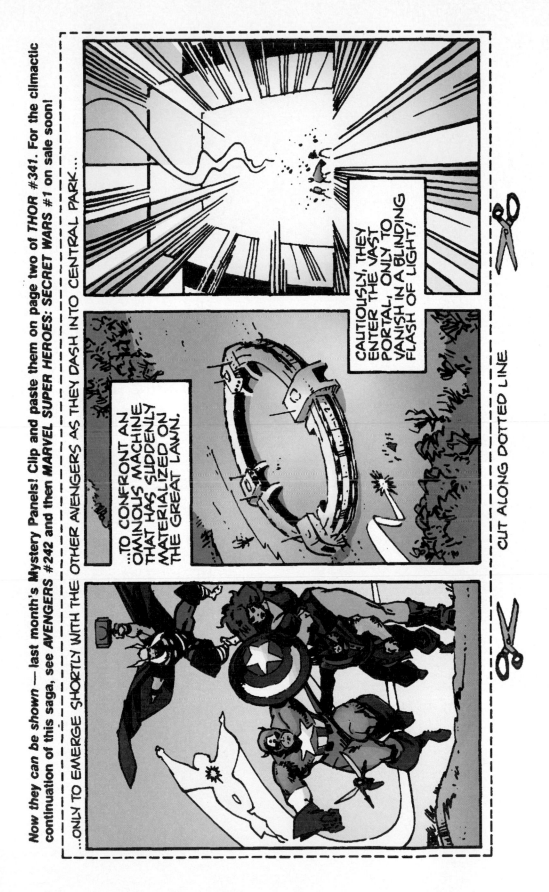

"Missing Panels" from *Thor #341*, which ran on the letters page of *Thor #342*, by Walter Simonson

Thor: The Ballad of Beta Ray Bill TPB (1989) cover painting by Walter Simonson

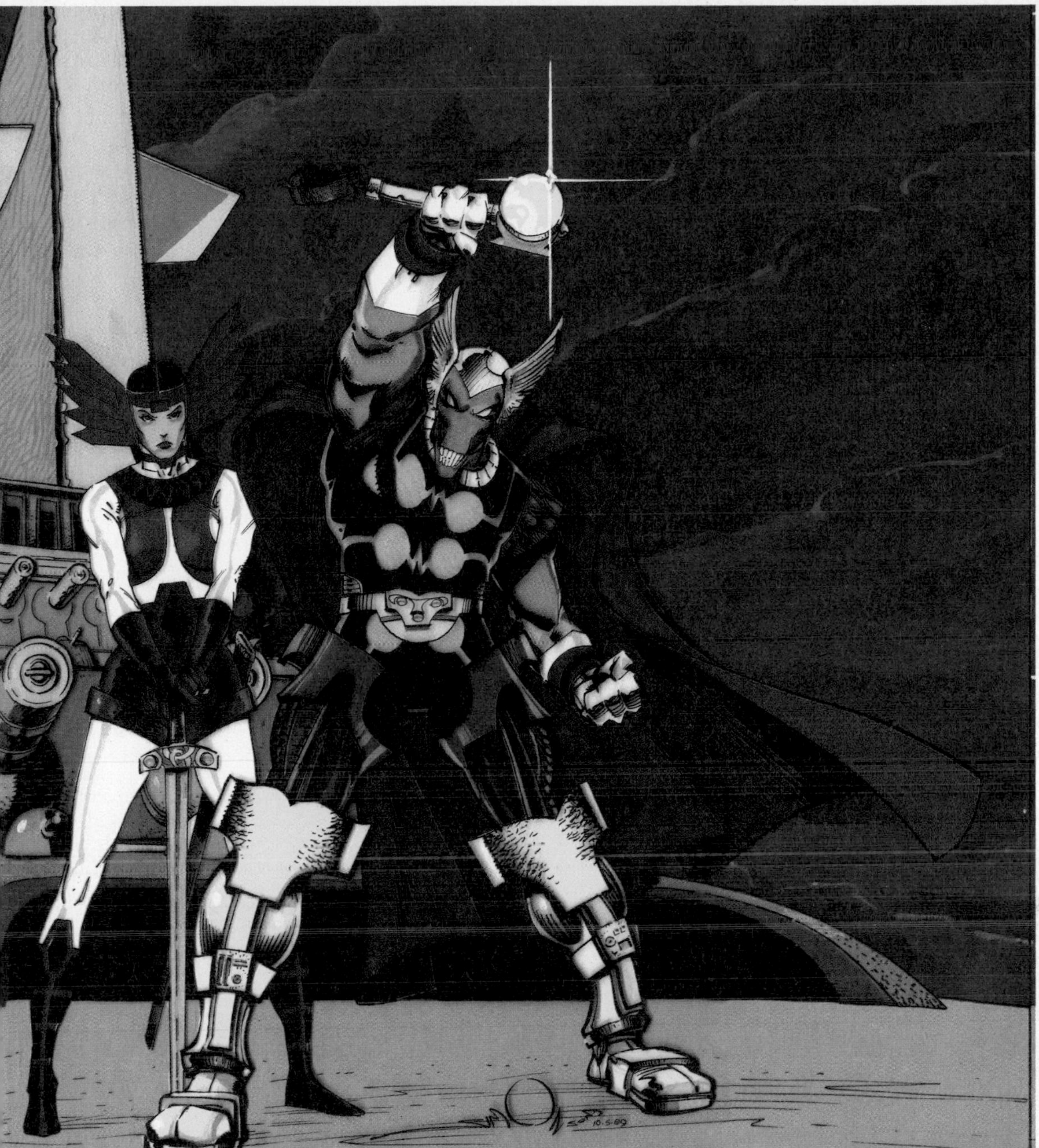
10.5.89

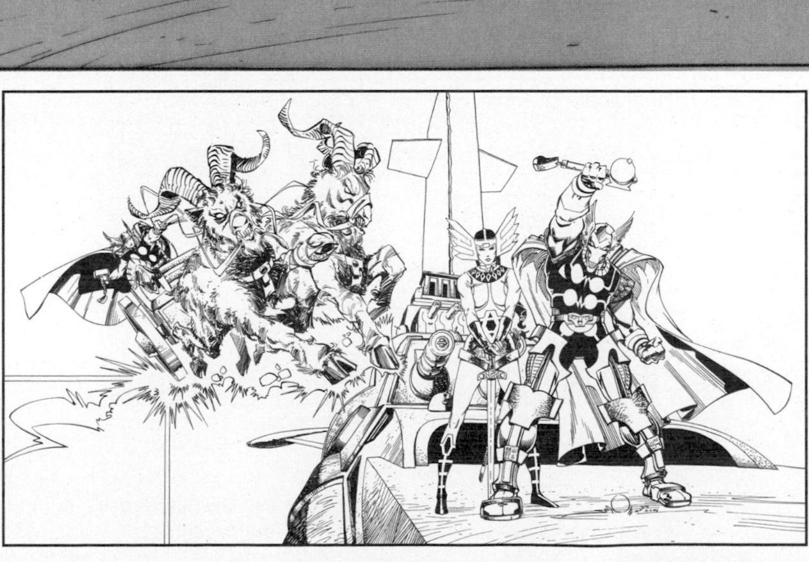

THOR: THE BALLAD OF BETA RAY BILL TPB (1989) INTRODUCTION

The ballad of Beta Ray Bill began as an idea.

I had been asked by then-editor Mark Gruenwald to take over *Thor* as both writer and artist and I wanted to start my work on the title with something unusual, something different, something unique. Something that had never been done in *Thor* before.

My model for such a beginning came from the work that Jack Kirby had done for DC Comics some thirteen years earlier. When Jack began his Fourth World tetralogy for DC, he took the name *Jimmy Olsen*, and revamped it completely. His first issue of Superman's Pal was as different from the preceding issues as chalk is from cheese! The issue was riveting. It exploded with new ideas, new characters, new situations. I didn't have as many ideas as Jack; no one does. But I definitely wanted to begin my run on *Thor* with as dramatic a break from the preceding issues as I possibly could.

Thor's enchanted hammer seemed like the right place to start. Besides Thor and Odin, no one had ever been able to lift it. The enchantment on the hammer, as longtime readers know, decreed that "Whosoever holds this hammer, if he be worthy, shall possess the power of Thor." It seemed like a good place to start. And that meant finding someone to hold the hammer who was not only worthy, but interesting, a character full of his own innate nobility, tragedy, and responsibilities. This was no opportunity to waste on some parochial hero.

Visually, Bill was designed to play against type. American comics are primarily a short story form. As a result, symbols are used relentlessly as an aid to shorthand communications in the medium. Which means that in the main, good guys look like good guys, and bad guys look like bad guys. An Adonis-like god who came to Earth and picked up Thor's hammer would surprise no one. A monster who did the same thing would be startling. I needed a monster. At the same time, the underlying nobility of the character could still be suggested. Bill's face was designed with a horse skull in mind. Few animals are so noble or beautiful as the horse.

Bill's name was another matter. I wanted a common name, a symbol of the hero's identification with every man, even if he himself was quite unique. And I also wanted something with a slight SciFi flavor. I had in fact originally thought of calling him "Beta Ray Jones" since Jones is such a stereotypical last name, but felt that as Marvel already had several Joneses in various comics (and editorial positions), I'd best look elsewhere for a name. And I liked the alliteration.

From such considerations was Beta Ray Bill born, a character unique even among his own kind, a combination of savior and pariah, noble enough to sacrifice himself and his happiness for his people, human enough to be hurt by their rejection. Most comics are a team effort and Thor was no exception. Thanks are due Mark Gruenwald and Mike Carlin who helped on the editorial side of the book. And I'd like to give a note of special appreciation to John Workman, whose distinctive lettering and sound effects gave the book so much of its graphic quality. Without the efforts of these fine folks, Bill's realization would have been a good deal less effective.

Walter Simonson
October 8, 1989

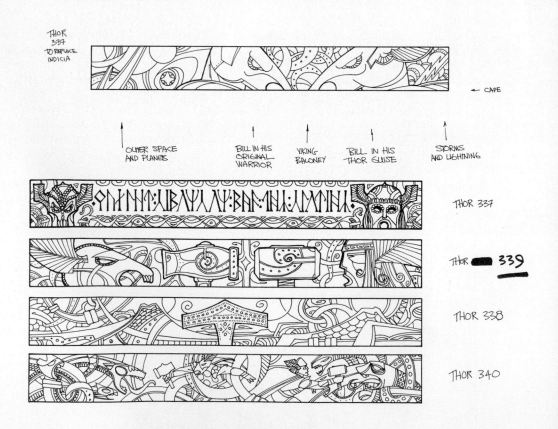

For *Thor: The Ballad of Beta Ray Bill TPB,* Walter drew new illustrations to fill the space where the indicias ran in the original comics.

THOR VISIONARIES: WALTER SIMONSON TPB (2000) INTRODUCTION

...For If The Odinsword Be Drawn!

I wrote that title in 1967 during the worst excesses of my efforts to imitate Stan Lee. Back then, I was a geology major in college, Vietnam was a looming shadow for every young man of draftable age in America, and Marvel was publishing about 11 comics a month. Which meant that I was measuring strikes and dips on the rocks below the Holyoke Dam, thinking tough thoughts about my future after graduation and purchasing every comic Marvel published.

Thor was my personal favorite. I'd already had an abiding interest in Norse mythology when I discovered Marvel's version. And Stan and Jack were telling wonderful stories. Stories I read so many times, I can still remember them better than I can my own. Off the top of my head — the Trial of the Gods. Thor's evolving struggle against Loki, the Norn Stones and the Destroyer, the Absorbing Man, the coming of Hercules, the treachery of Seidring the Merciless (I did think Odin missed the boat there; would you trust an advisor on your staff named Seidring the Merciless?), the titanic battle against Pluto and the forces of the Netherworld, the ultimate fate (at least for the first time) of Jane Foster, and the introduction of Sif coinciding with the War against the Trolls and their hidden ally, Orikal. (I never got the 'Oracle' reference there; I always thought the name sounded like some sort of decay-preventing dentifrice with an accent on the last syllable.)

Inspired by the comic, I wrote my own Thor story, an amalgam of Stan and Jack continuity sprinkled with a little Norse mythology, and overcooked in my heated imagination. The idea grew out of a pair of *Thor Annuals* Marvel published during the summers of the mid-60's. Somewhere along the way, I thought of doing a BIG Thor story, so big that it couldn't be contained in a single comic, and I structured it out along the lines of Marvel's publishing schedule. My imagined story would come out in the summertime. It would begin in one of the regular monthly issues of Thor, run through all the other Marvel titles the same month (they only had about 11 titles then, remember?), and finish up the following month with a double–length flourish in a *Thor Annual*!

I cast the fire elemental Surtur as my principal villain. Stan and Jack had already introduced him into the Thor comic by then but mostly, he was just one more really large bad guy. I wanted to go back to the mythology and recreate something closer to the Surtur I found there. A great being of fire who, at the end of time during Ragnarok, flings fire across the Nine Worlds with his really big sword, and burns almost everything to ashes. Including himself presumably.

And the Marvel Universe already had a really big sword.

In Tales of Asgard, a backup feature that ran in the early issues of Thor, Stan and Jack spun a story around the Odinsword (or Oversword as it was originally called). It was a huge blade fit for a giant that lay in a great sheath enshrined in the middle of Asgard. And it was said that if the sword were ever drawn, Ragnarok would fall.

Hooking the Odinsword up with Surtur didn't seem any great stretch given the prophecy. So I began building a story by assigning the sword an identity. I posited that it was Surtur's weapon, the very Sword with which he was destined to end the Nine Worlds. Odin had at some point in the deeps of time carried the Sword off to prevent Surtur from triggering Ragnarok prematurely. Over the centuries, the actual origin of the Sword had been forgotten and Odin's own name given to the blade. The prophecy was a faint echo of the sword's true nature. But of course, Odin remembered. As did Surtur.

My story began as Surtur magically retrieved his sword, calling it to his side and breaking the protective spells Odin had woven around it. But Surtur still had to set it alight in Asgard in order to bring about the final doom of the gods. And the way to Asgard led through Earth. Surtur's various minions would attack Earth throughout the Marvel Universe in the company's other titles, and finally, Surtur would attack Asgard directly, going up against Thor and then Odin himself in the final chapter, the *Annual*.

By the summer of 1969, I'd given up geology, failed my draft physical, and entered art school. And I had begun to draw my imaginary Annual. I was about 30 pages of pencils and inks into it before I concluded that my inking wasn't up to snuff. So I put the project aside, thinking I would return to it when my inks had improved.

I got my chance fourteen years later. Editor Mark Gruenwald offered me the chance to write and draw *Thor* for Marvel. By then, the Odinsword was gone, destroyed in an earlier story. I decided not to try to resurrect it. There didn't seem much point by then. But forging a new weapon wasn't a big story problem and after all those years, I finally got the chance to tell my original story, enlarging its mythological framework, and even layering in a little blacksmithing, some science fiction, and a bit of the Celtic fairy faith as well. I'd learned a few things since I'd imagined that original story.

There was an extra benefit from the gap between the story's conception and its execution. By the time I finally had the chance to do it, I'd given up trying to be either Stan Lee or Jack Kirby. Which meant among other things that I could abandon my original title for the saga. Until now. Just as well. I can't imagine what sentence that clause was supposed to be completing. And with luck, I'll never write a dangling phrase beginning with an ellipsis, a preposition and a conjunction again!

Walter Simonson
2000

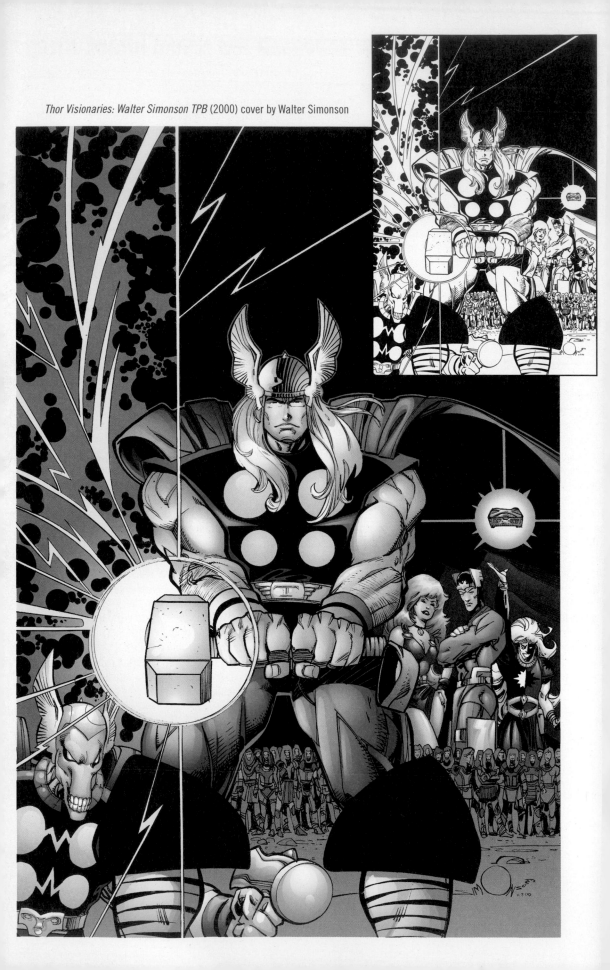

Thor Visionaries: Walter Simonson TPB (2000) cover by Walter Simonson

Pinup by Walter Simonson donated to charity

Pinup by Walter Simonson donated to charity

Thor by Walter Simonson Omnibus (2011) cover

COVER GALLERY

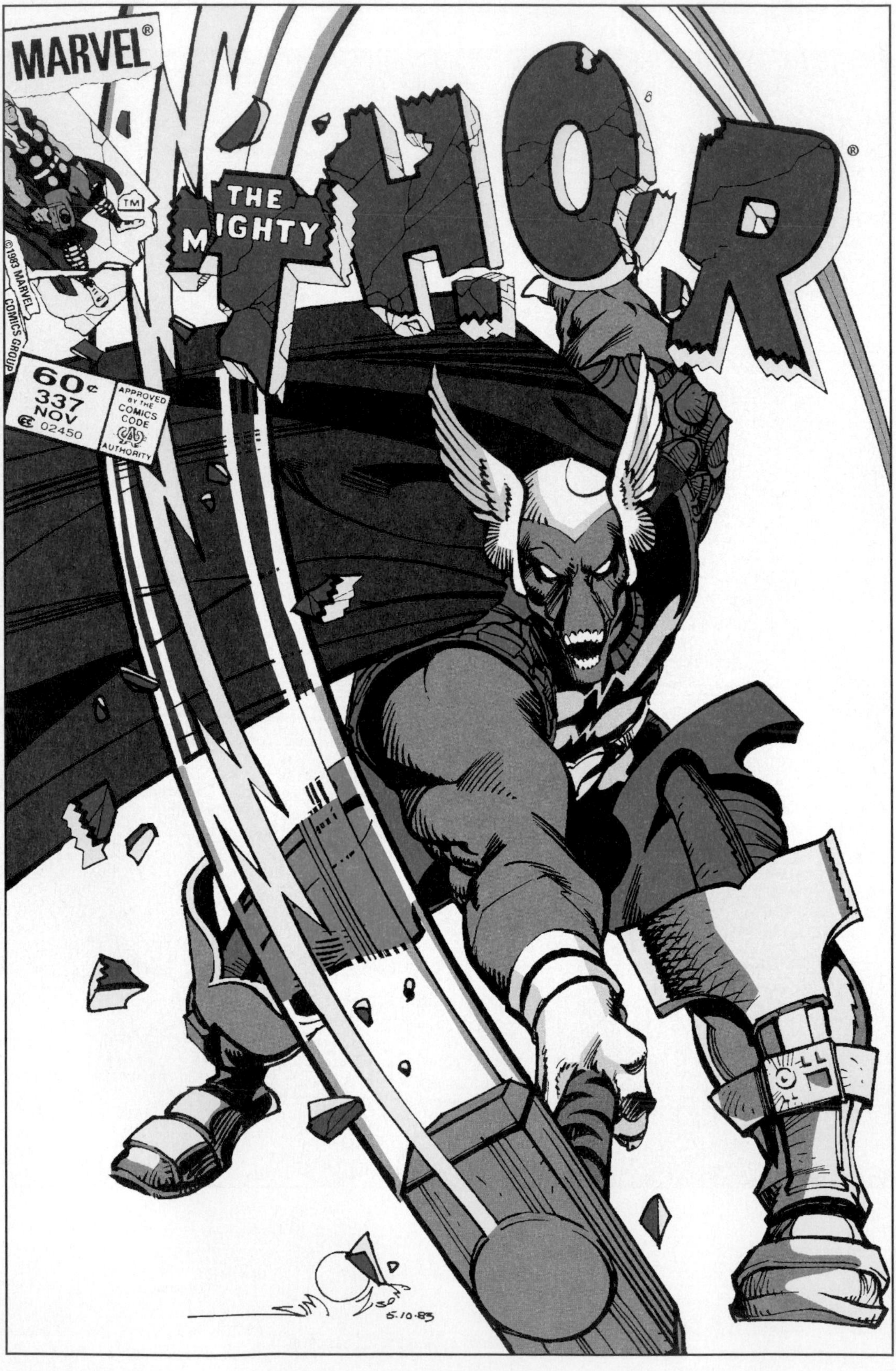
MARVEL®
THE MIGHTY THOR®
™
© 1983 MARVEL COMICS GROUP
60¢
337
NOV
02450
APPROVED BY THE COMICS CODE CA AUTHORITY
5.10.83

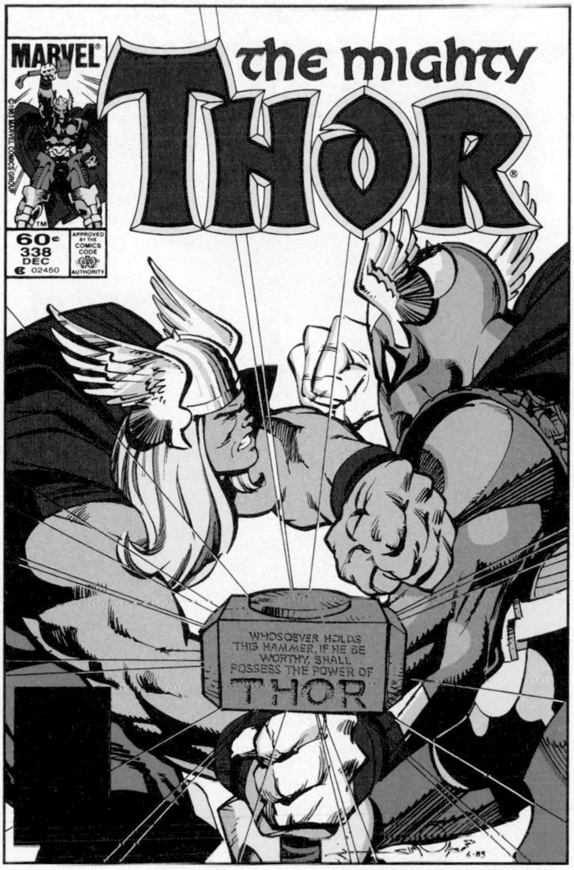
MARVEL
the mighty
THOR
60¢
338
DEC
02450
APPROVED BY THE COMICS CODE AUTHORITY
WHOSOEVER HOLDS THIS HAMMER, IF HE BE WORTHY, SHALL POSSESS THE POWER OF
THOR

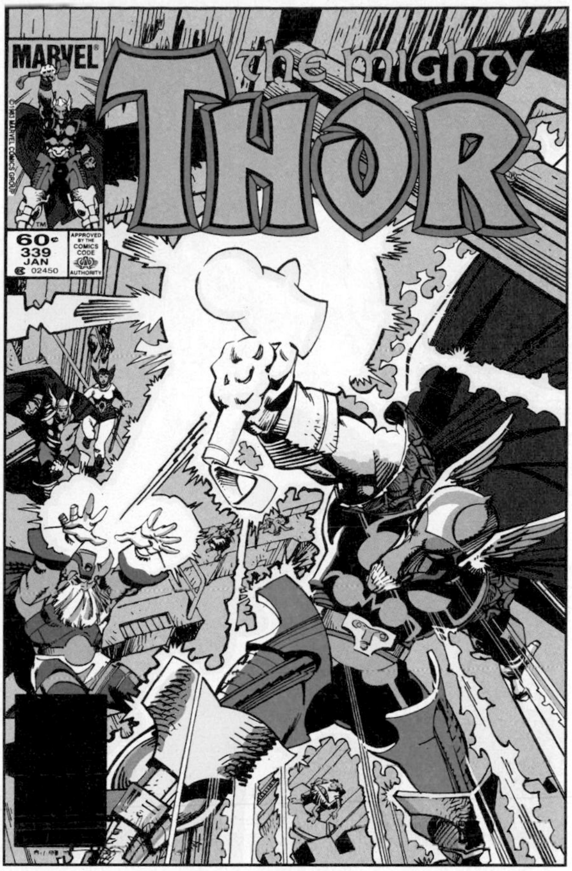
MARVEL
the mighty
THOR
60¢
339
JAN
02450
APPROVED BY THE COMICS CODE AUTHORITY

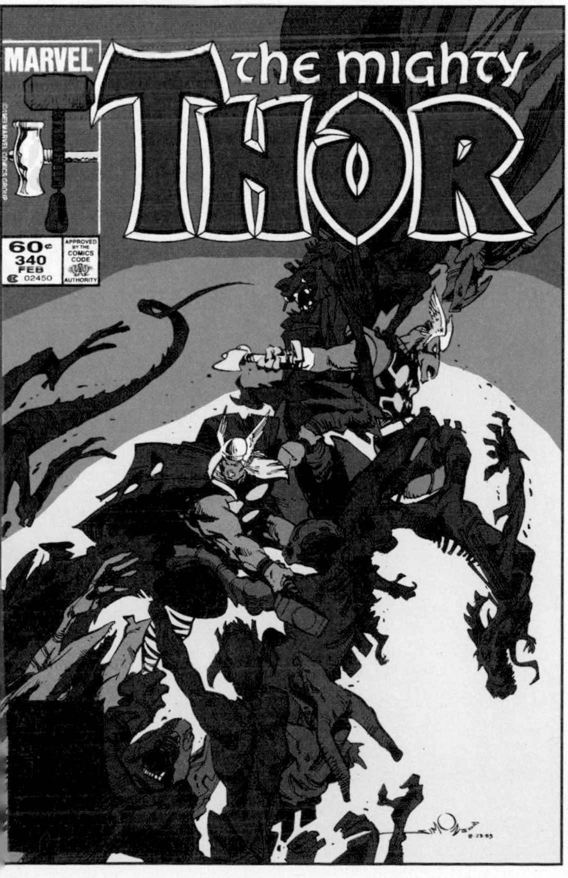
MARVEL
the mighty
THOR
60¢
340
FEB
02450
APPROVED BY THE COMICS CODE AUTHORITY

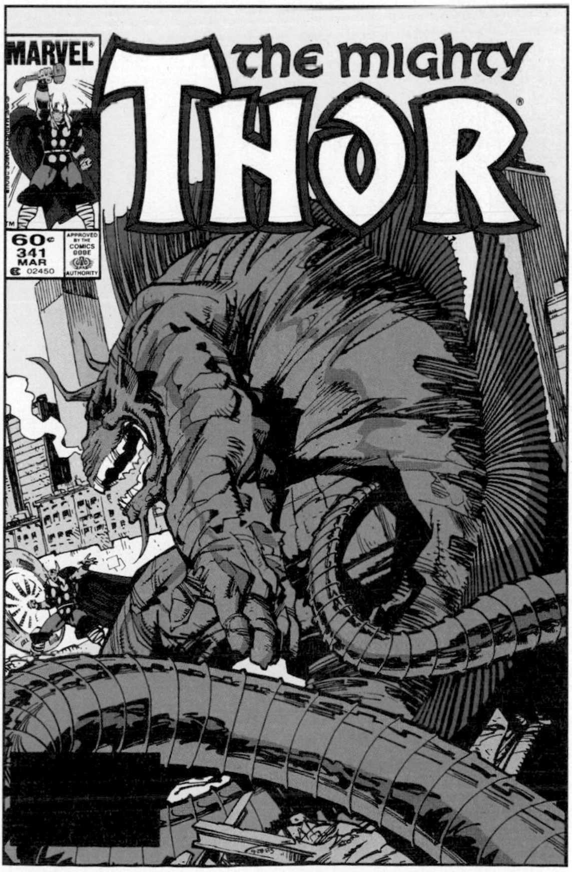
MARVEL
the mighty
THOR
60¢
341
MAR
02450
APPROVED BY THE COMICS CODE AUTHORITY

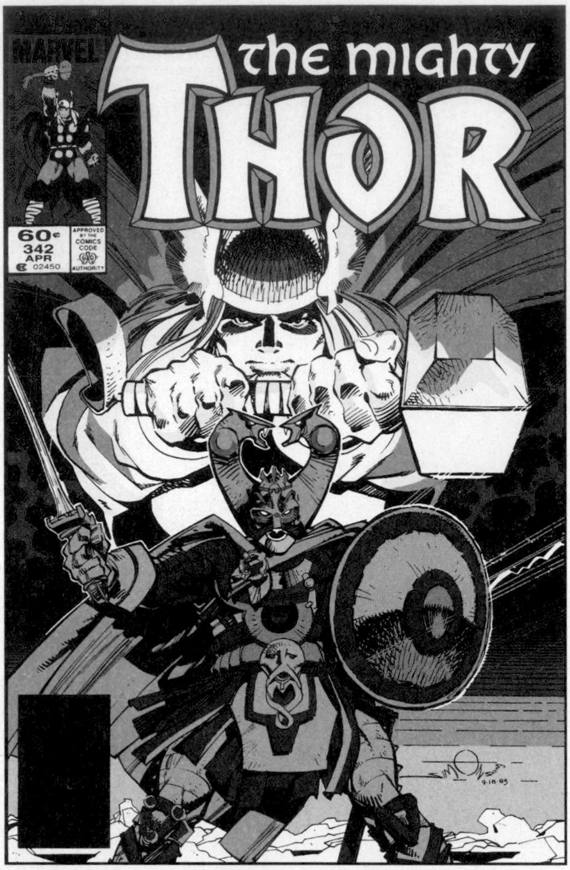
MARVEL
the mighty
THOR
60¢
342
APR
APPROVED BY THE COMICS CODE AUTHORITY
02450

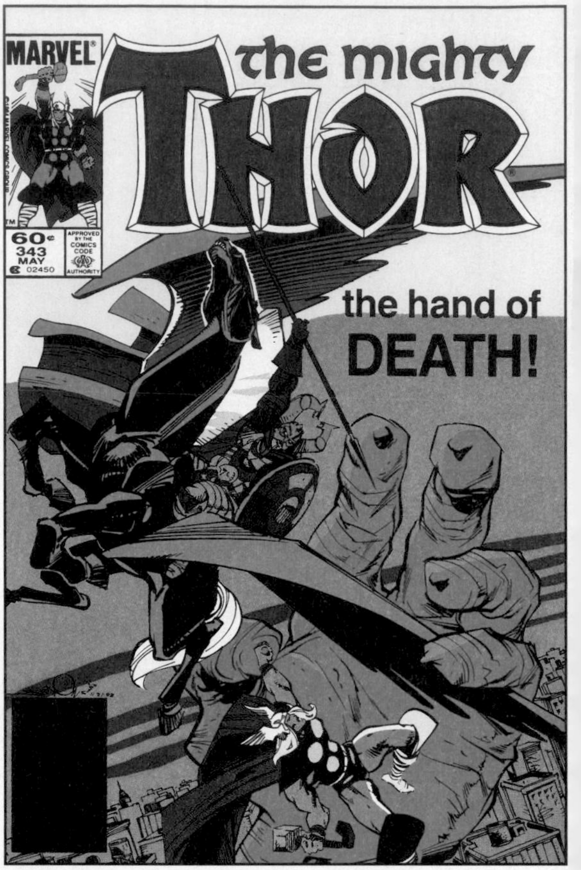
MARVEL
the mighty
THOR
60¢
343
MAY
APPROVED BY THE COMICS CODE AUTHORITY
02450
the hand of
DEATH!

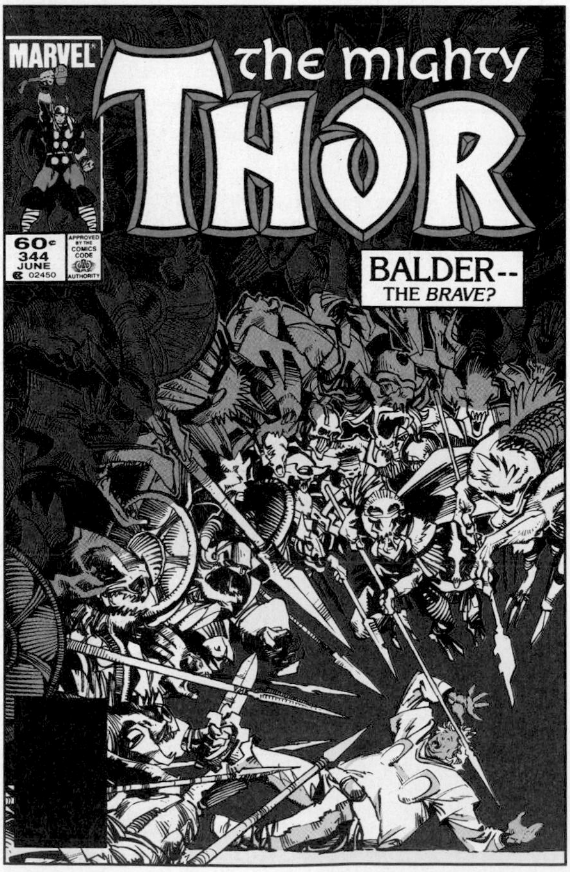
MARVEL
the mighty
THOR
60¢
344
JUNE
APPROVED BY THE COMICS CODE AUTHORITY
02450
BALDER--
THE BRAVE?

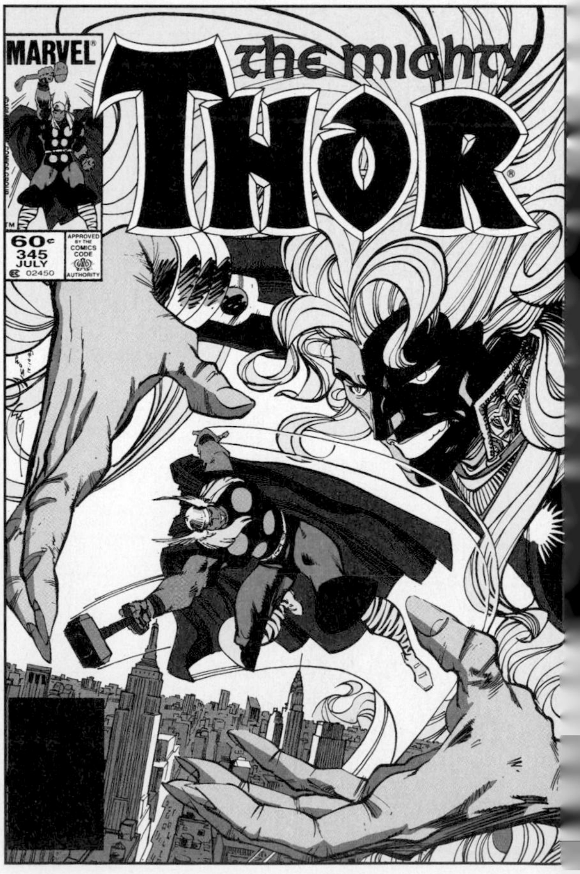
MARVEL
the mighty
THOR
60¢
345
JULY
APPROVED BY THE COMICS CODE AUTHORITY
02450